Mr Lawson's Gamble

Also by William Keegan

Who Runs the Economy?
(with Rupert Pennant-Rea)

Mrs Thatcher's Economic Experiment

Britain without Oil

Mr Lawson's Gamble

WILLIAM KEEGAN

To my sons

Harry and Bartholomew

First published in Great Britain 1989

British Library Cataloguing in Publication Data

Keegan, William, *1938–*
Mr Lawson's gamble. – (A John Curtis book).
1. Great Britain. Economic conditions
I. Title
330.941'0858

ISBN 0-340-50978-3

Published by Hodder and Stoughton,
a division of Hodder and Stoughton Limited,
Mill Road, Dunton Green, Sevenoaks, Kent TN13 2YA.
Editorial Office: 47 Bedford Square, London WC1B 3DP.

Photoset by Rowland Phototypesettng Limited,
Bury St Edmunds, Suffolk

Printed in Great Britain by
Mackays of Chatham plc, Chatham, Kent

CONTENTS

ACKNOWLEDGMENTS

I should like to thank everyone who has helped in the writing of this book. Sir Ian Gilmour, Dr Ray Richardson, Adrian Hamilton, Anthony Howard, Richard Brown and Adam Raphael read the manuscript and made valuable comments. My secretary Ruth Fisher typed the manuscript and held the fort.

My especial thanks go to Hilary Stonefrost, who has been a constant source of encouragement and support.

PREFACE

Nigel Lawson has been one of the most influential figures in British politics of the past ten years. First as the Financial Secretary to the Treasury in 1979–81, and subsequently as the longest-serving Chancellor of the Exchequer since the First World War, he played a central role in the formulation of British economic policy during the Thatcher decade.

Lawson was widely fêted by the Conservative Party after the June 1987 election victory – indeed, he was credited by many with having been the architect of that victory. When this was followed by the dramatic tax-reforming Budget of March 1988 (reducing the range of income-tax rates to two, and the top rate to 40 per cent) Lawson was hailed by some colleagues as 'the greatest Chancellor since Gladstone', and even tipped as a future leader of the Party.

That period from June 1987 to March 1988 contained the high points of Lawson's Chancellorship. From then on, things began to go wrong, with public disputes between the Prime Minister and her Chancellor, and the recall of Mrs Thatcher's most favoured economic adviser, Professor Sir Alan Walters, to Number 10 Downing Street. These political embarrassments reflected troubles on the economic front, as a rapid deterioration in inflation and the balance of payments led to a series of increases in interest rates aimed at cooling consumer demand and protecting the pound.

The aims of this book are to trace Nigel Lawson's influence on economic policy from 1979 onwards; to examine his diagnoses of the problems; and to understand why he took the actions he did. Lawson was a very powerful force in the Treasury when he was Financial Secretary: the decisions taken in economic policy at that time contributed in no small measure to the problems he faced later, when he made a commendable attempt at expansion.

His period of popular success as Chancellor was very brief: it was not until towards the end of 1986 that, with unemployment at last falling, and other indicators improving, economic conditions appeared sufficiently favourable for an election to be contemplated by the Conservatives with some confidence.

The consumer boom persisted long after the June 1987 election victory, and contributed to the subsequent problems with inflation and the balance of payments. But the seeds of the trouble were sown well before, in the de-industrialisation of the early 1980s, and the deregulation of the financial markets: the former adversely affected the 'supply side' of the British economy (offsetting the much-vaunted gains in productivity, or output per person); the cumulative effects of the latter were to produce a bigger and more sustained consumer boom than expected, and to frustrate efforts to control it.

The early chapters examine Lawson's views about the economy when he was working as a journalist, and in Opposition. An expansionist and a solid Keynesian in the 1960s, Lawson changed his allegiance from Edward Heath to Margaret Thatcher after the latter became leader of the Conservative Party in 1975, and later threw his energies into the newly fashionable economic doctrine of monetarism.

After disavowing Keynesianism and demand management, Lawson in office appeared to be on a continual search for simple 'rules' by which to run the economy. These rules varied from the pursuit of targets for various measures of the money supply, through an apparent obsession with the pursuit of a 'balanced budget', to a passionate campaign to put the pound into the exchange rate mechanism of the European Monetary System.

The quest for these successive rules involved impaling economic policy on a number of 'hooks'. The aim seemed to be to impress on the financial markets that this was a Government which declared its intentions and adhered to them, in contrast to its extremely pragmatic and flexible predecessors.

Yet in practice Lawson wanted flexibility, and spent a lot of time trusting to his own judgment rather than the monetary rules to which he paid lip-service.

Nigel Lawson emerges essentially as a pragmatist, responding to the way events and policies turn out, and happily discarding positions which had earlier been put forward as the economic gospel. Few of his statements are a good guide to his future actions; sometimes they contradict themselves relentlessly. He is always articulate at explaining the fundamentals of his policies, but as the underlying situation becomes more complex and subtle than expected, those fundamentals alter radically. Yet his confidence remains undiminished, and he moves on to a new enthusiasm.

The extent of the deflation caused by the 'primitive' monetarism of 1979–81 appears to have caught Lawson by surprise. The response was to rationalise by arguing that manufacturing industry did not matter that much, but also to modify the strict canons of the earlier policy. Later, when the extent of the consumer boom of the late 1980s (itself associated with the consequences of financial deregulation and the abandonment of monetarism) also took him by surprise, Lawson was only reluctantly pushed into taking countervailing measures.

The desire to offer a better monetary rule than the much-derided M3 was a factor which led him to pursue the goal of a fixed exchange rate within the EMS; but here the irresistible force of a Chancellor who dominated the Treasury came up against the immovable object of the Prime Minister herself.

One consistent theme of Nigel Lawson's since his journalistic days has been his belief in meritocracy and his opposition to anything smacking of egalitarianism. Another has been his associated opposition to incomes policy. As this book was being completed in July 1989, the course of earnings was raising questions about whether the United Kingdom's underlying wage inflation problems had been solved; and the main short-term preoccupation of economic policy was to hold the pound steady in order to ward off a devaluation which would make inflation worse. Another of Lawson's persistent themes – a bias in favour of lower public spending – had helped to produce a large Budget surplus; but the seriousness of the balance of payments position imposed severe constraints on the use of that surplus.

The conduct of economic policy in Britain has seldom been an easy matter, and there was certainly much disillusionment with the outcome of the economic policies of the 1970s. Mr Lawson and his colleagues came forward with great confidence to offer their solution. This book tries to address some serious questions about whether that confidence was justified.

ONE

Lawson the Expansionist

1956–72

Nigel Lawson was one of the star recruits to the *Financial Times* during the period of Sir Gordon Newton's editorship (1949–72). Newton had a policy of taking on one or two recent graduates a year (usually Oxbridge), as trainees. Among those recruited during the summer and autumn of 1956 when the country and Fleet Street were preoccupied with the Suez Crisis, were Nigel Lawson and Jock Bruce-Gardyne, both of whom went on to politics and became ministers in Mrs Thatcher's first Government of 1979–83.

The graduate intake into the *Financial Times* in the 1950s and 1960s seemed to divide into two camps: those who saw journalism as a career, and those who regarded it as a stepping-stone to the City, Parliament or even industry. The 'Class of '56' combined journalism and politics, sometimes alternating and sometimes simultaneously. But this was not necessarily out of choice. In practice journalism was a useful stop-gap when the slings and arrows of political misfortune were overwhelming. And, in Lawson's case, political ambition was something that developed: it was not obvious to his contemporaries either at Oxford or in those early days at the *Financial Times*. A colleague of Lawson's at the *Financial Times* in the late 1950s recalled: 'We seldom discussed our own political views, although I do remember Nigel once asking me over lunch which way I voted.'

The fact that Lawson studied economics and then went into financial journalism has led many Conservatives to describe him as the most technically qualified Chancellor since the war. This is the kind of sweeping judgment which Lawson himself, while happy to hear, might well dispute: Dalton, Gaitskell, Roy Jenkins – all were highly qualified. Perhaps the assertion is more true of the Conservative side – although Reginald Maudling was hardly economically illiterate either.

As for economic qualifications for the Chancellorship, Lawson himself loses few opportunities to deride economists, and experts in general. His 1956 joint-entrant to the staff of the *Financial Times*, now Lord Bruce-Gardyne, dates this contempt back to their first joint article, on the effects of the nationalisation of the Suez Canal by President Nasser. They were told by the Suez Canal Pilots' Association that the Egyptians would not be able to cope with running the canal, and the experiment would be over within days. 'Both of us emerged from that experience with a healthy scepticism about the advice of interested professionals,' Bruce-Gardyne has said.

Indeed, according to Lawson himself, his strong suit at Christ Church, Oxford, where he read Politics, Philosophy and Economics, was not economics, but philosophy. His particular interest in logic was a legacy of his principal interest at Westminster School, which had been mathematics. He once remarked, 'I knew that I would never be an outstanding mathematician. I knew I didn't have it in me.'[1] Harold Macmillan once said of his own education that, 'it helped you to tell when a chap was talking rot.' Lawson has said of his exposure to Linguistic Analysis at Oxford, 'it teaches you to think very logically and clearly, to listen carefully to what other people are saying and detect when they're talking nonsense.'[2] He got his First 'on the strength of my philosophy papers, not on my politics or economics, which just about passed muster, but no more.'[3]

Lawson would seem to have been almost uncharacteristically modest about his abilities as an economics student. He studied under Roy Harrod, a very distinguished Keynesian economist – indeed, the official biographer of Keynes. Harrod once commented that Lawson was the most brilliant pupil he had had; but Lawson himself, so often described as 'arrogant', attributes that 'over-generous remark' to the fact that he gave Harrod 'some help' with a new venture into philosophy.

Lawson has told many people that he learned more about the economy from his work at the *Financial Times*. 'I'm sure I wasn't the most brilliant economics pupil he ever had.'[4] Harrod's son Dominic (of the BBC) believes his late father was very generous with such remarks, and that there was a succession of former pupils who were told they were 'the most brilliant'.

While at Oxford, Lawson had thought of becoming a barrister, but did not take to either the company of lawyers or the food at Middle Temple dinners. He flirted with the idea of being a don, but decided the main attraction was Oxford itself, and that was not good enough. He tried the Foreign Office, did well in the exam but failed the 'country house' character interviews. This was a great blow, but would not surprise those – many – since then who have found him arrogant, difficult, prickly, pugnacious, private and moody. Those closer to him know that he is personally kind, witty, loyal and extremely good company, but acknowledge that his other reputation is not surprising, because he will, in the words of the journalist Christopher Fildes, 'cross the road to pick a fight'.

Lawson once told the story of how he had been sought out while at Oxford and interviewed by the British security services, with a view to a job. But Smiley's people were none too keen on his revelation that 'the living man I most admire would be Bertrand Russell', and from then on the interview was effectively over. 'In the silence that followed, the sense of astonishment and shock was palpable. I'm quite sure they had other good reasons for thinking me unsuitable . . .'[5]

Lawson's early interest and ability in economics may or may not have been remarkable, but there are some who have remarked on his early interest in financial matters. His friend Jock Bruce-Gardyne wrote, 'He has the chess-player's ability to see several moves ahead, and like the best poker player he relishes a gamble while at the same time calculating the odds.'[6] But Lawson himself has said, 'This poker thing has been greatly exaggerated. One of my lesser interests.'[7]

And his colleagues of the 1950s and 1960s recall that the budding Chancellor was always interested in money. He is credited with having inaugurated, as features editor, the *Financial Times*'s annual survey, 'The Cost of Living Around the World'. He also did a year as the principal writer of 'Lex', the investment column which concentrated mainly on developments in the City and individual companies, rather than on wider economic matters. In those days there were plenty of signs of Lawson's subsequent ability in politics almost to court unpopularity. As the *Financial Times*'s historian delicately puts it: 'Lawson, with his yellow waistcoat, green bow-tie and confident manner, had not been everyone's favourite person, but he had been an excellent features editor with a keen, open mind.'[8] (There was a theory in later years that, in seeing Lawson as a possible successor to himself, Gordon Newton, the editor, did not regard this unpopularity of Lawson's as, by any means, a disqualification for the job.)

Having made his mark within *Financial Times* circles, Lawson went on to make his journalistic presence felt in the outside world when he moved to the *Sunday Telegraph* in 1961. As City editor he was able to comment on the economy and develop his interest in specifically financial matters, including retaining the rising City financier Jim Slater to write a share-tipping column.

Lawson's *Sunday Telegraph* columns showed early indications of the gambles he was going to take later: there was an obsession with the need to introduce a value-added tax, which he appeared to regard as a panacea for the ills of the British economy; the risky, near-doubling of VAT in June 1979 was strongly advocated by Lawson.

Lawson covered a wide range of economic and financial matters in his *Sunday Telegraph* column: he wrote combatively, entertainingly and well. In those days, he was sometimes concerned and at other times dismissive about balance of payments deficits, which he has been sufficiently cavalier to dismiss as a 'problem of success' in the late 1980s, under his own Chancellorship. He also railed against high interest rates; but was prepared to tolerate them in the cause of an expansionary fiscal policy.

He was a great 'interventionist'. Thus on August 13th, 1961, he was castigating the then Chancellor Selwyn Lloyd's 'little Budget' as 'another dose of 7 per cent and all that' (7 per cent being a very high rate of interest in those days). He was urging 'export incentives' but noting despairingly, 'But any move in this direction will have to wait at least until next year's Budget. By that time heaven knows what our balance of payments position will be like. Whatever else happens, it is plain that something must be done to make the cost of money cheaper to the exporter, and done *now*.' He added: 'The obvious solution, to cut Bank Rate by 2 per cent . . . is so simple and so sensible that it can safely be considered a political impossibility.'

Lawson was also a great enthusiast for policies of economic growth. In March 1963 – when Reginald Maudling was Chancellor – he expressed the hope, in a pre-Budget article, that 'we may see the effective repudiation of stagnation (sometimes politely referred to as stability) as the prime aim of economic policy.' He added, in the true spirit of Keynes:

> Far too much is being made of the alleged lack of confidence (on the part of business and individuals alike) that is said to be at the root of our economic sluggishness . . . it is orders, not confidence, that business lacks. In fact, of course, the level of production is determined simply by the level of demand. And the management of the economy is more than just a confidence trick.[9]

His columns ranged from investment advice – more in the early days than later – through coverage of Common Market and GATT (trade) negotiations, to general economic advice for the Chancellors of the day – first Selwyn Lloyd, whom he castigated for his deflationary tendencies, and later Reginald Maudling, whose expansionist tendencies he encouraged. An investment column complimented investors as 'by and large a shrewd body of people' but added, 'if the market does have one weakness it is its susceptibility to fashion.'[10]

For a time his column was headlined 'Talking of Money', and returned frequently to the subject of stocks and shares. After capital gains tax (CGT) was introduced in 1962 Lawson showed an interest in ways of avoiding it – 'the determined speculator might well prefer to avoid stocks and shares altogether. Commodities – so it appears – only come into the gains tax net if they are commodities that are dealt with on a futures market. Where there is no futures market – in tea, for example, not to mention more exotic commodities such as rattlesnake skins – it seems as if you can speculate to your heart's content.'[11] (Lawson's father had been in the tea trade in the City of London, but it was his grandfather who was the 'great gambler' of the family.) In the context of speculation, Lawson enthused particularly about a book entitled *How I Made $2,000,000 in the Stock Market*, noting, when it comes to 'systems', the 'crucial incompleteness of the purely statistical approach.'[12]

Nigel Lawson has always been said by his colleagues to be a 'man of enthusiasms'. The attempt to get the British economy moving in the early 1960s led him many times, in an atmosphere where devaluation was not the done thing, to advocate various forms of export subsidy, most consistently a switch to value-added tax (VAT), with rebates available to exporters. One Sunday in 1961 found him advocating greater Government involvement in export finance, another proposing 'an invisibles export drive' to supplement the performance of visible exports.

Europe was an enthusiasm, and there are parallels with his advocacy of full entry of the pound into the European Monetary System's (EMS) exchange rate mechanism in 1988 as early as May 1961, when he wrote (at a time when our membership of the European Economic Community (EEC) itself was being debated):

> We can either wait and see how it develops . . . or we can join now, which would – this has to be faced – mean accepting the ultimate need for a common policy over a wide range of economic, fiscal and monetary matters to an extent that nobody can at present foresee. By taking this risk we would be able to exercise considerable influence over the particular type of common policies that emerge. By waiting and seeing we would lose this vital opportunity. This, basically, is the choice.[13]

The headline was 'To Plunge or Not to Plunge'.

The Sunday Telegraph period demonstrated an early preoccupation with the subject of taxation and tax reform. Ironically, in view of the inflationary effects both of the rise in VAT and the abolition of hire purchase controls by the Thatcher Government from 1979 onwards, the young Lawson was only too aware of the problems such moves could bring. Hire purchase controls had been abolished by the Conservatives in the late 1950s and reintroduced in the early 1960s, and Lawson wrote a spirited defence of h.p. controls as an economic weapon. 'It does nothing to change the cost-of-living index (unlike an increase in purchase tax which could lead to embarrassing wage claims), it takes no money out of the pockets of the public and – above all – it works and works fast. In short, this is an economic regulator which it would be sheer madness for any Government to eschew.'[14]

Lawson advocated making 'the dead hand of taxation at least *appear* less oppressive, particularly where incentive is most needed.'[15] He enthusiastically greeted the announcement in September 1962 that, under the Treasury's then rising star William Armstrong, there was going to be a study of *tax policy* – previously regarded as the jealous preserve of Inland Revenue.[16] In contrast to the position he was to adopt as Chancellor, Lawson was in those days in favour of allowing the Government 'more scope to use changes in tax to meet the most pressing economic needs of the day.'[17] He was fully in favour of the introduction by Selwyn Lloyd in 1961 of the 'regulator' – the power to vary indirect taxes by 10 per cent, upwards or downwards, at short notice. His pre-Budget advice to Lloyd in 1962 was 'to provide himself with even better regulators for the year ahead. These should include the power, not only to raise or lower purchase tax and excise duties by up to 10 per cent of the official rates, but also to raise or lower personal income tax by the same amount at any time during the year.'[18]

During his 1980s Chancellorship, Lawson was to show contempt for the previous consensus idea that tax policy should, if anything, be biased in favour of redistribution of income towards the poor. His views in the 1960s were apparent in a review of Professor Richard Titmuss's *Income Distribution and Social Change*: 'The author is evidently of the view that our society, as it progresses, ought to become steadily more equal (in terms of incomes). This seems highly questionable. It is when a commodity is scarce that rationing is most important. As a society becomes more affluent – and in particular as its poorest classes become richer – it surely becomes less and less important quite how rich the richest are.'[19]

In the early 1960s the future Chancellor saw tax policy so far as having been preoccupied with the Gladstonian task of raising revenue to cover expenditure, and the Keynesian one of varying Gladstonian principles in the interest of economic stabilisation. There was much else for it to do, he thought. There was 'the whole question of incentives – incentives to export or invest, incentives to save more or to work harder, and so on.' What, he asked, was the most effective form of tax incentive for business? Was it a cut in company taxation, or in high personal tax rates? He was even prepared to flirt with the possibility 'is it in fact an increase in personal tax to make people work harder to achieve a given standard of living?'[20]

When the enquiring journalist became the interested politician, he was not necessarily going to listen to those experts who told him that the incentive effect of lower marginal tax rates was difficult to discern. And he was certainly not going to show much concern for the effect of his 'incentive' policies on the plight of the poor.

Having advocated large tax cuts for Maudling's 1963 Budget, Lawson added:

> It may indeed be true that if the Chancellor does introduce the right kind of Budget for current conditions he may be forced to increase taxation in, say, a year's time. But there is nothing wrong with that.
>
> The kind of stop–go that is economically bad and politically damaging is an abrupt switch from 8 p.c. a year growth to stagnation. No-one minds a sharp touch of the brake to shift the economy from 5 p.c. growth to 4 p.c.[21]

There was also in this article an early indication of Lawson's regarding the trend of unemployment as important at least *politically*. 'On a purely political level, the polls show that it is not tax changes that influence votes, but the direction of the trend of unemployment.'

A headline on another of Lawson's pre-Budget articles of 1963 asked: 'Must Sterling Spoil the Budget?' The article itself was a remarkable signal of attitudes he was to adopt during his Chancellorship, when for a time he tied the value of the pound unofficially to the West German D-Mark – against the wishes of Mrs Thatcher. He wrote: 'Devaluation talk has been rife ever since the breakdown of the Common Market negotiations: it was widely – and, I believe, correctly – held that inside the Community sterling would have been stronger.'[22]

He continued: 'To this have been added further fears: of an expansionist Budget on April 3 leading to a balance of payments crisis in the autumn, and beyond that of the election of a Labour Government.'

The 'Lawson Boom' of the late 1980s invites comparisons with the 'Maudling Boom' of 1963–64, which ultimately became a source of embarrassment to the Conservatives – and not only the Conservatives: the balance of payments position inherited by Harold Wilson's Labour administrations of 1964–70 was to dominate economic policy for years to come. But just as Lawson was to dismiss concerns about the balance of payments in 1988 and 1989, so we see him in March 1963 urging Maudling on, and regarding the balance of payments as something that can easily be financed.

The young *Sunday Telegraph* commentator may have been more right about the justification of Maudling's dash for growth, however, than about his own subsequent effort: the eventual balance of payments deficit then amounted to only 1 per cent of gross domestic product, whereas the 1988 deficit was over 3 per cent. At all events, we find him quite relaxed about the prospect in 1963:

> Let's assume the very worst possible outcome: a really huge jumbo-sized run on the £ of as much as £1,000 million – more than half as bad again as in 1961. The bulk of this would of necessity return once confidence recovered – as it did in 1961 – and in the meantime there would be no need for panic action of any kind. For on top of our published reserves of £965 million (and reserves are there to be used) we can rely on some £500 million of short-term aid from foreign central banks.

After reference to other sources of borrowing, including the International Monetary Fund (IMF), he added, 'So there is no question whatever of Britain being forced to devalue – any devaluation would have to be a deliberate act of policy.'[23]

Lawson also offered a wise assessment of the willingness of other countries to provide temporary support, because they did not want us to devalue either. This was especially so of the Americans, who feared that trouble for the dollar would follow.

All this was by way of further advice to Maudling on the 1963 Budget, and he concluded with 'a simple four-point outline . . . one that will expand the economy and at the same time strengthen sterling.' The Budget must be 'dramatically growth-orientated . . . and this means large tax cuts.' The tax cuts must be presented 'as a determinedly expansionist fiscal policy' combined with high interest rates – or what were high at the time – 'Bank Rate to be raised to 5 p.c. to attract foreign money.' Higher interest rates would not be accompanied by credit controls. 'There would, of course, be no credit squeeze, and as an earnest of this the joint-stock banks should be allowed to reduce their liquidity ratios from 30 to 25 p.c.'[24]

The Maudling April 1963 Budget did include expansionist tax cuts, both in purchase tax (the precursor of VAT on consumer spending) and income tax. Lawson, while offering 'two cheers for Maudling', impatiently complained that the expansion was delayed until July, when the income tax cuts were due. For some reason he did not see the immediate purchase tax cuts as reflationary at all – 'the great need is for a boost for the economy *now*' he wrote, 'not in three months' time.' Again showing a pointer to the future, he was disappointed that the cuts in income tax, when they came, would take the form of higher allowances rather than cuts in what was then called the 'standard rate'. Maudling was castigated by his 'two cheers' supporter for seeming to have 'an innate distrust of the tinsel and showmanship of the public platform.' In this context Lawson complained that Maudling was the 'sort of man who would rally the troops on the eve of Agincourt with a dissertation on the need to apply an incomes policy to the armed forces.'[25]

Lawson's passion for the grand gesture was apparent in his conclusion that 'temperamentally Mr Maudling has shown himself addicted to gradualism. But there can be no doubt that the right way to manage the economy is to give the maximum away when spare capacity is at a maximum. And that means now.'[26]

The Maudling Budget had been introduced against the background of the early 'indicative planning' exercises by the Government in concert with the National Economic Development Council (NEDC), containing representatives of employers and trades unions. The general feeling was that Maudling wished to secure the co-operation of the unions over incomes, in order to help the quest for more rapid growth. Lawson was sceptical about incomes policies, saying, 'If Ned's whole growth programme is to be taken as realistic and not simply as a Utopian aspiration, it must convince by its relevance to an economy without a working incomes policy. This, after all, is the situation with which the Treasury has to contend.'[27] ('Ned' was an early nickname for the National Economic Development Office (NEDO) and Council, succeeded by 'Neddy'.)

Lawson pin-pointed a conflict between the Treasury's short-term objectives of policy and the National Economic Development Office's long-term growth projections of 4 per cent a year. We see here an early indication of Lawson's interest in a year-by-year target for the economy: 'It is vital that, as the French planners do, Ned now "breaks down" its five year growth programme into a yearly scheme of targets and objectives. Only if this is done can it hope to have any real influence on public opinion. A report on economic growth, not for 1961–66, but for 1963–64, is vital if Ned is to continue as a meaningful body.'[28]

The Lawsonian Medium-Term Financial Strategy of 1980 onwards was to have year-by-year targets. But these were to be in terms of financial objectives, such as the money supply, and the public sector borrowing requirement (PSBR). And the emphasis was to be on contraction first, after which it was assumed that expansion would follow. But in the 1980s there was to be less precision from Lawson about year-by-year growth targets for the economy than in the 1960s.

Not only was the Lawson of the early 1960s expansion-minded: he was also prepared to throw cost considerations to the winds in the interest of the greater objective. Thus 'if the Pilkington Committee's objective of higher quality commercial television is to be realised the last thing the Government wants is to encourage the programme contractors to cut their costs. They should be spending more money on programmes, not less.'[29] In order to achieve the chosen objective of reductions in the public sector borrowing requirement, Lawson would later throw his weight behind all manner of 'cost conscious' decisions which, by the same logic, would lead to lower quality.

The thirty-one-year-old Lawson was already keen on stirring up competition between the banks, and also on a more competitive attitude on the part of the building societies. He felt they did not compete enough for deposits, and if this meant higher interest rates for depositors – which in turn would cause higher lending rates – did that matter? Why should he pay only half a per cent more for his overdraft than ICI? 'Lack of competition has led to lack of flexibility . . . either I am paying too little or ICI too much.'[30]

Anyway, real interest rates were not too bad, because of the effect of 'money illusion': 'the equilibrium level of interest rates at a time of rising prices is never quite as high as it would be if we were hard-headed enough only to pay attention to the "real" rate.' This was why 'I would not wish to see completely stable prices, still less – *pace* Mr Maudling – falling prices.' Indeed, Lawson fancied that his objective of a more competitive banking system, involving higher interest rates to attract deposits, could be achieved, thanks to 'money illusion', without raising real lending rates 'as much as they would have to if prices were completely stable'.[31]

This was followed by a statement of Lawson's views on inflation which echoed those of many economists at the time, to the effect that, thanks to 'money illusion', a little inflation was no bad thing – indeed a help to growth. 'This is why a mild annual rate of increase in prices is such an effective stimulus to economic growth – and why falling prices would bring much nearer the danger of recession.'

However, his bias in favour of a small degree of inflation was not merely economic: 'The great social justification, to my mind, for a mildly inflationary economy is that a society in which borrowers do better than lenders of money is fundamentally more attractive than one in which the reverse is true.'[32] To anyone who took Lawson seriously in this belief, his relaxed attitude in practice to the inflation rate of 3½ to 4 per cent he inherited from Sir Geoffrey Howe some twenty years later was all the more understandable – whatever he actually chose to say about his objectives for 'zero inflation' when in office.

Another 1963 gem was an attack on the method of measuring the public sector borrowing requirement. Until the 1960s, the Budget accounts had been divided into current expenditure ('above the line') and capital expenditure ('below the line'). On the Conservative administration's proposal to scrap this dividing line, Lawson said: 'The Government's proposal is utterly misconceived. Lumping Government current account and capital account transactions together, and then on top of this to add loans to the nationalised industries to produce one jumbo-sized borrowing requirement, will be enough to scare the daylights out of every Swiss banker and inhibit all future Chancellors from taking adequate expansionary measures when these are needed.'[33]

There was much General Election talk during 1963. Lawson from time to time diverted himself from the economy itself to advising his readers on the stock market (more specific advice was given elsewhere in the section he edited).

Having noted that share prices had not fallen at all after the Labour victory of 1945 he was still sure that 'wild Socialist talk' could have an unsettling effect on the stock market in the run-up to the 1964 General Election. His gambling instinct appeared in the advice: 'I am equally confident that the prospective rise in equities if the Government wins is markedly greater than the likely fall on expectations of a Labour victory. This is no time to sell equities. It is a time to buy.'[34] More cautious temperaments might have recommended 'hold'!

Lawson's fear was that a Government led by Harold Wilson might not be sufficiently growth-conscious: 'Paradoxically, the greatest danger may be a Wilson government's lack of economic radicalism and desire to appear internationally respectable by pursuing unduly cautious economic policies.'[35] In July, Lawson was worrying that, 'It does not look as if the economy has really been recovering all that rapidly over the past three months.'[36] And he continually made reference to the association between the political popularity of the Government and the unemployment figures – unemployment had risen from 1 per cent in mid-1961 to 3½ per cent in the first quarter of 1963, and Labour had been in the lead in the opinion polls since the second half of 1961. But unemployment was now falling, and more rapid growth in prospect.

In August, Lawson was in confident form, noting that, 'According to the independent National Institute of Economic and Social Research – few of whose members can ever in their lives have voted Conservative, so it can scarcely be Conservative propaganda – output over the next 12 months is likely to rise by between 4 and 5 per cent.' He observed that, 'Expansionary policies bring about expansion.' But the improvement in the short-term outlook left fundamental problems unsolved – including 'the long-term course of exports, the regional problem, agriculture, the need for widespread reform of the tax system, the meaning of Tory planning, and – on a broader canvas – the world liquidity dilemma.'[37]

The future Chancellor was by now on his way to other things. He was about to join the 'war effort', leaving the *Sunday Telegraph* after a lively two-and-a-half-year stint, to move on to Conservative Central Office, which was already gearing itself up for the General Election – not yet announced – of 1964. Among his closing pieces there was a sceptical view of incomes policy, a subject which had come up at the Trades Union Congress in Brighton in September 1963. The TUC, encouraged by Maudling and the NEDC, had been discussing wage restraint. Lawson pointed out that nobody would have dreamed a year or two earlier that the TUC would come to discuss the pros and cons of wage restraint. After acknowledging that there might be *some* impact, in this new climate, on the rate of growth of wages, Lawson put down a firm marker for the future of his views on this subject: 'Brighton has made it clear that the prospect of an agreed incomes policy in the sense of a precise formula linking wages with prices, profits or whatever, or more generally as part of a package deal hammered out between the Chancellor of the Exchequer and the General Secretary of the TUC within the framework of Ned, is as remote as the moon. And I suspect that this is true whatever Government may be in power.'[38]

He believed that the TUC itself could not make such policies 'stick' with individual unions, and the leaders of the latter could not do so with the rank and file. During the years between his fairly definite conclusions on the subject in 1963 and his arrival in Government in 1979, there were to be sporadic efforts by both major political parties to make incomes policies work. They were also to have rather more impact than Lawson expected, at least for short periods. But the handling, or mishandling, of incomes policy by the Labour Prime Minister James Callaghan and his Chancellor Denis Healey in the late 1970s was going to allow Lawson as an Opposition Treasury spokesman scope to attack. His would be an influential voice deriding the concept of incomes policies; and the failure of the Thatcher Government to get to grips with wage inflation would return to haunt him as Chancellor in the late 1980s.

His objections to incomes policies have always been deep-seated. Even when welcoming the fact that 'planning has ceased to be a dirty word' (in the context of NEDC in early 1962)[39] he disliked incomes policies partly because he strongly objected to the possible damage to business from such a quid pro quo as restraint on profits or dividends, and partly because restraint on wages and salaries might affect something he has always believed in, 'incentives'. He disliked the idea of 'ascetic self-restraint'. The way to keep the growth of incomes and profits 'as far as possible' in step with the growth of productivity was 'through fiscal action by the Government on the *overall* level of incomes and profits.'[40]

Lawson has always seen the imposition of wage restraint as a threat to freedom. While the Treasury was describing incomes policy as mere 'common sense' in the early 1960s, he was saying 'it involves a degree of Government control that no free society has yet been prepared to accept'.[41] He saw the Neddy mechanism as having a possible use in spotting potentially inflationary labour shortages:

> Forget about your wages policy, Mr Lloyd. The type of planning we need in Britain is not what is generally thought of as planning at all. It is the co-ordination of the various expansion plans and projections that each company at present undertakes on its own behalf, under the common stimulus of a rate of growth of incomes (in real terms) greater than we have hitherto been accustomed to in this country.[42]

Lawson's formative views on the desirability of growth-orientated policies, and the undesirability of incomes policies, were intimately linked. In attacking the then fashionable view of Professor Frank Paish of the London School of Economics that there should be a sizeable margin of unused resources (sizeable, in those days, meant 2½ per cent unemployment as opposed to 1½ per cent) to keep inflation under control, he said this amounted to 'nothing more than a positive incentive *not* to modernise and *not* to invest, with all that that implies'.[43]

Another valedictory message from Lawson to his *Sunday Telegraph* readers reminded them of his fundamental belief in taking risks on the side of economic growth. 'I am willing to bet that it will not be long before someone, somewhere, solemnly warns Mr Maudling that the economy is going ahead too fast, and that he should start putting the brakes on now if he wants to avoid the débâcle that followed the late 1959 boom. It is, therefore, important to be quite clear why this would be palpably wrong advice . . .'[44]

Essentially, Lawson subscribed to an opinion, fairly common among Keynesian economists at the time, that, from the point of view of combating inflation, the faster the growth, the more easily wage increases could be absorbed, and the lower the actual rise in costs per unit of output. He wrote, 'The smaller the increase in production the harder it is to keep wage increases within it' and, 'The only justification for having an incomes policy at all is that, as a means of reducing the rate of wage increase, it is in theory preferable to the alternative method of restricting demand. To hold back demand, therefore, in order to try and make an incomes policy effective, is to defeat the whole object of the policy itself. I am not sure that Mr Lloyd ever fully realised this.' This was in July 1962, when Lloyd had just been replaced by the more expansion-minded Maudling, whom Lawson was continually egging on to be even more expansionist.[45] (It was in this article that Lawson coined a phrase much quoted ever since: of the Treasury over the previous seven years he said: 'Its actions fall neatly into four categories: too little, too late, and too much, too late.')

A characteristic headline on one of Lawson's many 'growth-orientated' articles of the time stated: '"Safety First" Can Be Dangerous'. He told Maudling, 'It is never safe, there are always risks to be taken; and unless these risks are run, the ultimate price to be paid will be far higher.'[46] He preferred driving fast towards a dangerous corner knowing that you could apply your brakes to driving at a pace appropriate to a vehicle with no brakes at all.

During his years in office Lawson was going to show considerable contempt for the vestiges of the 1960s planning efforts: indeed, if his voice alone had been listened to, the National Economic Development Office would almost certainly have been abolished. But this was one area in which the diffident Sir Geoffrey Howe, as Chancellor, overruled his ebullient Financial Secretary. One of Lawson's closing articles for the *Sunday Telegraph* manifested his general distaste for allowing the trades unions any say in Neddy-type planning, but showed qualified support for 'contractual' planning efforts, which were not made 'clandestinely', between Government and industry. In France, for instance, in return for certain incentives, industries would try to meet Government export targets.[47]

In so far as the inclusion of the trades unions in Neddy discussions was aimed at securing their co-operation in reducing wage inflation, Lawson thought the position was hopeless. There was not even a way in which their co-operation could somehow be 'traded' for economic growth, because the Government was committed to aiming at faster economic growth anyway, 'not so much by its own pledges, which are usually evasive, as by the fact that public opinion now demands growth.'[48]

The aim in those days was to raise the average growth rate from 3 to 4 per cent a year. In a reference to one of the leading trades union leaders of the day, Lawson said: 'It is doubtful if Mr Cousins has stopped to work out the compound interest implications of this over a long period, or the difference in real national wealth that these two arid percentages conceal.'[49] Others concluded that difficulties with the unions over incomes were a blow to many who supported 'planning for faster growth'. But, showing characteristic resilience, Lawson himself bounced back with the discovery that a distinctive feature of French planning efforts, much admired on this side of the Channel at the time, 'has been the total absence of any incomes policy and the degree to which organised labour has been excluded from the planning process altogether'.[50]

During his stint at the *Sunday Telegraph* Lawson also dropped one or two clues to his broader philosophical approach. He attached importance to economic matters in shaping both politics and history. He once wrote: 'We are all good Marxists now in the City. The great teaching of Karl Marx, you will recall, was that history is determined by economic forces. The fact that he misunderstood the economic forces, although unfortunate, should not be allowed to detract from this important discovery.'[51] And, in a review of a book by Michael Shanks, then industrial editor of the *Financial Times*, *'The Stagnant Society'*, Lawson expressed sympathy with Shanks's diagnosis that, in Lawson's words, 'the problem . . . is to be found in the complacent traditionalism, the well-fed sloth, the effeteness and lack of dynamism that characterises so much of Britain today.'[52]

But he concluded that sensible proposals for reform were not enough. In Germany the impetus had come from the shock of military defeat, in France from 'the collapse of a worn out democratic system combined with the inspiration of the ideal of European unity.' Even in the United States, according to Lawson, the 'shock of the Soviet sputniks' had led to the dynamism of President Kennedy. 'What national traumatic experience have *we* to undergo?' he asked.[53]

His final article for the *Sunday Telegraph* as City editor appeared in October 1963. Lawson was now off to Conservative Central Office to help research and write the Conservative Leader's economic speeches, but was already speculating publicly about the arrival of a Labour Government and the fate of its Chancellor. 'The Chancellor of the Exchequer entered the Cabinet Room. The poor man had been having a bad time. No longer a member of the Cabinet . . . he battled on bravely. "Our balance of payments is precarious, our reserves are running out, and sterling is steadily weakening," he cried.' This was part of a fantasy headed 'Alice in Downing Street'; the effect of the reality of 'Margaret in Downing Street' was to be felt some years later.[54]

The appointment within Central Office had been arranged by Lord Poole, joint chairman of the Conservative Party, the idea having been to beef up Macmillan's speeches on the economy. Harold Macmillan underwent a prostate operation and resigned the premiership; and Lord Poole also resigned. Sir Alec Douglas-Home honoured the arrangement (he had once confessed not to understand the economy at all, and to working it out with match-sticks), and Lawson developed a considerable respect for him, whom he admired as 'the perfect gentleman'. The move was a characteristic Lawson gamble: the announcement in the *Sunday Telegraph* stated: 'The appointment is a temporary one and will terminate after the General Election' and Lawson gave way to his successor, Kenneth Fleet. It was a 'characteristic' gamble, because, in terms of his friend Jock Bruce-Gardyne's assessment of a man who was always calculating the odds, Lawson would have had a reasonable expectation of an invitation back to the *Financial Times* if he did not like what he saw of politics in close-up.

Malcolm Rutherford of the *Financial Times* has pointed out: 'In those days political advisers, for that is what he became, were less in evidence than they are today. It was regarded as slightly indecent for an outsider to have the Prime Minister's ear and the relationship was somewhat surreptitious.' Lawson was officially based at Central Office in Smith Square, but, as Rutherford says, 'At one stage Lawson had a room in Number 12 Downing Street but could enter Sir Alec's office only by underground passage. Most of the rest of their exchanges took place while the Prime Minister was travelling, away from officials.'[55]

The director of the Conservative Research Department has recalled visits from Lawson during this time when 'looking like Napoleon in his youth [he would] march up and down the room, concentrating, telling me how everything ought to be done, firing words in bursts like a machine gun, with considerable pauses for ums and ahs as he thought out how he felt that morning, whether he thought I was being stupid, whether everyone else was being stupid . . . it started the day on a positive note – even if a bit late!'[56]

Lawson made a mark during this period. Quite apart from the industry and spirit he applied to speech-writing, he was considered to have made a major contribution to the 'war effort'. He was credited by the *Sunday Times* with having had a hand in the decision to delay the Election until the autumn of 1964, rather than the spring, on the grounds that the economy would be looking better. The result, a very narrow majority for Labour instead of the landslide many Tories had feared, seemed to justify the delay. Whatever the extent of Lawson's influence, the experience of close exposure to the inner workings of the Conservative Party certainly gave him a taste for the political life, a taste which came to him relatively late: unlike so many of his eventual colleagues in Cabinet, he had eschewed politics at Oxford, preferring to appear in undergraduate revues. Colleagues from the mid-1960s recall that he had a desire to rise fast, once smitten with the political bug. It was a case of more haste, less speed, however: in 1964 after his period working for Home he declined the directorship of the Conservative Research Department; and the impatient prospective Chancellor had no truck with the idea of earning his spurs going through the motions of contesting a safe Labour seat. The impression that he was an arrogant young man in too much of a hurry did not appeal to a succession of constituency parties, which turned him down. He apparently felt he had enough experience in this regard to warrant a book (which he never wrote) on the lines, 'The Life and Times of a Rejected Tory Candidate'.

While thus learning the hard way, Lawson was able to think aloud about his economic and political philosophy in first the *Financial Times* (to whose columns he returned as a weekly 'independent' contributor during 1965) and then in the *Spectator*, which he edited for nearly four and a half years from the beginning of 1966.

Like his earlier *Sunday Telegraph* columns, the 1965 *Financial Times* articles included continual pleas for faster economic growth and more expansionist economic policies. Since these were the days of Harold Wilson's first Government, the 'National Plan' and talk of 'the white heat of the technological revolution', such pleas were not exactly falling on deaf ears. But the eyes of the Government were, in Lawson's view, blinkered by the refusal to take one of the principal measures which would assist faster economic growth, namely the devaluation of the pound. Lawson rightly saw the refusal to devalue as a desire to please the Americans.

An early column, 'The Myth of Internationalism', praised the French President General de Gaulle for seeing that 'the only meaningful political entity is the nation state', castigated the British for paying more attention to the international role of sterling than to national self-interest, and described the 'now sadly one-sided *special* relationship with the United States' as 'the Custer's Last Stand of the atlanticist internationalists'.[57] Much fuss had been made about the way the Americans had helped to prop up the pound, but that was only because they did not want attention to switch to the dollar, he wrote in another article.

Just before the spring 1965 Budget, Lawson told his *Financial Times* readers that this was 'No time for deflation', and took the opportunity to aver his belief in managing demand in the economy – a belief he was to abandon, for a time, as Financial Secretary, nearly twenty years later. 'No one,' he then wrote, '(except, perhaps, Mr Enoch Powell) is opposed to the regulation of the economy . . . what has gone awry so often in the past is that the timing has been all wrong . . .' Deflating home demand on its own could only 'buy time' through a 'once for all' reduction in imports, 'it cannot put our balance of payments right.'[58]

Apart from backing the idea of a quick 'freeze' on incomes to assist a devaluation to work, Lawson continued to develop his deep-seated opposition to the basic concept of incomes policies. It was not so much that incomes and costs were out of line with other countries as that productivity was too low. To improve productivity one needed the product differentiation, improved design and technical advance that went with 'a dynamic, expanding economy'. Indeed, he preferred a policy which would be 'concerned solely with productivity "on the ground" and which welcomes exorbitant wage increases if they secure genuine increases in productivity . . . The goal of economic policy must be the achievement of a high wage, high productivity economy.'[59]

Time and time again, during his journalistic days, Lawson made strong pro-European noises. He was contemptuous of schemes of 'association' with the EEC – 'There is no halfway house to Europe. We are either in the Common Market; or we are out of it . . . European unity is not a first step to anything. It is an end in itself.'[60]

If there was a choice between America and Europe, Britain had to choose Europe. The 'transatlantic umbilical cord' had led the Government to support America's 'highly dubious' Vietnam policy, and to accept 'a cripplingly expensive military role East of Suez.' The time had come to sever the cord. But, from the point of view of Conservative policy formulation, it was convenient that the present (Labour) Government had taken over the 'special relationship', East of Suez, and incomes policy, which had hamstrung the previous Government. 'This is particularly fortunate for the Conservatives, who instead of being left holding three unwanted babies have found a willing adoption society in the most unlikely – but useful – place.'[61]

Lawson thought the conventional 'Left–Right' dichotomy was, in regard to the great economic issues of the day, such as economic growth and the Common Market, 'utterly meaningless'. Oppositions, he wrote, won elections not by the persuasiveness of their policies but by the failures of the Government's. 'A wise Opposition, therefore, waits until it has become clear where the Government's major failures lie, and then exploits them for all it is worth.'[62]

As far as he was concerned, there was not 'a single ideological spectrum ranging from extreme Right to extreme Left': the parties divided 'on a mixture of historical, sociological, psychological, emotional and intellectual grounds.'[63]

Lawson was especially contemptuous of calls for 'a move to the Right'. He said: 'At the present time, those advocating a move to the Right are likely to mean one of at least three totally distinct (and indeed contradictory) directions: the liberal Right of the *laissez-faire* Powellites, the illiberal Right of the anti-black, anti-satire brigade [he had made *Private Eye on London* his "book of the year" at the *Sunday Telegraph*], and the traditional Right of the protectors of sacred cows . . . none of these extremes is capable of uniting the Tory Party, let alone the nation.' He firmly rejected the idea of 'careering off in this wild direction'.[64]

The future architect of Conservative monetarism was scathing about that early Tory monetarist, Enoch Powell. 'The basis of the economic doctrine of

Powellism is that the role of Government should be confined to promoting competition and preventing inflation,' he noted. Then, having pointed out that these propositions were not actually connected, 'It is perfectly possible (at least, in theory) to have untrammelled, *laissez-faire* capitalism without price stability or the other way about.' Lawson then stated, 'It is a pity that Mr Powell so uncompromisingly prefers price stability to expansion and full employment and it is also rather strange.'[65] (Lawson had in an earlier *Financial Times* piece said he believed high unemployment was not desirable in itself, and political suicide anyway. He was also to describe it as an 'evil'.)

Lawson added that it was the people themselves who preferred a rising standard of living and full employment to stable prices 'and it is Mr Powell, the arch-priest of the democracy of the market-place, who presumes to tell them that they are wrong. It would be interesting, too, to know how much unemployment Mr Powell – if he were Chancellor – would tolerate in order to achieve price stability by the method he advocates: the deflation of monetary demand.'[66]

The future 'non-interventionist' Chancellor also attacked Powell's view that 'regional subsidies' were a distortion of the natural workings of the market-place. Not only was life more complicated than assumed by Powell – people might prefer to remain in Scotland even if there was more work in the South-East – but also the 'social costs', in congestion, of allowing industry to be concentrated in the Midlands or South-East were plain. He complained later of 'the valuable physical capital that is wasted in declining areas.'[67]

Nor was Lawson in those days noticeably fierce about public spending. In an article 'Could the Conservatives Really Cut Taxes?' he noted that, in that period (before the introduction of VAT), the principal effect of inflation on taxation was to reduce the burden of indirect tax and increase that of direct taxes – 'a wholly undesirable combination.' Cutting taxes hinged on reducing the percentage of gross national product (GNP) taken in public spending, but 'this is a good deal easier said than done . . . so much of public spending is on what must surely be the growth "industries" of the second half of the 20th century – roads, because there are more cars; pensions, because there are more old people; education; housing; and so on – that to hold back its growth . . . would be perverse and wrong.'[68]

Here, writing in October 1965, Lawson had remarkable foresight about one route to reducing public spending that was to be taken under his Chancellorship after 1983 – 'gradually to remove as much as possible from the public sector to the private, as the Tories did with housing in 1951–64.'[69] The word 'privatisation' had not yet been coined; nor, it seems, had it then entered

Lawson's mind that wilful neglect of the public sector, by curtailing its growth, was desirable in itself. Yet the Thatcher administration, under his Chancellorship, was to do both.

One curiosity of the mid-1960s-Lawson was his open avowal of the desirability of low interest rates – a proclivity he was to display, but without much success, during his much-publicised battles with Number 10 Downing Street in years to come. 'If the Tories ever allow themselves to become the bankers' party they are lost,' he wrote in May 1965. 'The Conservatives must be on the side of the borrowers not just because there are more of them, but because economic growth depends on it.'[70]

On what he called 'the social counterpart of an efficient, free economy' Lawson does not appear to have wavered much over the years. He saw Labour as egalitarian and the Conservatives as believers in a hierarchical society – 'a difference that will, I believe, increasingly come to be seen at the heart of the political debate.'[71] Although Labour had successfully presented itself as being both egalitarian and the party of the meritocracy, there was a fundamental conflict here. 'My own belief is that Britain cannot afford an egalitarian society, and that very few people want it anyway.'[72] In fact, in the 1960s, when many Tories were flirting with ideas of further redistribution of income towards the less well off, Lawson was already unashamedly a meritocrat, indeed a 'Thatcherite', in arguing 'for free economy to work efficiently, the incentives and rewards for success at all levels *need to be heightened and not eroded.*'[73] (My italics.) This was asserted rather than argued: there was no suggestion that perhaps the ambitious would prosper without the need for extra rewards. But Lawson was remarkably prophetic of what would eventually prove politically tolerable in the 1980s. 'If [the Conservatives] . . . can demonstrate that it is more natural to graft the meritocracy on to the traditional order than to make it adjust to an egalitarian society, if they can convince the new men that the Conservative Party believes in an open and not a closed hierarchy, then – and only then – the future is theirs.'[74]

On trades unions Lawson's libertarian and economic views merged in a way consistent with what we have seen so far: where individual members of the work force were victimised, this was a simple matter of human rights which had to be sorted out. He was much more concerned about strikes over restrictive practices than over wage claims – 'It is not excessive wage claims, but resistance to new techniques, that damages the nation most.'[75] And he was by no means one-sided in his attribution of blame: 'Ultimate responsibility in industry, whether for efficiency, industrial relations, or whatever, lies fairly and squarely with management. The most outrageous restrictive union practices have only grown up because management – past or present – has allowed them to.' He put the emphasis not on weakening unions, and making life easier for bad management, but on removing the obstacles to good management.[76]

Attacking the Confederation of British Industry for supporting incomes policy, he said 'it failed to realise that, while the avoidance of inflation is primarily the responsibility of the Government, the pursuit of greater productivity is primarily the responsibility of industry.'[77] (For good measure, Lawson at about the same time praised the Transport Workers' leader and Labour Cabinet Member Frank Cousins because 'although often muddled, he genuinely believes in increasing productivity and in the advance of technology'.)[78]

Lawson was fundamentally Keynesian in his *Sunday Telegraph/Financial Times* days. He shared the consensus view that 'the real point at issue . . . is simply this: to what extent, in what way, and for what purpose should the State intervene in the working of the economy?'[79] He took for granted, as generally agreed by all parties, 'that the State should intervene to maintain full employment, prevent undue inflation, preserve the exchange rate, and generally iron out, so far as possible, the fluctuations in the trade cycle.' Indeed, he added, 'nor is there a fundamental dispute about how this is to be done.'[80] He also believed the State should 'intervene actively' to promote economic growth, whether by 'substantial investment incentives' (tax incentives were important in order to bring self-interest into line with national interest) or through export subsidies. Lawson cited the practice of Dr Erhard in West Germany between 1951 and 1955 in this latter regard.[81]

Lawson's constant themes in 1965 were therefore the need for faster growth, and the urgency of removing such impediments to this goal as too high an exchange rate, and excessive commitments overseas. As for incomes policies, wages and salaries accounted for three-quarters of the costs of British goods, and the most that could be hoped from such policies was that 1 per cent a year would be lopped off the growth of incomes – 'It would take at least 13 years of continuous success with incomes policy to achieve the same effect as a 10 per cent devaluation would have overnight.'[82]

Time and time again, Lawson advocated devaluation as the solution to the British balance of payments problem. If there was a country Britain should emulate, it was France, which had shown that 'while posturing on the world stage is the quickest road to national bankruptcy, policies of economic and political realism, so far from forcing a great nation to turn its back on the world, can lead to greater opportunities for influence, eminence and genuine prestige in international affairs than we have known for many a year.'[83] If there was a man he would like to emulate, an early hint was that he admired

'Dr Erhard, the chief apostle and most successful practitioner of the free market in Europe' – he also noted that Erhard 'claims to have invented the art of psychological economics.'[84]

Although Lawson spent the early part of his career writing about the news rather than making it, he did manage to get into the headlines himself over a mortgage deal in 1966 in a way which people were to recall in 1988 and 1989, when the main plank of his monetary policy was a series of increases in mortgage rates. The episode took place during the tail-end of this period as the *Financial Times*'s 'independent contributor', when it was already known that he had been selected to succeed a leading Conservative politician, Iain Macleod, as editor of the *Spectator* in January 1966. Having advertised his house in Markham Street, Chelsea, for sale at just under £20,000, he applied for a mortgage of £20,000 from Kensington and Chelsea Council in order to buy a larger house in Hyde Park Gate. £20,000 in those days was equivalent to well over £100,000 during his 1980s Chancellorship, and at the time the well-heeled Lawson was married to the even better heeled Vanessa Salmon, of the J. Lyons family. The idea of such a person receiving such a loan from the local council on such a house caused a minor political scandal, and associated Lawson's name with mortgages in the public mind. He took the opportunity to defend himself in characteristically vigorous fashion in the 'Notebook' column of the first *Spectator* he edited, in January 1966. 'I used the public sector only because the private sector, in the shape of our Victorian and only semi-commercial building society movement, is (to coin a phrase) failing the nation,' he said.[85]

Lawson had applied for the loan shortly before the then Chancellor, James Callaghan, had advised local authorities to cut spending. And Labour minority members of the Kensington and Chelsea Council, which approved the loan, complained that more deserving cases would not receive loans as a result. In a riposte to Labour members who maintained that the favourable rate of interest on local authority loans was for those who would otherwise be unable to borrow, Lawson said: 'Making a commercial, unsubsidised, mortgage loan, so far from costing the Council anything, actually makes a profit for the often hard-pressed ratepayers.' He added, in a remark that made interesting re-reading during the period of 13-per-cent-plus mortgages under his later Chancellorship: 'It's news to me that the Labour Party now regards 6 per cent as a "favourable rate".'[86]

Lawson edited the *Spectator* for over four years, first under the proprietorship of Sir Ian Gilmour, and later of Harry Creighton. It was always a lively read under his editorship, with many distinguished names writing. Apart from the 'Notebook', which he wrote for quite a long time, he did not produce many signed articles. But he wrote most of the leading articles, in which he campaigned long and hard for a devaluation of the pound (which came in November 1967), for measures to ensure that the devaluation 'worked' – that is to say, that sufficient restrictions were placed on domestic demand in the economy to make room for exports (or import-saving) in order to correct the balance of payments – and for Britain's entry into the European Community. It is noteworthy that he championed many liberal causes, including the kind of reforms instituted by Roy Jenkins as Home Secretary which were to be cited (for reasons that were never convincingly explained) by Mrs Thatcher and Mr Norman Tebbit subsequently, as the source of Britain's social problems in the 1980s. He also uninhibitedly supported the Biafran cause in the Nigerian Civil War.

The principal signed economic and City column in the *Spectator* in 1966–70 was that of the veteran economist, Nicholas Davenport. Davenport had been a friend of Keynes and was a populariser of his policies, with particular bees in his bonnet about the need for 'cheap money' and the vulnerability of the economy, when in balance of payments difficulties, to flows of short-term 'hot money' from abroad. These two obsessions were linked by his particular loathing for paying high rates of interest on inflows of hot money from abroad. Like Lawson, Davenport was an expansionist, and always in favour of keeping interest rates low to encourage business investment. For Lawson himself, it was now less the level of interest rates that mattered than the general expansionist atmosphere, to give confidence to industrialists contemplating future investment plans.

Many people were to comment in later years that Lawson's early grounding was a natural preparation for his eventual Chancellorship. Although he was now actively looking for a seat to fight in what was to be the 1970 General Election, there is no record of what ambitions were in his mind when he wrote, of the sacking of the French Finance Minister in a 1966 reshuffle, that the French were playing 'the traditional English game of "when things go wrong, sack the Chancellor".'[87]

A certain gambling instinct was apparent to his colleagues at the *Spectator*. Alan Watkins, then the paper's political columnist, has told a story of how he expressed surprise on learning that Lawson did the football pools, and Lawson replied, 'Well, the sum you might win is absolutely enormous.' To which Watkins said: 'But the odds are enormous too.' Lawson then countered: 'Yes, I know, but it's worth doing just for the money, just for the possibility of getting this enormous sum.'[88] From time to time Lawson was interested in the betting on various events, but covered himself: thus, while suggesting an outside bet to readers on a top Treasury official of the time, at 33–1, for the

Governorship of the Bank of England, he did counsel a 'saver' on Lord Cromer, the hot favourite at 3–1 on, who in fact got the job.[89]

An early article on the malaise in the Conservative Party told readers not to blame the new leader, Mr Edward Heath, and said the problem was the Party no longer had an '*idée force*' in which it could believe and on which it could crusade.

The Empire had gone, and the Commonwealth – for which Lawson has at nearly all times expressed contempt – was no substitute. But 'old fashioned liberalism (individual liberty, free trade, *laissez-faire* and the market economy) needs too many qualifications today to pass as an *idée force* for anyone except Mr Powell. Europe, perhaps alone, could still be an *idée force* . . . but the time for that is yet to come.' Meanwhile, he suggested, the Tories should concentrate on 'the real mistakes that this pragmatic and often Conservative government' (that of Mr Wilson's Labour administration) 'is actually making' rather than standing back to attack 'the vices of theoretical socialism.'[90]

A statement of the line he was to pursue relentlessly in his *Spectator* leaders was provided in February 1966:

> The central problem of the management of the economy is, after the achievement of peace, the most important for any government. It is also the most difficult. A credible policy today demands a fresh look at our overseas commitments, at the sterling area, and at the exchange rate itself. This, and not the incomes policy, is what the Tories ought to be arguing among themselves today. To oppose the exploded policies of the early sixties with the exploded policies of the late fifties is no substitute.[91]

There was much in this kind of analysis that was shared with the diagnoses being made on the Left at the time. And Lawson's leaders were strident about the absurdity of eschewing devaluation in favour of 'accepting a rate of economic growth and a level of unemployment that the public would rightly, because it is unnecessary, regard as unacceptable.'[92]

The Chancellor who was to be such a passionate advocate of putting the pound fully into the European Monetary System in 1988–89 staked out his basic position in 1966–70, when Britain was still some years from joining the European Community itself. The country faced a clear choice – 'the choice between becoming a leading member of a strong and independent Europe that is an equal partner in a new-style Atlantic Alliance, or degenerating to the status of an American satellite.'[93] But it had a 'strategy of weakness': it supported the Americans in Vietnam in return for loans to prop up the pound, and it was too weak to join the European Community.[94]

Lawson told his readers that they should distinguish between a 'topic' and an 'issue'. The cost of living was a topic, not an issue. There had been no correlation between the rise in prices and Government popularity over the past few years.[95] On the other hand the *trend* of unemployment was important to electoral success – not the absolute level; provided the Government of the day remembered the elementary rules of Keynesian economic management, there was no compelling reason why it should ever be defeated at a General Election. Indeed, Keynesian economic management was almost too much of a good thing – it was a threat to the two-party system: 'Parliamentary democracy in Britain looks like becoming the foremost casualty of the Keynesian revolution.'[96] As for Professor Nicholas Kaldor, a leading Keynesian economist of the time, and a butt of much ill-informed right-wing comment, Lawson said he was 'a delightful and civilised person'.

In addition to favouring the social reforms of the then Labour Home Secretary Roy Jenkins, Lawson was also at this stage developing the pleas for greater freedom for the consumer which would figure so prominently in his policies later. Correspondingly, he regarded State regulation of prices and wages as a diminution of personal freedom, unacceptable in peacetime. But there were limits – 'the simplest way to go about losing money is to yield to the temptations of avarice,' he said in relation to people who had lost money in a notorious insurance swindle of the time.[97]

Lawson's obsession with the balance of payments led him at one point to state that the Government would be judged not only by the speed with which it succeeded in eliminating the balance of payments deficit, but also by 'the cost in terms of slow growth and sacrificed prosperity.'[98] The July 1966 measures were criticised for hitting investment in modernisation. What was wanted were measures which simultaneously deflated domestic demand but introduced a corresponding expansion in exports by devaluing the pound.[99]

It was always known that the Wilson Government had ruled out devaluation as an option from an early stage when it was elected in 1964, and that this was applied to internal Whitehall discussion too. It has more recently emerged that this was part of a formal, and secret, deal with President Johnson.[100] But the subject was also little discussed in the newspapers, partly because of ignorance of the issues, but partly out of a self-denying ordinance, in response to Government pressure. At one stage a Lawson leader referred to 'the lonely furrow the *Spectator* has been ploughing' in advocating devaluation. 'Only when we have put our balance of payments right – the overriding priority – will we have earned the time, and be able to devote our efforts to tackling the really long-term and deep-seated deficiencies in the economy.'[101] There was a reminder of one Labour comment after the devaluation of 1931, which helped the UK to recover faster from the slump than most other countries:

'Nobody told us we could do this.' ('What Sidney Webb Wasn't Told' said Lawson's headline.)[102]

Lawson's *Spectator* leaders built on the 'meritocracy' theme he had adumbrated in his *Financial Times* articles: he advocated 'a total embrace of the idea of meritocracy, which is utterly opposed to egalitarianism and can be happily grafted on to the Tories' concept of social order.' The associated freedom and independence in the social field 'means a total denial of the small-minded egalitarianism . . . in education, incomes policy, taxation and foreign travel.' (The foreign travel was a reference to the £50 'allowance', or 'restriction' as Lawson preferred to call it, then operating as one of the measures – alternative to devaluation – to assist the balance of payments.)[103]

His advocacy of measures to assist freedom and independence led him to say: 'This requires, paradoxically, the greater redistribution of wealth, but a much smaller redistribution of income.'[104] There were probably more paradoxes here than even he intended. One can see the seeds of the 'popular capitalism' by which Lawson was to set so much store in the 1980s, in the reference to 'greater redistribution of wealth' and one can see that the freedom of those who have no wealth is inhibited, and ought to be enhanced by greater redistribution – a point that Labour politicians were to take up in the late 1980s.

But the redistribution Lawson seems to have had in mind does not, to judge from his subsequent actions as Chancellor, ever appear to have been from the rich to the poor, or less rich. Taken with the view expressed earlier in the *Financial Times* series, it can be seen that the redistribution was to take the form of reallocating assets owned by tax-payers as a whole to those who subscribed for them in subsidised 'privatisation' issues.

Again, the advocacy of 'a much smaller redistribution of income' was not quite what it seemed. One can see that Lawson and his school regard redistributive taxation as an infringement of the liberty of those who have to pay the high taxes (welfare or utilitarian economists might argue that the gains to the poorer from redistribution far outweigh the losses to the rich); but the phrase in effect meant, as we were to see in practice during the 1980s, a redistribution of post-tax income from the lower echelons of income earners to the highest.

Perhaps Lawson gave away more than he realised of his innermost feelings in a Christmas leader: 'At Christmas, as the dustmen claim their annual bribe and carol singers swing their polythene Oxfam boxes, we do our best to think of others, especially overseas, less fortunate than ourselves. Even if the thought alone does not count for so much, it is at least a healthy mental and spiritual exercise.'[105]

The editor of the *Spectator* certainly made no bones about his belief in helping those who could already help themselves. In three successive signed articles, 'A Tract For the Tories', in 1967, Lawson spelled out the views on freedom and inequality which were undoubtedly to influence his taxation and public expenditure policies all those years later. He actually preached that the Tories 'must put the *principle* [his italics] of inequality – and, in particular, the creation of new inequalities in response to new achievement – above the ossification of existing inequalities.' While continually praising the European ideal, and particularly de Gaulle and Erhard, and railing against the 'special relationship' with the USA, Lawson was nevertheless prepared to cite American society with approval as being an example of the way that holding out the prospect of 'new inequalities' was, in the long run, 'probably the only way of preventing existing inequalities from falling victim to political extremism.'[106] Everybody can become a millionaire or President if they try . . .

'If the negative aspect of freedom is absence of restrictions,' he wrote, 'the positive aspect is the possession of sufficient private means to allow of a modicum of independence. Once again, it is only through a reform of taxation that this vital source of independence can be more widely distributed among the people.'[107] Again, redistribution was being used in the sense of a redistribution from public spending and public goods to the private individual, certainly not from richer to poorer.

He added that failure, as well as success, should be 'recognised', in the sense that 'indiscriminate paternalist subsidies' should be jettisoned in favour of 'a lavish financial scheme for the relief of poverty, based on manifest need.' This was an early indication of a theme which was to dominate much Conservative political discussion in the 1970s and 1980s – but which still somehow ended by leaving the impression that poverty was getting worse, not better . . .

For Lawson in his 'Tract', democracy was preferable to repression or revolution, but did not necessarily bring wiser government. It replaced the oppression of the majority with the oppression of two minorities – the successful, and the really poor: 'The Conservatives should seek to appeal simultaneously to both these minorities.'[108] As it was, they stood in danger of appearing either as the party of the 'individual' – 'a noble but to most people an austere and forbidding creed' or of the middle classes – 'which condemns them to a permanent minority'. They had also replaced the Empire with 'the chimera of the Commonwealth instead of a Gaullist-type belief in Britain.'[109]

But economic failures held everything back. The theme that emerges strongly from Lawson's 'Tract' is that he is searching, rather like the 'planners' of the 1960s whom he found so philosophically repugnant, for ways of removing 'obstacles to faster growth'. He did not see the answer then in economic liberalism – or Powellism, as it was often known at the time. Indeed, he castigated the Powellites – 'Uncertain as to what a Tory government ought to do in the economic field, they fall back on the answer that it should do nothing at all – or at least as little as possible, leaving as much as possible to the free play of market forces.' This approach was 'plainly inadequate' – modern corporations were oligopolistic, and 'miniature states' responsible for the welfare of their subjects, not the free competitors of the Manchester Liberal model. And the slumps of the past showed that complete *laissez-faire* was anything but the solution to the economic problems of the nation or the world. 'There must remain a major Government role in the management of the economy.'[110]

For Lawson the distinction was that Tories should simply aim at faster economic growth itself, leaving the consumer to decide the shape, whereas Labour not only wanted a different balance between the public and private sectors, but 'within the private sector itself there tends to be a distinct Socialist pecking order, with striped toothpaste and similar decadent manifestations of the so-called candy floss economy (such as foreign travel, shops and offices) at the end of the queue.'[111] He wanted to expand the economy 'as fast as our physical resources allow' and was not too rigid about the inflation targets:

> If we really were dedicated to the total elimination of inflation – to prices not rising at all – then no doubt there would be a basic conflict with faster economic growth. But if, as is surely more reasonable, we are to confine ourselves to the more modest aim of keeping the rate of inflation within tolerable bounds – creeping rather than galloping, and in particular in line with the rates of inflation among our main competitors overseas – then it is difficult to believe that (once we have reached a sound competitive base to start from) this is the root of our problem.[112]

The 'sound competitive base' meant an initial devaluation, of course. The UK's problem was that 'imports have a persistent tendency to rise faster than exports' and, if anything, the balance of payments deficit 'has been increasing from one economic cycle to the next.' (He could have been writing an internal Treasury memorandum in mid-1989.) Here he managed to suggest that, without paying excessive homage to 'liberal economic beliefs', the Tories could make market forces and the price mechanism work better, in the interests of growth, by letting the pound float to 'find its own level', and free the country of the 'tyranny' of an overvalued currency. 'The role of the state,' he said, 'is not primarily to provide an engine for expansion – that is inherent in man himself – but rather to remove the obstacles to faster growth; and at the present time the biggest obstacle is our chronic balance of payments weakness.'[113] Deal with this, and the Treasury would be free to run the economy 'in a responsible manner on sound Keynesian lines'.[114] Lawson even fantasised about the prospect of an export boom leading businessmen to invest in new capital equipment to meet the next export boom – the 'virtuous' circle.

The pound was eventually devalued in November 1967. The aftermath of Lawson's great campaign for devaluation was something of an anticlimax. He found himself persistently criticising the new Chancellor, Roy Jenkins, for being dilatory in taking the necessary measures to curb consumer spending so that devaluation could be 'made to work'. In November 1968 he urged that, since the Chancellor had failed to control the consumer, he should do something about public expenditure, which had, he said, been increasing twice as fast as consumer spending during the Labour Government's tenure so far.[115] Jenkins in fact ended up with a Budget surplus before the General Election year of 1970. But the economy appeared to be reviving in spite of a cautious Budget, and so did Labour in the opinion polls. The last *Spectator* leader under Lawson's editorship, written when he himself was campaigning against Joan Lestor for the seat of Eton and Slough, sounded a despairing note that 'unrestrained wage inflation' seemed to be bringing Labour to the brink of Election victory again.

In fact Labour lost the Election of June 18th 1970, and Lawson himself suffered a defeat, with the votes in his constituency going against the national trend. His proprietor Harry Creighton took the opportunity to write to him suggesting he take a rest – the two had never got on, especially over Lawson's pro-European policy – and that was the end of his *Spectator* editorship.

TWO

The Conversion

1972–79

When Nigel Lawson decided in 1964 that he would like to move from journalism to politics as soon as possible, he had patience thrust upon him. The national swing to the Conservatives in their unexpected victory of June 1970 was 4.5 per cent, but Lawson himself managed only 1.8 per cent in Eton and Slough. He decided to continue the search for a safe seat, and meanwhile opted for freelance journalism, rather than the editorship of the *Investor's Chronicle* (which might have led to the editorship of the *Financial Times*). He was increasing his stakes in the bid for a political career.*

He did not have to wait much longer. In January 1972 he was selected for the new constituency of Blaby, in Leicestershire, near where the M1 and M6 motorways now meet. It was reckoned to be a safe Conservative seat, containing three-fifths of the previous Harborough constituency, where the Conservatives had a 20,000 majority in 1970. Lawson had written for the *Sunday Times* and *London Evening Standard* in 1970–71, and *The Times* in 1971–72, on a freelance basis. He now took up a research fellowship at Nuffield College, Oxford, in 1972–73, before returning to Conservative Central Office to work for yet another Prime Minister, in this case Edward Heath. Indeed, he wrote the February 1974 election manifesto for the Conservatives.

The Election which brought Lawson into Parliament took place after the breakdown of the Heath Government's incomes policy in 1973–74; in the midst of the associated miners' strike, Heath had called the General Election

* He was also losing stakes: in the early 1970s he entrusted an inheritance, and some of his then wife's money, to a professional investment manager, who, in Lawson's words, 'pretty well lost it all'.[1]

on the issue of 'Who Governs the Country?' Many Conservatives felt disillusioned and bitter over the Heath Government's experiences with incomes policy; and Labour had been going through a phase where, to differentiate its product from the Conservatives, it was against incomes policy itself.

After first trying to tame the trades unions, Edward Heath had then attempted to woo their co-operation, by offering them a stronger say in the consultative process surrounding economic policy decisions. The breakdown of this process, and the miners' strike in particular, led many Conservatives to revolt against what they labelled 'corporatism'; subsequently they were reinforced in this stand by observation of the close consultations which took place between the Labour Government and the trades unions in 1974–75.

Lawson was among those – Sir Keith Joseph and Mrs Margaret Thatcher were others – who alleged that the Heath–Wilson attempts to bring the TUC and the Confederation of British Industry into economic policy-making had made Britain into a 'Corporate State'. This became a great pejorative term, and parallels were drawn with Mussolini's Italy. It could equally have been said that members of the Government, CBI and TUC were eating, drinking and breathing, and that this too was reminiscent of Mussolini's Italy. The Heath and Wilson administrations of the 1970s may have had their faults, but comparisons with Mussolini were over the top.

Lawson had been very much in favour of the expansionary policies of Heath and his Chancellor Anthony Barber at the time, and both Mrs Thatcher and Sir Keith Joseph had, at the Departments of Education and Health and Social Security respectively, been among the biggest spenders of the Heath administration. It is difficult to imagine that there would have been quite such an outcry against the 'corporatist' tendencies of Edward Heath if he had not lost the Election.

Lawson himself thought the issue 'Who Governs the Country' in February 1974 was a bogus one: with characteristic frankness he once said, 'We called the election because we thought we would win.'[2] The February 1974 Election result, associated, as it was, with the apparent failure of incomes policy, undoubtedly strengthened the hostility within the Conservative Party towards incomes policies. Lawson himself, who would seem, to a later generation, to have been a highly unlikely author of a Heath manifesto, has commented thus:

> I was a great supporter of Ted Heath over things like the abolition of resale price maintenance and joining the European Community. But I always disagreed with him on macroeconomic policy. I wrote to him that I was totally opposed to the course he was taking; a statutory incomes policy is the worst kind of all. But of course I wanted the Conservatives to win the election, and so in the manifesto I tried to put the best case I could for the policies that were being pursued.[3]

Incomes policy, incomes policy . . . it continued to be Lawson's economic *bête noire* during the 1970s, but the beast was to be joined in the cage by others before the decade was done. Two months after his election to Parliament on February 28th 1974 Lawson became a member of the Commons Expenditure Committee. In August that year the all-party committee endorsed a report by its General Sub-Committee attacking incomes policies as a policy instrument. This was not just as a result of the new Member for Blaby's powers of persuasion, given the general climate. He was notably vociferous on the subject at the time, but he was not a member of the Sub-Committee, although his friend Bruce-Gardyne was, along with Nicholas Ridley.

At about the same time, Lawson wrote an article in *Encounter* in which he said, 'The most important task of government today is to introduce acceptable measures that will, directly or indirectly, curb, deter and tame the use of trade-union power.'[4] This was against a background where a return to 'free collective bargaining', and a system under which wage earnings were being increased automatically in line with cost of living 'threshold agreements' (themselves influenced by the impact of the first 'oil shock') led to inflation at an annual rate of nearly 20 per cent during the first six months of 1974.

'If we are serious about halting the new inflation,' he wrote, 'there is nothing for it but to curb, or at least deter, by a series of carefully-chosen legislative measures, trade-union and shop-steward power.' Such was the existing power of unions that 'we may well need a National Government, in the sense of a genuine coalition drawn from both major parties, to do the job.' He thought 'the problem of trade-union power is the most serious constitutional crisis and challenge the modern democratic state has yet had to face.' He was against 'a crude, all-out, frontal assault' on the trades unions. 'Indeed,' he said, 'governments will need to be almost machiavellian in the care and subtlety with which they pursue this end.'[5]

Lawson's basic views on policy were enunciated in his journalism of the 1960s. His analysis of the British Government and its power structure came in a book published jointly with his old *Financial Times* colleague Jock Bruce-Gardyne, in 1976, entitled *The Power Game* [Macmillan]. *The Power Game* examines the background to four decisions relating to economic policy during the 1960s – the Concorde Saga, the 'doomed departures' in the direction of the Common Market, the abolition of resale* price maintenance, and the saga surrounding the 1967 devaluation of the pound. It shows a fascination with the interplay of ministers, Civil Service departments, the Bank of England and pressure groups, accompanied by the disclaimer 'Nor for the purpose of this

* It would now be called 'retail'.

inquiry, is it of any concern to us whether the decisions made were right or wrong.'

Despite this disclaimer, there is nothing to suggest that even at this distance Lawson had changed his mind about the rights and wrongs of the devaluation issue – the whole tenor of that section is of how a Prime Minister determined to 'divide and rule', Harold Wilson, managed to put off a necessary, sensible – and ultimately inevitable – decision for three years, and how such procrastination damaged Labour's other priorities. In some ways the book can be seen as an advance study (and warning) for the practice of the Chancellorship, with due note being taken of how Harold Macmillan put the 'amenable' Selwyn Lloyd into Number 11 so that he himself could intervene in Treasury matters (which raises the question whether Lawson, in his *Sunday Telegraph* attacks on Lloyd, had been focusing on the right target), and how Macmillan overrode the Treasury with regard to the vast commitment of expenditure to the Concorde project. Lawson had plenty of warnings from his study of the Westminster/Whitehall power game of how difficult a Chancellor's position could be made. And, if anything, he is critical of Treasury officials at the time for being too supine over the devaluation issue, although later as Chancellor he was not to show open admiration for those who disagreed with him. He is also dismissive of the Treasury's obsession with incomes policy. 'Whatever else the three-year non-devaluation saga may have been, it was not a case of mandarin power' the authors observe. But, while knowing that the 'no devaluation' policy was in part designed to please the Americans, the authors did not have access to the papers uncovered later by Clive Ponting, which proved that there had been a secret deal between Wilson and Lyndon Johnson.[6]

Lawson and Bruce-Gardyne lament that there was insufficient public debate over the devaluation issue, and even have a good word to say for the country's economists, whose views did not surface much, but who were two to one in favour of devaluation. They lament that 'there was no Keynes to challenge the prevailing orthodoxy' and aver 'it requires more than the failure of a policy to bring about its reversal: it also requires – in practice – the development of an uninhibited public debate.' Wilson is castigated for having given the editor of the *Observer* a 'severe dressing down' for being unpatriotic over sterling. Yet in his days as Chancellor, Lawson was often going to take issue with newspapers in private over such differences of opinion.

Lawson and Bruce-Gardyne made some judgments in *The Power Game* which are intriguing in the light of the former's experiences at the heart of the power game of the 1980s. 'British Prime Ministers are surrounded by men who want their job,' they wrote, 'usually including one or two who have already challenged them for it!' Again, 'The Governor of the Bank can frighten Labour governments, whereas Tory ministers think they know all about the foreign exchange markets.' There is also the judgment that 'the popular conception of politicians as creatures of Party, and civil servants as open-minded individuals is, operationally, if anything the reverse of the truth. It is ministers who tend to think and act as individuals (the isolation of ministers from each other in modern government, the type of man who chooses politics as a career, and personal ambition all play a part), while it is the civil servants who (in general) acquire power by sinking their individuality in a corporate ethos: in this way they both build up a departmental *esprit de corps* and limit the range of policy options from which ministers are invited to choose.' A better clue to Lawson's subsequent personal approach to the business of relations with his department is difficult to find. He was determined to impose the policy options himself, and dominated the Treasury in a way few of his predecessors had achieved.

The authors conclude with the aphorism:

> Interest groups cajole, the Bank of England warns, the civil servants guide, the backbenchers plot, the departmental ministers propose, and the Prime Minister disposes. But so often it is pure hazard which tips the scales in the end . . . There is only one certainty, and that is that both the true nature of the distribution of power and influence in the British policy, and our understanding of it, are constantly evolving.

And they sound a warning note about so-called 'corporatism' – the way that both the Heath and Wilson Governments had brought the TUC and CBI into the economic consultative process in order to square them for co-operation on incomes policy.

Lawson described his share in *The Power Game* as 'the belated fruit' of his 1972–73 research fellowship at Oxford, which preceded his work for Edward Heath before the February 1974 Election.

Lawson became an Opposition Whip in 1976, and was made a spokesman on Treasury and Economic Affairs in November 1977. Before then he had played an active part in Commons debates, sometimes very active – on one occasion, in March 1975, he was reported to have got so heated in a debate over Government help for a motor-cycle company that he slapped a member of the Government in the face with his Commons Order paper. In November of that year he spoke up again for the tax-payer, over the Government's rescue operation for the Chrysler car company. 'If this is such a good investment,' he said, 'the people have a right to ask before any decision is taken, how much of the quarter-of-a-million pounds plus that Mr Wilson received for the newspaper serialisation of his incredibly dull memoirs is he personally prepared to invest in Chrysler?'[7]

During the mid-1970s Lawson was one of a group of politicians, economists, journalists and City figures who were attracted by the doctrine of monetarism, whose most influential proponent was Professor Milton Friedman, then of Chicago University. Lawson regarded the economic problem of the 1960s as stagnation and the threat of world recession. With the rate of inflation in Britain rising to over 25 per cent in 1975, his attention switched to inflation, as the *Encounter* article quoted above had already signalled.

He was hardly alone in this; nor was concern about inflation confined to the 'monetarist' group which formed itself around Sir Keith Joseph and then Mrs Thatcher. The crucial difference was that whereas the conventional Keynesian establishment tried to adapt and augment basic Keynesian economic policies to cope with a more inflationary environment, Lawson and his colleagues were attracted by the claims of the monetarists that first, the deterioration in inflation was largely the result of Keynesian policies, and second, monetarism offered the cure to inflation that Keynesian policies could not provide.

To Friedman and his followers the prognosis was attractively, and deceptively, simple. Inflation was a monetary phenomenon: control the supply of money and you control inflation. To Keynesians, inflation was a more complex phenomenon, the result of competing claims on limited resources, with increases in wages above the rate of growth of productivity playing the crucial role. Incomes policies of some sort were essential, and, if these had been mismanaged in the past, the proper approach was to try to manage them better, not give up altogether.

When Lawson and his close friend Samuel Brittan had been writing for the *Financial Times* during the 1960s (Brittan was principal economics commentator from 1966, after a period in Whitehall) they had tended to be contemptuous of the concern shown about inflation by the 'older school' of financial journalists. Lawson later said:

> What they talked about, warned against, didn't match any experience which I had had during my lifetime. I was far too dismissive of their warnings. When inflation took off in the late Sixties and early Seventies, my views about it changed very rapidly. An accelerating rate of inflation presents a threat to society itself. From then on there has been a natural evolution in my views as a whole.[8]

It was the experience of the Seventies that really mattered. Even in one of the last *Spectator* leading articles for which he had been responsible, just before the June 1970 General Election, Lawson seemed more concerned that wage inflation would help Labour to win – which it did not – than in attacking inflation *per se*; the emphasis was still on the lack of *expansion, vis-à-vis* overseas competitors.[9]

We have seen how strong was Lawson's repugnance for incomes policies. After the breakdown of Heath's incomes policy – and, later, of Callaghan's in 1978–79 – this became a revulsion. He was also impressed by the argument of Samuel Brittan (among others) that demand management no longer worked, because more and more of any injection into the economy of monetary demand was absorbed by price increases rather than real economic growth.

Thus in 1977 Lawson wrote a letter to *The Times* taking issue with a letter from the man on whom he had once urged even more expansionist economic policies, Reginald Maudling. Maudling had himself criticised *The Times*'s espousal of monetarism, on the grounds that too slow an expansion of aggregate monetary demand would cause needless unemployment. Lawson countered by arguing: 'This is one charge that cannot possibly be valid, since the essence of the "monetarist" analysis is that, in modern circumstances, a more rapid expansion of aggregate monetary demand will *not* in fact lead to any sustainable fall in unemployment, but merely to a rise in the rate of inflation.' He said dismissively that Maudling was 'straying down the primrose path of an inflation of aggregate monetary demand.'[10]

But Lawson still avowed his own beliefs in economic expansion. He added that Maudling was:

> absolutely right to be concerned about economic expansion. Unfortunately, the whole drift of recent legislation in, for example, the fields of housing, social security, taxation, and even employment itself (*vide* important sections of the Employment Protection Act) has been both to boost unemployment, by interfering with the efficient and economic working of the labour market, and to blunt the personal incentives which, in a free society, are the sole engine of economic expansion.[11]

'Sole' in this context was rather strong, especially in the light of Lawson's beliefs of the 1960s. While he had certainly been a consistent advocate of 'incentives' and reforming the tax system, he had also been a great believer in the ability of the Government to manage demand. It may reasonably be argued that demand was *mis*managed in the 1970s, but it was an extreme reaction to go from this conclusion to the belief that it should not be managed at all.

One of the commentators preaching monetarism at this stage was Peter Jay, then economics editor of *The Times*. The Bank of England, which actually printed the money, became the whipping boy for Jay, Lawson and others. In April 1976, Jay made the revolutionary proposal that control of monetary policy should be entrusted to an independent 'Currency Commission', and completely removed from the Government of the day – which would also have meant denuding the Treasury and the nationalised Bank of England of their monetary powers. The Currency Commission would be instructed to regulate the money supply under strict rules for its growth, fixed by statute.

The British economic establishment may have been under pressure in those days, and, indeed, suffering a loss of morale – so that the burgeoning monetarist pressure group was faced with less resistance than one might reasonably have expected. But if there was one thing that got short shrift, it was Jay's Currency Commission. Whitehall and the Bank of England closed ranks immediately, and were so successful in laughing the proposal out of court that they did not even have to fight a serious battle on this specific issue. But it was certainly one of a number of monetarist thrusts which contributed to the disarray of the Keynesians.

Lawson, in a letter to *The Times* later in April, was on to the main point with his comment: 'The important step, of course, is not so much the creation of a commission as the statutory enactment of the rules.' He added that this 'is the only way of restoring any degree of parliamentary control over monetary policy.' He had earlier that month explained in the Commons that 'Parliamentary control over monetary policy means that the policy would be expected to follow certain rules – whether they be rules of the gold standard, or rules for a certain increase in the money supply as propounded by Professor Friedman, or the ideas of Professor Hayek.'[12]

This search for 'rules' was going to dominate Lawson's professional life in the following years – both in the run-up to office and in office itself. This penchant of Lawson's has often been put to me by others who have worked with him as a quest for panaceas, and – more unkindly, but not necessarily less accurately – a desire to be impaled on hooks. Subsequent developments suggested that this enthusiasm for Professor Friedman's simple rules could not be attributed to the mischievous spirit of a man who, as it happened, was speaking in the Commons in the early hours of April Fools' Day 1976. He went on to say: 'The question at the bottom of this is whether the Government are prepared to accept any external constraints on their actions in monetary matters . . . At present control of the money supply is left entirely at the discretion of the Government.'[13]

Colleagues of Lawson's at various stages of his career attest to his intellectual curiosity, and to his tendency to adopt new enthusiasms. Some also maintain that he is at heart 'pragmatic', in the modern sense of adaptable and flexible. The problem with the enthusiasm for a fixed monetary rule is that it was by definition a commitment to an unpragmatic approach. At least at this stage, however, there is also a cautious streak in Lawson: the calculating poker-player added, 'Parliament would be asked to approve derogations from these rules in exceptional circumstances.'[14]

Interest in monetarism was also being shown at the time by certain Treasury and Bank of England officials, and indeed targets for monetary growth were introduced in 1976. But there was a world of difference between adding monetary targets to the battery of weapons for trying to control the economy, and abandoning the management of demand in favour of strict adherence to a preordained monetary rule, to which all other aims of economic policy were to be subordinated.

There is bound to be a conflict within people who at the same time search for fixed rules and cannot resist interfering in legislation, or in taking all sorts of new initiatives. In June 1977 Lawson became well known for his 'amendment to an amendment' in the Finance Bill. Two Labour backbenchers had moved an amendment under which personal tax allowances would automatically be indexed for the previous calendar year's inflation each Budget-time. This 'Rooker-Wise' amendment became the 'Rooker-Wise-Lawson' amendment when Lawson moved in the course of the Finance Bill committee that the Chancellor still have the discretion not to index allowances in this way if he so chose. Apart from anything else, this still suggested a yearning for flexibility and the freedom to manage demand in the economy. But Lawson also supported the principle of indexation, and did so in large part because he objected to a situation where tax revenues automatically rose simply because of inflation, thereby facilitating 'a further shift of resources from the private sector to the public sector'.

Lawson's activity in the Finance Bill impressed Mrs Thatcher, who had herself attracted attention initially in the Commons through her Finance Bill work. It was hardly a surprise when he was appointed a front-bench Treasury spokesman in November 1977, and became increasingly involved as an adviser to Mrs Thatcher on the economy. He was not at this stage as close to her as others in the Shadow Cabinet; and, indeed, his libertarian views on everything from hanging onwards meant that he could not fully be, in Mrs Thatcher's famous phrase, 'one of us'. But it was to be Mrs Thatcher's growing respect for him which brought preferment: Lawson did not belong to any particular faction of the Conservative Party.

In his début as front-bench spokesman Lawson vigorously attacked the Chancellor Denis Healey for not abolishing exchange controls. Labour had been through the traumas of the 1976 collapse of the pound, and the enforced approach to the International Monetary Fund for a loan; now the pound was much stronger, and people had begun to notice that North Sea oil was going to assist the balance of payments. Exchange controls were one of the 'constraints on freedom' about which Lawson felt strongly, but he had had to accept the need for them because of the weakness of the balance of payments during the 1960s, when the main object of his wrath in this sphere had been the fifty-pound travel 'allowance' imposed by Labour. Now he argued that companies and financial institutions should be free to invest overseas as they chose, and repeated a newspaper report suggesting that only the TUC was preventing the Government from relaxing controls. But Healey made it clear that he thought such relaxation threatened to divert much-needed investment in Britain.[15]

In January 1978, Lawson made a rare appearance in his old periodical, the *Spectator*. Here he put down some important markers for his future approach as Chancellor. One passage which seemed a relatively innocuous debating point at the time was a contemptuous reference to the quality of the economic forecasts on which the Treasury's and the Organisation for Economic Co-operation and Development's analyses for that year were based. As Lawson became more monetarist, and showed less respect for the traditional preoccupations of those concerned with 'the real economy', he was to be one of those ministers who in the early 1980s encouraged a 'cost-saving' reduction in the quality of economic statistics; this would prove increasingly embarrassing to the Treasury in the course of the 1980s.

Lawson referred in this article to the 'all-important inflation front', adding, 'the crucial question is whether the Chancellor continues gradually to reduce the rate of monetary growth in the economy, which is essential if inflation is to be genuinely curbed, or whether he relaxes the pressure in order to accommodate the renewed increase in inflation.' This statement suggests a certain confusion in Lawson's monetarism at this stage: if inflation was entirely a monetary phenomenon, then there could have been no question of 'accommodating' an increase in inflation – an increase in inflation could only occur if monetary policy was previously relaxed. Lawson here seems still to be assuming, in Keynesian fashion, that the question is whether wage-inflationary pressures are 'accommodated'.[16]

Some months earlier he had written, 'High pay settlements do not necessarily lead to high inflation.'[17] Now, in his *Spectator* article, he was already seeing through the kind of policy dilemmas he himself advocated, by predicting that Healey, faced with wage-inflationary pressures, would in fact accommodate them 'hoping to disguise it by moving from a fixed monetary target to so-called rolling guidelines, and by pinning still more faith on a permanent incomes policy as the sovereign cure for inflation.'[18]

By March, Lawson was calling on the Treasury to set 'a statutory target' for monetary growth, asking for the growth of the money supply to be brought back within its target range, and urging that one way of doing this was by relaxing exchange controls and encouraging an outflow of capital. One of the Treasury ministers, Denzil Davies, said a statutory target for monetary growth was not practicable 'although it seems now to be a commitment on the part of the Conservative Party.'[19]

The January 1978 *Spectator* article gave a clear indication that, even if Lawson's monetarism was still confused, he had wholeheartedly abandoned his advocacy of running the economy at the highest possible pressure of demand. And, interestingly, he had done so at a time when the one factor that in the 1960s he had regarded as a constraint, namely the balance of payments, no longer appeared to be a problem. He even adapted Belloc on the subject:

> Whatever happens, we have got
> North Sea oil, and they have not.

He ventured: 'I am not of that austere school who believe that even this black manna will prove a curse in disguise. In the long run, it will at least make us marginally richer than we would otherwise be – although Mr Healey's claim in the current *Socialist Commentary* that "the most important single advantage it will give us is that we shall be able to run the economy at a higher level of demand for longer periods than we have known since the war" is crude inflationary nonsense.'[20]

The irony was to be that, in the first few years of the Thatcher Government, the economy, despite the complete absence of a balance of payments constraint, was to be run not only not at a higher level of demand, but at the *lowest* level in post-war years. Later on, under Lawson's Chancellorship, it was to be run at a very high level of demand indeed, notwithstanding the way he scoffed at Healey – so high that Lawson himself was going to be accused of committing the very 'inflationary nonsense' he complained of on this occasion.

North Sea oil was to benefit the economy in two ways: not only would Britain be a net exporter of oil in the 1980s, but oil royalty and tax revenues would assist the Government's finances.[21] Lawson made it clear he thought that, rather than be 'frittered away on so-called social spending and still further politically-skewed state intervention in industry', they should be used 'constructively to cut the high levels of direct taxation . . . which at present sap and sour the hard work, enterprise and attitudes of both management and labour on which the success of any free economy ultimately depends.'[22]

On the crucial question of the effect on the pound, Lawson was contemptuous now of the very idea of 'exchange rate policies', saying, 'The tune will be called by market forces, and the only question is the Government's response to them.' Lawson showed himself sensitive still to the effect of more than a modest rise in the pound on export profitability; to avoid a dangerous erosion of export profitability, he advocated 'a progressive relaxation of exchange control'. And in a prophecy that was wrong for the right reasons he said, 'If likely economic events are any guide, it looks odds on an autumn election, before things are too obviously seen to be going wrong.'[23]

Lawson's worries about Government encroachment on freedom were intensified by a revelation in early 1978 that Labour had a 'blacklist' of companies that would be penalised for breaching its then 10 per cent limit on pay increases by not receiving official assistance or Government contracts. He got on to the front pages by accusing the Government of speaking with 'the language of despotism' and comparing these methods to those of the Mafia, with the Prime Minister James Callaghan as 'the Godfather'.[24]

Lawson was beginning to make his name now as a pugilistic character who did not mind whom he took on, or whom he offended. People began to think of him as a Conservative Denis Healey. He used to turn up in the Commons, or at Central Office meetings when the Election manifesto was being prepared, bubbling with new ideas and new enthusiasm, and manifesting little sensitivity towards anybody else, whose ideas he was happy to dismiss with disdain. Healey subsequently recalled: 'When he was a young man in the House, he was extremely lively and boisterous, and I used to enjoy his speeches. He always reminded me a little bit of the Cad of the Remove in a schoolboy story or Steerforth in *David Copperfield*.'[25] On the other hand, one official who worked with both Healey and Lawson commented: 'Deep down Healey is a softy, whereas Lawson is not.'

But Lawson certainly resembled Healey in not going out of his way to build up a personal following in the Commons. Indeed, he had at times seemed to take an almost malicious pleasure in putting down his backbench colleagues and giving the impression that he would not suffer them gladly. One of his closest associates has commented: 'The thing about Nigel is that he devotes a lot of time and energy to cultivating people who can do him no good at all, and happily kicks in the teeth all sorts of people who can do him harm.'

He early antagonised the then Mr Whitelaw with his brusque manner of 'not suffering fools gladly'; and by making an enemy of Whitelaw he undoubtedly delayed his own subsequent progress to the Cabinet. In June 1978 the *Observer*'s political columnist Alan Watkins, in an article entitled 'Maggie and Her Silly Billies', commented: 'Mr Nigel Lawson, though clever, is silly, in that he will always contrive to produce the wrong political answer by the exercise of the most rigorous and impressive economic logic.'[26]

Among the calls made by Lawson in the summer of 1978 was one for the indexation of the tax system for capital gains (which the Conservatives did subsequently introduce) and an increase in the amount of a mortgage which should be eligible for tax relief (this did happen once under the Tories, but it was something on which Lawson was to change his position when in office, possibly a rare example of the Treasury influencing *him*). Lawson was even more active in the Standing Committee on the Finance Bill now that he was a front-bench spokesman, and had great fun in teasing Labour about its failure to control the money supply – good practice for when they were going to do the same to him.

By August 1978, when official figures were showing a rise of 15 per cent in wage earnings (against the 10 per cent guideline), Lawson complained that this was 'a monument to the folly of the Government's incomes policy.'[27] And during the winter of 1978–79, as Labour tried forlornly to impose a 5 per cent limit on wage settlements and industrial unrest grew into what was widely termed 'the Winter of Discontent', Lawson felt increasingly reassured that he had been right all along about the alleged folly of incomes policies. As for the subject of the reform of trades unions, this was now firmly on the Conservative agenda.

His long-held interest in Europe brought a salvo in the autumn of 1978, when the Labour Government was considering whether to put the pound into the new European Monetary System. Lawson called for all the Treasury's background papers to be published so that there could be an informed public debate (he was somewhat more secretive about such things once he joined the Treasury), and asserted: 'This is no mere technical detail or Euro-pedantry: it is a decision which could be as momentous for our economic future as was the Bretton Woods Agreement of 1944 or the return to the Gold Standard in 1925.'

'Momentous' indeed. The Callaghan Government flirted with the idea, but decided to join the new EMS without putting the pound into the exchange rate mechanism; in other words, it became an instant absentee from the new Club. Lawson, with his zeal for 'rules', became interested in the EMS from the mid-1980s. His eventual passionate enthusiasm for the EMS was to become a very public bone of contention with the Prime Minister when he was Chancellor.

For the time being, however, inflation was the subject which interested him most, its conquest having risen in the scale of preferences from, on his own criterion, a 'topic' to an 'issue'. Monetarists were offering an easy solution to inflation; and it was only when monetarism proved flawed that he turned his mind and energies to the EMS.

Reminiscing in 1985, Lawson harked back to an article he had written in *The Times* 'shortly before we came into office in 1979, setting out what I thought the economic strategy of a new Conservative Government ought to be.' He added, disarmingly, 'I'm not sure whether many people read it at the time – although it did elicit a fan letter from Hayek, whom I scarcely know.' He went on:

> Anyway, the first element in the strategy – and it sounds trite to say it now – was that there must be a medium-term strategy which should take the place of living from year to year and from day to day . . . the other [element] is that it had to be a strategy about finance. Why? First, because the great problem for economic policy, as it is potentially at any time for our sort of society, is inflation, and inflation is a *financial* problem. Nothing can be more financial than your money and mine losing its value rapidly. So there had to be a *financial* strategy. Second, in a free society, the only levers at the Government's command are financial levers. Thus it was essential that we had a strategy which concerned itself with something that Government can actually control.[28]

What were these financial levers? Control of the money supply and the budget deficit. 'The essence of the Medium Term Financial Strategy was, first, to produce over the medium term a gradual reduction in the rate of growth of the amount of money in the economy, as a means of getting inflation down; and second, to buttress this with a gradual reduction in the budget deficit,' he added.[29]

The simple logic of this – day-to-day living bad, therefore medium-term strategy; inflation financial, therefore financial strategy – had all the superficial attraction of the kind of Powellian argument that Lawson used to deride as being naïve and unrealistic in the 1960s. The logic was more linguistic than conceptual – perhaps the kind of trap in which even a man with a passion for logic can be ensnared. One wonders whether his linguistic philosophy also equipped him to detect when he himself might not be talking sense. Events were going to remind Lawson of the complexities of economic life. But there is another interesting aspect to his reminiscences in 1985 of his article in *The Times*: in his memory, time had understandably elided events.

The article was in fact written in 1978, not 1979 (when *The Times* was on strike); and the strategy outlined was neither described as 'medium' nor 'financial' – that was to come later. Nevertheless, the seeds of the 'Medium Term Financial Strategy', or MTFS, were sown in *The Times* article, which proposed 'a long-term stabilisation programme to defeat inflation, re-create business confidence, and provide a favourable climate for economic growth.' Two economists at the London Business School, Terence Burns and Alan

Budd, had already advocated a medium-term financial plan (in October 1977) and they were subsequently in touch with Lawson.

He wrote in *The Times* article: 'At the heart of such a programme must lie a firm commitment to a steady and gradual reduction in the rate of growth of the money supply until it is consistent with our best guess at the potentially sustainable real rate of economic growth. Only in this way can inflation be wrung out of the system.' The article started with a derogatory reference to the way the Prime Minister, James Callaghan, had recently questioned, in a broadcast, whether a General Election the coming winter would make 'the great domestic issues that the country now faces . . . any better.'

Lawson immediately expostulated: 'It is this obsession with the short-term that has been the bugbear of economic policy-making in Britain in recent years, and emancipation from it is the *sine qua non* of economic success.' He said wage controls were the consequence of the obsession with the short term, and caused governments to tailor all their other policies 'to the presumed needs of wage control'. Excessive budget deficits destroyed confidence: what was needed was 'something operationally and psychologically akin to the old balanced-budget discipline'. And then came what many of his future colleagues – who might or might not have been among the handful he thought had read *The Times* article – were to observe time and again during the 1980s: Lawson's obsession with finding a 'rule'. 'The secret of practical economic success, as overseas experience confirms, is the acceptance of known rules. Rules rule: OK?'[30]

Economics, he said, was about markets, and markets could not be fine-tuned. And, alongside 'a coherent long-term approach' to the demand side of the economy, there should be a long-term approach to the supply-side. This would take the form of 'a really significant reduction in personal taxation, at all levels, in order to re-create the incentive to take risks, to acquire skills, to expand and, above all, quite simply, the incentive to work.' This could be financed in part by a shift to indirect taxation and in part by growing revenues from the North Sea. At this stage Lawson saw a necessity 'to hold back public expenditure', but only to achieve a reduction in the Budget deficit, not to finance tax cuts. Cutting budget deficits would restore confidence; that would assist wealth-creation, which implied 'at the end of the day, a higher – not a lower – level of public services.'[31]

This vision was attractively simple, or deceptively simplistic – depending on one's view of monetarism. The emphasis which Lawson put on getting away from the short-term 'chopping and changing' of policy and from 'a climate in which business and industry find it difficult and discouraging to operate', was ironic in the light of the shocks to the system which monetarism and medium-term stabilisation plans were to bring in their wake after 1979. But, as Lawson said in his 1985 interview about his intentions in 1978, the idea behind the strategy was that 'the Government must declare it and announce its commitment to it in writing, as it were. Unless the Government does so, it won't be on the hook, and no one will believe it.'[32] Those officials who felt they were being mischievous or unkind in observing that Lawson seemed to like getting himself impaled on hooks need not have worried: he said so himself.

Some years later, in 1987, Jock Bruce-Gardyne was to comment: 'Precisely because he did understand monetary policy . . . he was quite prepared to play fast and loose with it.'[33] The first game was to down-grade a 'long-term stabilisation programme' into a 'medium-term financial strategy'. Other games would follow. But it is worth emphasising that a consistent theme of Lawson's is his antagonism towards incomes policies; that the seeds of the MTFS were sown against the background of the incomes policy being operated by the Callaghan Government. And that that incomes policy broke down in the winter of 1978–79.

It is arguable that it was not so much incomes policy itself that was discredited in the winter of 1978–79 as the Government's tactics in handling it. They were over-ambitious in their target, and Callaghan himself lost the confidence of trades union leaders by appearing to give them the impression he would have an Election in October 1978, and then hanging on too long until the spring of 1979, with the Government itself looking increasingly ragged. Most students seem to believe that the result of the May 1979 Election was a case more of dissatisfaction with the Government than outright enthusiasm for the Conservative manifesto. And, in any case, there were two Conservative manifestos: there was the official one, which bore the marks of the restraining influence of the men who were to become known as the Tory 'Wets'; and there was the more radical zeal of people like Mrs Thatcher and Nigel Lawson himself.

By this time Lawson had won considerable respect in Mrs Thatcher's eyes, and guaranteed himself an appointment as Treasury Minister. He was always more at home in the economics debate than the Shadow Chancellor Sir Geoffrey Howe, but the latter was more senior in the Party, with a lot more experience, and Lawson was going to have to wait his turn. But even before the General Election of May 1979 Lawson had laid his own private line to Mrs Thatcher, and was taken more seriously by her in economic matters than Sir Geoffrey himself.

What Lawson called 'The New Conservatism' was not fully explained during the Election campaign of 1979 – it might have lost votes. But he delivered a lecture to the Bow Group in August 1980 which was a kind of apologia for his conversion to monetarism and the New Right (on certain issues) during the 1970s.

Lawson felt sufficiently proud of 'The New Conservatism' to have it reprinted in pamphlet form by the 'Think Tank' which played an important role in the rise of Mrs Thatcher – the Centre for Policy Studies. It is an interesting document for several reasons: it shows, in his own words, Lawson's apostasy from Keynesian economics; it confirms, for today's reader, after some years during which the pure milk of monetarism has been diluted, that Lawson had then adopted ideas which were simple to the point of naïvety; yet it also contains passages which show that Lawson was considerably less naïve than some of his colleagues about the relationship between the money supply and wages, although any recognition of the connection between wage increases and inflation was, by this stage, 'The love that dare not speak its name.'

For many colleagues and observers of Lawson in the 1960s and 1970s (and there were many who were admirers but not friends) the recurring question with regard to his period in office and strong association with monetarism has been: does he really believe it – or did he just hitch himself to the bandwagon? The late Lord Kaldor – about whom Lawson had written with great respect in the *Spectator* – once observed: 'I can understand why Minister X believes in these policies – he is stupid; I can understand why Minister Y believes them, because he too is stupid; but Nigel Lawson – Nigel Lawson is an intelligent man.'

Monetarism, as we shall see, was much adapted and eventually abandoned as a creed by the Government of which Lawson was first Financial Secretary and later Chancellor of the Exchequer. Lawson was undoubtedly a 'disillusioned Keynesian' by the mid-1970s. Whether, in spite of what he preached for several years, he was genuinely converted to monetarism is a more difficult question. His passion for fast economic growth was certainly frustrated by the 1970s world of difficult trades unions, high inflation and increasing Government intervention. He was as energetic as any politician in trying to persuade his colleagues of the virtues of monetarism, and he was credited – if that is the appropriate word – by many Tory MPs with having given chapter and verse to Mrs Thatcher's raw prejudices. But close scrutiny of his texts suggests he always had some doubts, and there are those who wonder whether he simply – or, rather, complicatedly – nailed his colours to the monetarist mast which was sailing in the direction of ministerial office for N. Lawson.

The tract published in August 1980 spelled out the results of the conversion of the 1970s. 'At the macroeconomic level, our approach is what has come to be known as monetarism, in contradistinction to what has come to be known as Keynesianism . . . at the microeconomic level, our emphasis is on the free market, in contradistinction to state intervention and central planning.' He said these two strands fitted easily together, but were in fact distinct: it was possible to be a monetarist and a central planner, and Keynes himself had invented Keynesian economics as a way of avoiding central planning. The monetarism which he and the 'New Conservatives' had adopted consisted of two basic propositions. 'The first is that changes in the quantity of money determine, at the end of the day, changes in the general price level; the second is that government is able to determine the quantity of money.'[34]

These are bold, bald assertions, although the phrase 'at the end of the day' was not to be taken too literally. Monetarists talked of 'long and variable lags', but the most common assertion at the time was that there was a two-year gap between changes in the quantity of money and in the price level.

One way of approaching this intriguing matter is to apply what the Americans call 'the duck test' – 'If it looks like a duck, talks like a duck and walks like a duck – then it is a duck.' (Richard Darman, President Bush's Budget Director, answered those who asked whether Bush really meant what he said about promising not to raise taxes, by citing the duck test – 'If it looks like a tax . . . then it is a tax.')

By this criterion, Nigel Lawson during the latter part of the Conservatives' 1974–79 spell of Opposition, and, more crucially, in his time as Financial Secretary, 'looked like a monetarist, talked like a monetarist and walked like a monetarist.' His years as Chancellor suggest, as we shall see, that the monetarist phase was but another passing enthusiasm – entered into in disillusionment, but espoused with sufficient vigour to contribute significantly to the curious policy-mix of 1979–80 which inflicted lasting damage on the economy – damage which was to affect his own return to expansionist policies in the post-1983 Chancellorship.

Lawson once said in an interview that it was not a question of suddenly seeing the light on the boat to Chicago (where the monetarist economist Milton Friedman had been based). We have seen how Lawson in his journalistic days was always in favour of 'incentives', trades union reform and other policies to foster efficiency and productivity – what is now known as the 'supply-side' of the economy. Lawson was among those in the Conservative Party – Sir Keith Joseph and Mrs Thatcher were others – who thought that the Heath Government had been wrong to draw back from its 1970 manifesto commitments in this sphere; indeed, Lawson's old friend and colleague Jock Bruce-Gardyne wrote a book expressing much of their disillusionment with the Heath period, entitled *Whatever Happened to the Quiet Revolution?*

None of this was particularly 'monetarist', except in the sense that monetarists did tend to adopt the 'supply-side' rhetoric, and through such bodies as the Institute for Economic Affairs and the Centre for Policy Studies there was a mingling of the 'New Right' and the monetarists. Lawson saw the policies he came to espouse in 1979 as essentially the result of an evolutionary process: he and his colleagues were much influenced by the adoption of monetarism by Samuel Brittan in the *Financial Times* and Peter Jay, then at *The Times*, and by other reading. Monetary policy generally was more in vogue worldwide as a result of higher inflation, and this encouraged his thinking in this direction. So did the Labour Government's decision to adopt monetary targets in 1976, and all the drama surrounding Britain's approach to the International Monetary Fund to solve its mid-1970s balance of payments crisis.

But Lawson – rightly – regarded Labour's greater stress on monetary policy as grudging and half-hearted. He was, characteristically, to throw himself into it all with more enthusiasm. And he was especially influenced by the fact that the Conservative Party had come to grief in 1974 on his old *bête noire*, the issue of incomes policy, as it applied to the miners. Monetarists were preaching the attractive message (to him) that incomes policies were unnecessary anyway.

We have seen how permissive was Lawson's attitude to the admittedly much lower levels of inflation in the 1960s. But he now believed: 'Today the intolerable social consequences of the present high levels of inflation, and the still greater dangers to the fabric of society that would stem from any further acceleration, have combined with the economic dislocation caused by inflation to reinstate the old [pre-Keynesian] conviction that the prime economic duty of government is to maintain the value of the currency.'[35]

He conceded that 'there is, perhaps, rather less agreement on the means to this end,' adding, 'Our conviction that the means themselves must be monetary in no way denies the existence of a political dimension to inflation.' Thus Lawson, unlike some of his monetarist colleagues, did raise the question of *why* Governments had printed too much money: 'It may well be that political forces have played a prominent part in this. And in so far as they have, it is legitimate to strive politically to weaken those forces. But that in no way derogates from the crucial economic role of monetary policy.'[36]

He appeared to be thinking here principally of the trades unions – which Professor Friedman and other monetarists regarded as irrelevant to inflation – also, possibly, of public sector borrowing – indeed, in a later passage he said, 'Although they did not express it in these terms, the essence of [the Keynesians'] belief was that an increase in the supply of money via a budget deficit would have a sustained and indeed predictable expansionary impact on real things such as output and employment. By contrast, monetarists hold that, at the end of the day, what a Government does to the supply of money will produce purely money effects – although there may well be brief interludes during which monetary policies produce real effects.'[37]

Having conceded in one section that 'political forces' might play a part in inflation, Lawson elsewhere bowed to the standard monetarist line at the time that excessive wage increases could not cause inflation, they could only cause unemployment: 'So far, since the collapse of the previous Government's wages policy and its formal abandonment by the present Government, wage settlements have been running at a higher level than is sensibly compatible with the Government's monetary framework, with unhappy consequences for the level of unemployment.'[38] Even this was capable of the interpretation that Lawson still had his doubts about there being *no* connection between wages and inflation – there could be unhappy consequences for the levels of unemployment *and* inflation.

The truth seems to be that Lawson had tied himself in knots over the crucial question of the mechanism of inflation in Britain. Before his monetarist 'conversion' he had believed that there was a connection between excessive UK inflation and recurrent balance of payments crises, but he had also had a deep-seated, emotional antipathy towards incomes policies. He had resolved the dilemma earlier – given that he also, in those days, objected to higher unemployment – by arguing that all efforts must be made to raise output and productivity, so that the inflationary effect of the classic British wage increase would be correspondingly less.

He was now justifying his opposition to incomes policies on the grounds that they interfered with the workings of the labour market: 'If wages are controlled then imbalances arise with shortages of labour in some areas and excess supply – that is, unemployment – in others, and there is no way in which labour can be attracted to profitable firms.' Yet there is little evidence that in countries such as Japan and West Germany, where great attention is paid to ensuring that the 'norm' for wage increases is low and not inflationary, there cannot be scope within a sensible incomes policy for all sorts of market differentials.

Lawson's 'conversion tract' is more convincing in stating that the defeat of inflation has become the priority than in explaining how monetarism is going to achieve this. He states the assertions of the new-found faith, but suspects in his heart of hearts that life is more complicated. He then makes a resolute effort to assume all the complications away. And, this man who had in the past so contemptuously dismissed the simple, nineteenth-century liberalism of Enoch Powell, is not at all convincing in his attempts to explain how the New Conservatism is a perfectly logical extension and development of the Old.

There is one rather ironical passage in which he quotes the Conservative historian Lord Blake on Conservative 'distrust . . . of Utopian panaceas and of "doctrinaire" intellectuals' – a distrust that, of all things, should have been applied to the monetarist doctrines Lawson was now propagating.

Expansionary Keynesian economic policies had been Lawson's first panacea for the British economy. When balance of payments problems impeded these, devaluation and the removal of the balance of payments constraint had become the next panacea. Inflation having risen to levels which were higher than the 'mild' inflation he thought conducive to economic growth, its removal became the next priority, and monetarism the panacea to effect this. 'One of the more important contributions of the New Conservatism has been to show the damage that wages policies do' – monetarism, on the other hand, offered a simple syllogistical solution: inflation is caused by excessive growth in the money supply; governments can control the growth of the money supply; by controlling the growth of the money supply the Government can eliminate inflation.

Lawson had in the past, as we have seen, fully accepted that the State had a significant role to play in the economy; he had chided the Powellites for failing to recognise the economic concept of 'public goods' – that there were many activities, including subsidies to regional development, where Westminster, or the Man in Whitehall, could iron out the imperfections of the unfettered market-place. In 'The New Conservatism' he made the reasonable point that 'while markets are undoubtedly imperfect, so is the State'; but he proceeded from this observation to conclude that, 'So far from ever more State intervention being justified by virtue of the admitted imperfections of the market, a greater reliance on markets is justified by virtue of the practical imperfections of State intervention.'[39]

He thus abandons his previous belief that a certain level of State intervention is not only tolerable but actually to be encouraged, and constructs a 'man of straw' consisting of 'ever more State intervention' in order to justify moving back from the existing level. He couples this with the assertion 'the bad in society is so intimately and unknowably linked with the rest that an intention to deal with one specific and agreed evil may well do more harm than good.'[40]

'May well' but may well not. This is a counsel of despair which suggests, in the popular saying, that we may as well all go home – if indeed, as the State withdraws, we have a home to go to.

As the *Guardian*'s Ian Aitken commented at the time:

> Resounding stuff, to be sure. But it is the argument which, in one form or another, was used throughout those golden years of 'traditional' conservatism (not to

mention liberalism) to justify keeping women and children down the pits and tiny, half-starved infants slaving endlessly in the mills. Yet Mr Lawson disarmingly claims that even Benjamin Disraeli, inventor of the phrase 'the Two Nations' and patron saint of the 'Wets', would now approve the New Conservatism.[41]

He manages to convince himself that all this is 'very much in the broad historic tradition of Conservatism', which includes 'a profound scepticism about the likely results of state intervention in every aspect of our lives; scepticism about radical new plans of any kind . . . [and] a preference for gradualism in politics.'[42]

There was not much that was gradual about the monetarist policies that were introduced. Nor did Lawson appear to be aware of the paradox that here he was, lauding scepticism about State interference, while giving full backing to State adoption of the monetarist creed.

The adoption of monetarism was such an about-turn for a man who had been a Keynesian in his journalism that he felt it needed a lengthy historical explanation. Having taken consensus Keynesian economics as a natural reaction to the economic horrors of the inter-war years in his *Spectator* articles, Lawson now went back over the period and decided that: 'On the macroeconomic front there is a sense in which the monetarist policies espoused by the new Conservatism represent a belated unlearning of what were mistakenly believed to be the lessons of the war.'[43]

What was wrong in the inter-war years, he said echoing Friedman, was not the use of 'orthodox monetary policies' but their misuse. In the USA there had been too much monetary contraction between 1929 and 1933; in the UK the return to the Gold Standard in 1925 had also led to severe monetary contraction. 'In both countries, a marked departure from the orthodox canons of monetary policy, which inevitably had a severely disruptive effect on the real economy, was wrongly interpreted as proof that the orthodoxy itself was mistaken.'[44] As for the association between Keynesianism and intervention, that was a legacy of the historical accident that Keynesian policies emerged from the wartime years, when all sorts of controls were necessarily in force.

This is more of a desperate attempt at rationalisation than a serious justification. The debate between the 'old orthodoxy', which Lawson now wanted to return to, and the Keynesians raged throughout the 1930s. It was only because of the Keynesian contribution and its acceptance that people began to understand what had gone wrong with policy in the 1920s and early 1930s, and why. In arguing that the original orthodoxy was right all along, just mishandled, Lawson resembles here a man who wants to go back to the horse and cart and disinvent the internal combustion engine.

As for the legacy of the war years, the kind of 'mixed economy' which

Lawson took for granted in the 1960s had had plenty of time to evolve. The Conservative Governments of 1951–64 had every opportunity to dismantle 'wartime controls'; they chose to dispense with those aspects of State intervention they found anathema in peacetime – such as rationing – but to maintain a considerable degree of State intervention on purely pragmatic grounds: it might have its problems, but on the whole it worked, and it was what the electorate wanted. As for intervention to manipulate the levers of economic policy in order to achieve a reasonable balance between the aims of full employment, price stability and balance of payments equilibrium – that kind of intervention was the essence of Keynesian economics as taught by the master himself.

In his re-examination of Keynesianism, Lawson states that 'the excesses of the Keynesian delusion' were held in check by the fixed exchange rate system and by the fact that the numeraire, the dollar, was managed by a country that, until the Vietnam War, pursued non-inflationary policies. For Britain, foreign exchange crises served as 'a proxy for monetary disciplines'. The inflationary financing of the Vietnam War undermined the dollar standard and the fixed exchange rate system, 'while the necessary transition from a fixed to a floating rate regime removed the only existing proxy for overt monetary restraint.'[45]

Lawson himself, of course, had been a passionate advocate of floating exchange rates. We find in this argument a tendency to throw out the baby with the bathwater – Keynesian economics had run into trouble, let us abandon it altogether – or, with extreme sophistry, when it did work, it was 'a form of monetarist policy . . . pursued in a Keynesian guise.'

The monetarist message was that you did not need Keynesian demand management: sensible, steady, non-inflationary growth of the money supply would provide the conditions necessary for the private sector to prosper, and, with it, growth, output, employment and so on. On the other hand, 'Monetarists also believe that excesses in monetary policy – whether in the direction of an expansion or a contraction in the supply of money – will cause a greater or lesser degree of economic collapse and large-scale unemployment. A modern economy simply cannot function without reasonable stability of money.'[46]

The implied assumption is always that the Government can control the money supply. It is spelled out directly in one passage, where, after deriding 'Keynesian fine-tuning and State intervention in the economy', Lawson states that what his new monetarist policies are all about is confined 'to charting a course for those variables – notably the quantity of money – which are and must be within the power of government to control.'[47]

It had been a consistent theme of Lawson's that governments could not create economic growth; the trick was to remove the conditions inimical to it.

He repeats this point in 'The New Conservatism' – only this time it is inflation which is inimical to economic growth.

Monetarism will do the trick of removing inflation, and thereby the greatest obstacle to economic growth. That would be the stick; the carrot would be tax incentives.

THREE

Lawson as Quasi-Chancellor: the Medium Term Financial Strategy *1979–80*

In the summer of 1988 Nigel Lawson, having been the Chancellor of the Exchequer for five years, let it be known to press and public that he was the longest-serving Treasury minister of the century. The question arose whether the Whitehall machine had spontaneously informed him, or he himself had initiated the enquiry. The answer was: 'The latter.'

The pride Lawson took in this minor piece of constitutional history, and the attention to detail that prompted the thought, were typical. Note the careful consideration: it was not yet time to announce that he was the longest serving *Chancellor* of the century. Quite apart from Lloyd George's seven years (1908–15), Denis Healey, for Labour, had been Chancellor for over five years as recently as 1974–79.

But Lawson had, as Financial Secretary, been the number three minister at the Treasury in 1979–81, under the Chancellorship of Sir Geoffrey Howe. Add the two and a bit years of that stint to the subsequent Chancellorship, and you got the 'record'.

Yet the inclusion of his period as Financial Secretary in Lawson's 'record' is appropriate: during 1979–81 Nigel Lawson was a forceful presence in the Treasury, and in some important respects acted, during a crucial phase of the Thatcher Government's early economic policies, as a quasi-Chancellor.

Under the official Chancellor, Sir Geoffrey Howe, who was happier discussing the objectives of Conservative economic policy – lower inflation, faster economic growth, more obedient unions, a shift in the balance between the public and private sectors – than the means of getting there, Lawson spotted a vacuum in economic policy and filled it. Within a short time of arriving at the Treasury he surprised senior Treasury officials by turning up one Monday morning in the summer of 1979 with a paper he had written over the weekend calling for a 'Financial Plan' for the economy.

This was beyond the normal call of the Financial Secretary's duties, and reflected the thinking about 'long-term stabilisation' that he had been doing in Opposition, and communicating to the readers of *The Times*.

A long list of routine duties for the Financial Secretary included the European Community budget; Parliamentary financial business; and the 'disposals of assets'. He would also: 'assist the Chancellor on monetary policy, banks, building societies, National Savings, exchange controls and export credits.'[1]

For 'assist the Chancellor on monetary policy' a more accurate description might have been 'to take monetary policy over'. The most dramatic impact he had on Government policy was the forcefulness with which he introduced the Government's Medium Term Financial Strategy – the embodiment of his and his colleagues' conversion to monetarism – and the consequences this had.

His main achievement during his two and a half years as Financial Secretary was, according to the *Financial Times*, 'to lead a wholesale transformation in Government debt operations, which he saw as the main weakness in monetary control'.[2] And much of Lawson's work during the period of his Financial Secretaryship was in fact related to the Bank of England and to the technical changes in the marketing of gilt-edged stock. The *Financial Times*'s bland account of his achievements curiously omits the measure which many of Lawson's supporters would regard as his greatest moment: the abolition of exchange controls in the autumn of 1979.

An early indication of Lawson's determination to be 'his own man' at the Treasury had been given by his part in the appointment of his own Private Secretary. Jock Bruce-Gardyne, his long-time friend, arrived as a junior minister in the Treasury in the autumn of 1981, after Lawson had left for the post of Energy Secretary. According to Bruce-Gardyne, 'The Treasury was still humming when I got there with the remarkable tale of Nigel Lawson's Private Secretary.' In 'Sir Humphrey' fashion, Lawson had been offered a short-list, chosen by the Treasury, of candidates. The one man Lawson wanted, someone now in the Treasury who had previously worked for him in Opposition as a research assistant, was not on the list. Lawson insisted he was the only person he would take. He was told the man was not available, and that the 'appointment of his former research assistant would smack of political preferment which conflicted with the *mores* of the civil service.' He still insisted, and over several months won the battle, which had eventually been taken to the then head of the Civil Service, Sir Ian Bancroft himself.[3]

Lawson's Private Secretary, from October 1979 to April 1981, was Stephen Locke. He has stated:

> He did have a very close line to Number 10. There were plenty of requests from Number 10 for him to go over and talk to the Prime Minister about particular problems that had arisen. It was actually a problem at times because it sometimes put his more senior colleagues' noses out of joint. There was, for example, John Biffen, who was in the Cabinet. He got somewhat bypassed in some of those areas, which was often a source of some friction.[4]

Asked about Lawson's political qualities, Biffen has commented: 'Aggression . . . aggression in spades. He is pugnacious. I don't think that he enjoys any situation unless he can prosecute his point of view in a very robust fashion indeed.' Biffen saw in Lawson a lack of 'the underlying quality of loyalty and ability to work with a team, as a member of the team.' He was 'too individualistic'.[5]

Lawson upgraded the role of Financial Secretary rather further than had been officially planned. The Chancellor of the Exchequer has responsibility for economic policy as a whole, and the Chief Secretary to the Treasury is in charge of negotiations with other departments on the level of public expenditure. Both are members of the Cabinet. The Financial Secretaryship has been a variable role over the years, and can at times appear to amount to little more than that of the Chancellor's dogsbody. But Lawson, who was not a signatory to the Conservatives' economic manifesto 'The Right Approach to the Economy' (1977), managed to inaugurate a 'Financial Plan' which embraced the whole of economic policy, and to enforce it on his Chancellor and the Treasury itself. This involved bringing in a sympathetic monetarist economist, Mr (later Sir) Terence Burns, from the London Business School, as Chief Economic Adviser to the Treasury, in January 1980, and together they supervised the drawing up of the 'Medium Term Financial Strategy' (1980).

The MTFS was deliberately presented as the central element in what was to become known popularly as the Thatcher Government's 'monetarist' approach to the economy. Until then, both the Treasury and the Bank of England had tended to think essentially in terms of 'real' targets: the desirable level of output and employment figured prominently in political and official thinking; and while an acceleration in inflation or a deterioration in the balance of payments might occasionally divert the emphasis from 'real' to financial matters, such instruments of economic policy as targets for the money supply or the level of public sector borrowing were not normally considered ends in themselves, nor always as overridingly important means.

Nigel Lawson's spell as Financial Secretary changed all that, and contributed in no small measure to the deflation which took place in the British economy during the period 1979–81, leading to a fall of 4 per cent in gross domestic product between 1979 and 1981, and a rise in unemployment to 2 million and later 3 million. This occurred principally because most other aims of economic policy were subordinated to the attempt to achieve preordained targets for the growth of the money supply and the level of public sector borrowing. Although the MTFS was first unveiled in 1980, the June 1979 Budget contained elements of it. An important aspect of this policy was the way interest rates were continually raised – or allowed to rise: it was part of the new Government's philosophy that interest rates were 'determined by the market' – in an effort to cut down the demand for money. Interest rates of 16 and 17 per cent in the period 1979–81 led to a vast inflow of money from overseas into London, which served to aggravate upward pressures on the exchange rate from the growing balance of payments surpluses associated with North Sea oil. The resulting 'strength' of the pound induced severe weakness in British manufacturing industry, which could no longer compete effectively in overseas and domestic markets.[6]

The MTFS had been applied to an economy where inflation was rising fast: although Lawson and his colleagues had inherited an inflation rate of about 10 per cent (which they had promised to reduce) their initial policy changes included a near doubling of VAT, and allowed sharp increases in nationalised industry prices. These had a swift effect on the retail price index (RPI), the annual rate of increase of which shot up from 10.3 per cent in May 1979 to 15.6 per cent in July, with repercussions on the many wage deals which were geared to the index.

Lawson and his colleagues had been warned by Treasury officials that the VAT rise was likely to have a marked inflationary impact because of the way wage bargaining was conducted in Britain. But they paid more attention to monetarist economists who told them that in theory the move should not be inflationary, particularly since wage bargainers were also offered the benefit of offsetting cuts in income tax in the first Thatcher/Howe/Lawson Budget of June 1979.

When told that the RPI was bound to deteriorate, Lawson decided to invent a new index, which he hoped would put the situation in a better light. It was constructed, but amid considerable scepticism and resistance from the economists and statisticians involved, many of whom thought it was of dubious purpose and validity, and would be largely ignored. Many another junior minister would no doubt have been impressed by the force of Whitehall resistance. But Lawson fought it through, and on August 17th, 1979, the new 'Tax and Price Index' (TPI) was unveiled.

Lawson stated: 'It provides, in one figure, a measure which combines both tax changes and movements in prices, and so for taxpayers in general – which means the vast bulk of the population – gives a better indication of changes in total household costs than does the RPI on its own.' He added: 'Two broad points emerge from the TPI and RPI figures published today. The first is that in contradistinction of the sharp movement on the RPI in July, there was no increase in the TPI at all . . .' The second point was that, as measured by the TPI, the increase in household costs 'over the past year' was some two points lower than the RPI.[7]

There is not much evidence that people voluntarily negotiate lower wage and salary increases than they can get, simply because they have received tax cuts. Not much notice was taken of the TPI then; nor, although it continues to be published to this day, has much notice been taken since. It is not a concept used in the statistics of other industrialised countries; it was a political trick which failed, despite the attention Lawson tried to draw to it. It was noteworthy that rather less stress was placed on the TPI in the early 1980s, when an increase in the tax burden meant – as Lawson's officials warned him it eventually would – that the TPI started rising *faster* than the RPI.

One of Lawson's colleagues during the 1979 TPI episode commented: 'Nigel Lawson has always had a cavalier attitude to statistics. When he was Financial Secretary he invented the TPI because he thought it would be better for inflation. Nobody took a blind bit of notice.' Nevertheless, even if they think a Minister is doing something especially silly, Civil Servants tend to be impressed by shows of determination, and the episode helped Lawson to make an early mark on the Treasury.

The cavalier attitude towards statistics had another, more serious result. Because Lawson and his colleagues had convinced themselves that the 'monetary' economy was more important than the Keynesian 'real' one, and because the 'real' statistics were producing such a gloomy message in those early days, it was but a natural inclination to blame the messenger, and question the quality of the statistics. And once they had convinced themselves that the statistics were both unreliable and embarrassing, it was also an easy step, especially when the emphasis was on cuts in Government spending and the numbers of Civil Servants, to begin to economise on the use of statistics. Since many statistics came from industry in the first place, this could also be conveniently justified as 'lightening the load on industry'. The fruits of this exercise were to become apparent later in the decade, when many people, including Lawson himself, started complaining about inadequacies and inconsistencies in the official economic statistics. One Whitehall official commented: 'They cut the Central Statistical Office to ribbons. It was a serious mistake.

They genuinely believed you only needed "money" numbers – not the National Income figures.'

There was one phase during 1980 when Lawson, as Financial Secretary, and other ministers started to explain away the deterioration in the 'real' economy – output falling, unemployment soaring – by recourse to the 'Black Economy' (transactions not declared to the tax inspector). The fact that the Black Economy had been there before the statistics began to deteriorate did not seem to worry them. Lawson actually argued in private at the time that the existence of the Black Economy justified the Government's monetary policy, because Keynesian policies only aimed at 'misleading National Income arithmetic'. But while Lawson was dismissing demand management as out of date, his closest officials were saying things like, 'We are going to need a lot of demand management to get down to the monetary target – you cannot just set the monetary target and leave the economy to run.'

Lawson seemed for a time to be more concerned about vague concepts such as 'the right environment for business' than he did about the manufacturing base itself; it seemed to some observers that the Government was so obsessed by the wonders of small businesses that their ambition was to turn every big business into a small one. Had not new and small businesses provided most of the new jobs in the USA during the previous ten years? they asked. (Yes, but they were satellites to the world of big business.) In his memoir of the period, the then Employment Secretary James Prior says:

> All through the early period of Margaret's Government I felt the Treasury team were out of their depth. They were all theorists – either barristers or, in the case of Nigel Lawson, a journalist. None of them had any experience of running a whelk stall, let alone a decent-sized company. Their attitude to manufacturing industry bordered on the contemptuous. They shared the view of the other monetarists in the Cabinet, that we were better suited as a nation to being a service economy and should no longer worry about production. I could not see how this could be reconciled with the employment of a potential workforce of around 23 million people on a small island.[8]

But it was not only the 'real' statistics for the economy that were embarrassing in 1979. The fact was that in the second half of 1979 the main index of inflation was soaring. Having thus exacerbated inflationary expectations, the Government had that much bigger a task in deflating them. Indeed by the time the MTFS was unveiled as the centre-piece of the March 1980 Budget, the annual rate of inflation, now further augmented by inflationary 'catch-up' pay awards in the public sector, had reached 19.8 per cent.

The 'Financial Statement and Budget Report' (FSBR) is not a document that receives much attention outside a small circle of *aficionados*. It is published on the same day as the Budget speech, and though signed by the Financial Secretary, it traditionally incorporates decisions made principally by the Chancellor and Chief Secretary, as well as an economic analysis of the past year, and forecasts (with explanations) of the year to come.

As Financial Secretary Lawson presented the FSBR on June 12th, 1979 (Sir Geoffrey Howe's first Budget) and March 26th, 1980 (his second). The earlier document bore all the hallmarks of having been written, in the driest and most cautious possible tones, by rigorous economists and officials, determined not to stick their necks out. A typical sentence reads: 'The prospect is for rather little change in real personal disposable incomes over the next year.' There was no obvious sign that Lawson had imprinted anything other than his good name on the document.

By contrast, the FSBR of March 26th, 1980 was intensely political, a mixture of Lawson's views and aspirations for the economy, and official Treasury analysis. It was one of what were to become many publications from the Thatcher Government which blurred the traditional distinction between dispassionate Whitehall analysis, and political gloss. And it was the compromise outcome of a long struggle between Lawson and his Treasury and Bank of England advisers – made easier for Lawson by the support of Terry Burns from January 1980 – in which officials sought to modify the plan the new Financial Secretary had sketched out at home one weekend in the summer of 1979.

By this time the Financial Secretary had become quite a dominant figure in the Treasury, reluctantly admired even by officials who disagreed with him on policy, for his intellect and industry. There were already those who thought he should be substituted for Howe. Such admiration was not in all cases going to endure, especially after he returned as Chancellor in 1983. In particular, they would dislike the way in which Mrs Thatcher and her ministerial colleagues such as Lawson developed the habit of working with 'coteries' of sympathetic officials, who did not always tell them what they did not want to hear.

There was plenty that Lawson did not want to hear from officials in the winter of 1980. Their main concern was that here was an intelligent but naïve politician, apparently wanting to give hostages to fortune by committing himself to an impossibly rigid 'Plan'. During his period in Opposition in the 1970s Lawson had, as we have seen, associated what he regarded as the economic failures of the Heath and Wilson/Callaghan Governments, and also of Whitehall itself, with neglect of the dangers of inflation. 'They are obsessed by the "real economy" and do not pay sufficient heed to things financial' was the tenor of comments made by Lawson and his colleagues in those days. Lawson had also developed a certain contempt for politicians and officials who believed in 'pragmatism'. This had become a dirty word to his ears – an excuse for caving in to the demands of the trades unions, an excuse for not being steady on parade in the face of the counter-inflation inspectors.

Lawson's determination had been shown first by a spirited announcement within weeks of his appointment that the Government was studying ways of easing exchange controls. He talked about 'gradually lifting' them, but the eventual announcement in November 1979 of the complete removal of controls was a very dramatic step indeed; it was considered adventurous to the point of foolhardiness at the time by those who feared that, notwithstanding North Sea oil, Britain had not necessarily said goodbye for ever to its traditional balance of payments problem.

But Lawson's determination to have a fixed monetary plan – the MTFS – alarmed even those officials who were firmly behind his move on exchange controls. One adviser recalled:

> I should not have used the word 'pragmatic' in association with him in 1979. He had an absolute enthusiasm for rules. He gave the impression it did not matter what it was as long as he had an absolute rule, totally in black and white. His attitude then was that his M3 [money supply] target was going to be achieved, come hell or high water.

Some of those who worked closely with him attributed this characteristic of seeming determined to be impaled on hooks as an almost masochistic reaction to his own perception of the failures of the politicians of the previous decade. One colleague said, 'You can't put yourself gently on a hook. It misses the point, as it were. Trying to put yourself on a hook in the monetary field is bound to be uncomfortable. Even with the best will in the world, and the maximum of determination, the monetary system is so volatile that failure is inevitable.'

How deep was Lawson's revulsion towards pragmatism in economic policy is an open question. Indeed, as we shall see later, in practice Lawsonian anti-pragmatism was a short-lived phenomenon; but it lived long enough to wreak considerable damage. The revulsion may be seen in retrospect to have been a reaction against pragmatism as indulged in by others – in which case, it may even fit into an established pattern of political opportunism whose antecedents comfortably pre-date monetarism.

The 'certainty' provided by the monetarist doctrine was highly convenient for a politician who wished to remove 'uncertainty' and offer businessmen the freedom to plan their investment, in the knowledge that they would not be impeded by traditional 'stop–go' activities of pragmatic governments.

To this end, economic agents could be assured that the Government would be relentless in its battle against inflation. Instead of the insipid introduction to his first Financial Statement and Budget Report, Lawson's March 1980 FSBR proclaimed:

> The Budget is a further stage in the Government's medium-term policy of reducing inflation and improving the supply-side of the economy. The central feature of the anti-inflation policy is the gradual reduction of monetary growth. To achieve this reduction without intolerably high interest rates public sector borrowing will be reduced over the medium term. The Budget is intended to achieve a real level of public sector borrowing in 1980–81 significantly lower than in 1979–80.

The wiser counsels of official Treasury and Bank of England advice prevailed to a limited extent: instead of the firm limits which Lawson would have liked to announce for monetary growth, the MTFS offered 'ranges for the growth of the money stock'. (This was to come down progressively from 7 to 11 per cent in 1980–81, to 6 to 10 per cent in 1981–82, 5 to 9 per cent in 1982–83 and 4 to 8 per cent in 1983–84.)

The Bank of England also managed to slip in a footnote that looks especially judicious with the passage of time, warning that 'the way in which the money supply is defined for target purposes may need to be adjusted from time to time as circumstances change.'

Despite the fact that the economy was already manifestly heading for a recession (this was indicated by the more conventional forecasts that accompanied Lawson's new Financial Plan), targets were published for a continual reduction in public sector borrowing, both absolutely and as a proportion of gross domestic product (GDP).

At least these were generally interpreted as targets, although the small print of the MTFS described the course of the PSBR as, 'A projection . . . based on the assumed growth of GDP and present public expenditure plans that should be broadly compatible with the monetary objectives.' Treasury and Bank of England caution also led to the inclusion of a warning that all sorts of things could go wrong, so that 'to maintain a progressive reduction in monetary growth . . . it may be necessary to change policy in ways not reflected in the above projections.'

To conventional economists, the idea of deliberately aiming at reductions in the PSBR at a time of recession seemed bizarre. The normal Keynesian assumption was that it was perfectly healthy for public sector borrowing to rise during a recession, as an 'automatic stabiliser' for the economy. Indeed, not only was this healthy if it happened: it was something to aim at, especially if consumer spending was depressed by a high rate of personal savings.

Despite the small print, however, the intention to reduce the PSBR come what may was emphasised again and again in ministerial speeches. Even their guru Milton Friedman felt it necessary to point out to them that a higher PSBR was perfectly respectable in time of recession.[9]

Lawson, under the influence of even brief experience of reality, showed an early hint of flexibility in this regard in a speech to a *Financial Times* Conference in late January 1980. He acknowledged, in advance of the formal publication of the MTFS, that the PSBR would tend, in a recession, 'to increase through diminished tax receipts and increased social security benefits, other things being equal.' But this had to be seen against the background of the 'secular downward trend' to which the Government was committed. 'Taken together the cycle and the medium-term trend might be expected to produce a "stepped" public sector borrowing profile, with borrowing not changing as much as a proportion of Gross Domestic Product in recession years, but falling sharply in non-recession years.'[10]

This point was to be repeated in subsequent speeches, and represented a difference between Lawson and the Chancellor, Sir Geoffrey Howe, who believed that the PSBR should be brought down in all circumstances. But in the atmosphere of the times, it hardly seemed a great concession: the real question was whether the PSBR should be allowed to rise as a proportion of GDP during a recession. And the general tone of the speech in which the concession was made brought headlines in the serious press on the lines of: 'New hint of curbs on public sector borrowing' and 'Mr Lawson pledges tight hold on PSBR'.

Whatever the riders about the effect of unknown (or known) events on the finances of the public sector, the text of Lawson's FSBR was unambiguous about the basic monetarist beliefs which lay behind the MTFS: 'Control of the money supply will over a period of years reduce the rate of inflation . . . there would be no question of departing from the money supply policy, which is essential to the success of any anti-inflationary strategy.'

(One ironical comment on the success of the inflationary strategy so far was provided by the fact that the FSBR had risen in price by 150 per cent in the nine months since June 1979, whereas the increase in pagination required to accommodate the MTFS was 50 per cent.)

Although there has been a tendency in the Lawson camp to rewrite history and see economic policy since 1980 as a perfect continuum, never intended to be too rigid, at the time the Bank of England had to fight hard to convince

Lawson even to include the footnotes implying that there might conceivably have to be a degree of flexibility. One interesting aspect of the struggle the Bank had is that the Bank itself had been the original proponent of adding monetary targets to the weaponry of the previous Labour Government. For the Bank, it was not so much the MTFS itself, as the absolute commitment to the target figures, over several years, that caused concern. But Lawson was himself reacting, in his basic approach, to the kind of pragmatism the Bank represented. As far as Lawson was concerned, in this particular phase, if one was going to have a rule to influence expectations, one might as well have a rigid rule.

The impression Lawson intended to get across was that the tide of expectations could and would be turned, and that this Government, unlike any other, would adhere to its principles. Expectations were to be changed; and this was how they would be changed. But instead of providing the intended stable background to businessmen and their investment plans, the MTFS in fact created a very gloomy climate: it was rightly interpreted as a deflationary plan and, against the background of that deflation, and in particular the high exchange rate, the spirit of business confidence waned rather than waxed. It is doubtful whether many businessmen studied the minutiae of the MTFS but they certainly reacted to events by cutting back on capacity.

The period between 1979 and 1981 saw a fall of 15 per cent in the output of manufacturing industry, and of about a third in its investment levels. During this time there was a sharp reduction in the industrial base of the British economy;[11] and the bad effects of this were not offset by a surge of investment in the newer technologies and industry. On the contrary, expansion plans generally were curtailed, and the response of industry to the deflationary squeeze was to cut back on the kind of research and development required to nurture the newer technologies. Studies by the National Economic Development Office showed that Britain in the early 1980s had an even smaller share of world trade in the newer 'growth' areas such as information technology than the old, and that its share of new patents taken out in the USA (one of the best tests of technological dynamism) was comparatively low.[12]

The monetarist obsessions of Nigel Lawson as Financial Secretary or 'quasi-Chancellor' contrasted sharply with many of the things he had said as an economic commentator in his journalistic days. He had once castigated those who aimed at lower public borrowing in order to achieve a balanced Budget, arguing that one should ignore 'the Eisenhower school of economic commentators who see some mystical significance in an overall balance, since this is a muddled amalgam of Gladstone and Keynes without the logical consistency of either.'[13]

The MTFS, and the money supply policy from which 'there would be no question of departing', happened to be launched at a time when a more pragmatic – even philosophical – approach would have been helpful. The 'simple rule' enshrined in the MTFS was that if the money supply was expanding faster than the target range, then interest rates should either not be lowered, or should be raised further in order to bring the supply of money under control. It did not allow for the possibility that monetary policy could be tight even if the key indicator – M3 – measuring bank deposits plus notes and coin in circulation, might suggest that it was loose.

As Financial Secretary, Lawson had a big part in Treasury, Bank of England and Number 10 Downing Street discussions during 1980–81 on attempts to improve methods of monetary control. He was at first attracted by another simple panacea – the idea that through directly controlling the size of the monetary 'base' (M0) of the economy – the balances that the banks hold at the Bank of England, as well as banks' 'till money' and notes and coins in circulation – the Government could exercise greater control over monetary policy than by aiming at M3. The idea was always repugnant to the Bank of England – which takes its primary function of being 'lender of last resort', to the banking system, more seriously than the achievement of any quantitative target – 'the authorities have always stood ready to provide liquidity in the form of balances at the Bank of England, in essentially unlimited quantities though at a price of the authorities' choosing.'[14] And Lawson was impressed by the weight of official expertise suggesting that under a system of monetary base control interest rates would be much more volatile.

One change in methods of monetary control that Lawson did favour was the abolition of the so-called 'corset' on the growth of bank deposits, introduced by Labour in 1978. In keeping with his belief in greater freedom, and in relaxation of controls, Lawson pushed strongly for the many developments during the 1980s which came under the general heading of 'deregulation'. The 'corset' itself was removed in the summer of 1980, and had a dramatic expansionary impact on the monetary statistics. Greater competition among banks, between banks and building societies, and between overseas institutions and British ones, was all encouraged as part of the new 'philosophy' which he so passionately approved. But such developments were greatly going to complicate the task of controlling the money supply – the pivot of the anti-inflationary policy. And the abolition of exchange controls, which had already taken place, weakened the Government's ability to impose quantitative controls on bank lending.

The Bank of England managed to get a reference into a joint Treasury–Bank consultative paper on monetary control in March 1980 about taking 'other measures' into account in monetary policy, not just M3. But the basic weight of the Government's reputation lay on control of M3, and Lawson emphasised in a post-Budget press conference after the MTFS had been formally unveiled that the principal commitment was to a declining target over the years for the growth of M3.

For all his political attachment to this simple goal, however, by May Lawson was manifesting distinct signs of concern about complications to come: he told the Building Societies Annual Conference that if they sought to compete more aggressively with banks for deposits 'obviously we should have to consider switching the focus of policy more to the wider aggregates, which includes building society shares and deposits'. And the special tax treatments of the societies would have to be reconsidered. (The building societies were already expecting the banks to compete more vigorously with *them* after the abolition of the 'corset'.)[15]

The toing and froing of the relatively lowly Financial Secretary between the Treasury and Number 10 Downing Street was causing widespread comment within the Treasury during 1979–80. Because they had associated him with policies of the previous Labour Government, Sir Douglas Wass, the Permanent Secretary to the Treasury, was regarded with some suspicion initially by both the Prime Minister and Lawson. Eventually Wass won Mrs Thatcher's respect, but there were times when the lines of communication were out of order, and, as one of Sir Douglas's colleagues commented, 'Lawson was behaving like the Permanent Secretary.'

But he was also a thorn in the flesh of Sir Geoffrey Howe, the Chancellor himself. Although, as the political architect of the MTFS, he was selling his medium-term plan to a willing buyer, his 'high profile', and obvious desire for the top job, were irritants to Howe. In particular, Howe was put out when, while he himself was trying to get across an atmosphere of austerity in his March 1980 Budget (which was not, in the circumstances, too difficult), Lawson could not resist telling a press conference that, if all went well with the MTFS, within two years the basic rate of tax could be brought down from thirty pence to twenty-five pence. This was, in fact, going to take a lot longer – and in the end Lawson himself would get the full glory, under his own Chancellorship, for the move. Another irritant to the official Chancellor was that Lawson was part of a (for a time) 'secret' group of the faithful that met Mrs Thatcher for breakfast, and included the Chief Secretary John Biffen and Norman Tebbit.[16]

He certainly, during 1979–80, began to display another characteristic that was to become a feature of his Chancellorship – a perennial optimism that things would improve in a few months' time, or not be so bad as others were saying. While this kind of optimism is almost standard for most politicians, it seems to have been especially prominent in Lawson – unlike his Treasury colleague Biffen, who in one speech spoke openly of the prospect of 'three years unparalleled austerity' (medium term, indeed . . .).

An expansionist at heart, an expansionist who had not only bought a suspect economic doctrine but successfully sold it to his colleagues, Lawson at first rationalised away the mounting economic damage, and later argued that it was a necessary prelude to British economic renaissance. The MTFS embodied the spirit of the monetarist policies that had been in operation from Day One (some would say 'the attempt at monetarist policies'), and the real economy was deteriorating even before the formal unveiling in March 1980. The trouble was that it promised a lot more of the same, if one took the targets even half seriously. And in this respect, a ready inclination to get off hooks as well as on to them would not necessarily help. Getting off hooks in a dignified manner takes time. And sometimes the way in which policy was changed was going to be so obfuscatory that British industry – whose better performance was meant to be at the heart of the monetarist experiment – did not necessarily notice, or act accordingly.

Sometimes Lawson's rationalisations during 1980 simply reflected his enthusiasms and his enquiring mind. He was genuinely interested in new theories (or old theories in new bottles) – not least if they promised to deflect criticism. Thus the idea that the decline in manufacturing did not matter, because the future of our economy lay in services, had a natural appeal to him; so did the rationalisation that, because they were supposed to be changing the climate of opinion and expectations, the gloomy Treasury forecasts of recession need not be believed: they were the result of past assumptions, based on experience when the appalling Socialists were in power – things were now going to be different.

What the MTFS had failed to take account of was the crucial importance of the exchange rate. If the pound is too high, this has an adverse effect on the ability of British industry to compete against manufacturers from overseas – both in export markets and at home. The output and profits of industry were being squeezed in this way in the period 1979–81; but because the figures for the growth of money supply were running well above the targets in Lawson's MTFS, interest rates were kept high, attracting overseas funds to London, and maintaining the pound at a level where it continued to cause serious damage to industry. Monetary policy was in fact tight, but not according to the MTFS.

The winter of 1980–81 saw the first occasion on which Lawson was to come up against Professor Sir Alan Walters. The Bank of England had, since the summer of 1980, argued that monetary policy was too tight; and, indeed, two reductions in interest rates – from 17 to 16 per cent on July 3rd, and again to 14 per cent on November 15th – were made for essentially pragmatic reasons, in spite of the evidence of the figures for M3. The Financial Secretary insisted, however, that there should be no reference in the Bank's public comments to the way concern about the exchange rate had influenced these decisions.

Professor Walters has suggested that the pragmatic Bank at this stage was more interested in the survival of British industry than in controlling inflation.[17] In fact it was concerned about both.

When Walters arrived at Number 10 Downing Street as the Prime Minister's Economic Adviser in January 1981, he threw his weight behind a campaign to get the exchange rate down to a more realistic level, and argued that monetary policy had indeed been too tight in 1979 and 1980. Walters and his colleagues in the Number 10 Policy Unit had an overriding influence on discussions preceding the March 1981 Budget, whose object was to lower interest rates and the exchange rate.[18]

Close observers felt throughout the 1979–80 period that Lawson desperately wanted to be Chancellor himself, and to this end wished to impress the Prime Minister with his credentials. There are many who think there was no real 'intellectual' justification for the kind of economic policy decisions taken in 1979–80 – but in so far as there was, Lawson was generally credited with having provided it as backing for the Prime Minister's deep feelings that the nation should be run in accordance with her ideal of the Grantham household.

Not generally being thought of as a politician who was particularly sensitive to other people's feelings, Lawson, with his obvious ambition to be Chancellor, and with a private line to the Prime Minister, had not necessarily played his early cards too well with Sir Geoffrey Howe. After eighteen months of devoted service to the cause, he was appointed a Privy Counsellor in the January 1st, 1981, New Years Honours List. There was then a reshuffle in which John Biffen, who had generally been considered to have a relaxed approach to being Chief Secretary (and part of whose duties on public expenditure were from the start put into Lawson's hands), was moved to the Leadership of the House of Commons. Lawson was furious to see the number two job of Chief Secretary go to Leon Brittan, brother of his friend from *Financial Times* days, Samuel Brittan, the economics commentator, but closer to Howe than to him.

Lawson was not consulted about the appointment of Leon Brittan, and was telephoned with the news at home in his constituency just before the public announcement was made. Sir Geoffrey Howe was unavailable at the Treasury to witness Lawson's wrath the following day, having an urgent appointment in Northern Ireland. Samuel Brittan was quoted as saying: 'I was delighted that my brother got into the Cabinet. But I was worried that it was at the expense of Nigel, who I regard as the only government minister with the slightest understanding of economic policy.'[19]

One colleague at the time said, 'Lawson simply went into a sulk for days. He was furious, saying Howe preferred appointing his friends to rewarding talent.' But it was not simply opposition from a Chancellor who thought he was in too much of a hurry. Willie Whitelaw, in effect Deputy Prime Minister at the time, and somebody to whom Mrs Thatcher listened, was also against Lawson's promotion to the Cabinet, having been 'rubbed up the wrong way' once too often by his junior colleague. Lawson actually went to see Mrs Thatcher at Number 10 to protest.

FOUR

Lawson as Quasi-Chancellor: the Zurich Speech and the 1981 Budget

January–September 1981

There was a fair amount of 'nursery behaviour' in the Treasury in January 1981. It was the beginning of the run-up to the Budget, and the snubbed Lawson went off to give a major speech on economic policy in Zurich, without even warning Howe, who was furious. Lawson and his close colleagues often refer back to the Zurich speech as an example of early 'pragmatism', but it contains flagrant examples of non-pragmatism, notably in regard to the exchange rate. It also demonstrates political obstinacy in so far as, while recognising the problems with the 'hooks' on which monetary policy was now impaled, it expresses the determination to remain firmly impaled on M3.

Lawson composed the Zurich speech on what colleagues described as 'his old battered typewriter'. It was a last-minute affair, so that officials could not have much chance to act to tone it down very much; and the Chancellor did not see it until afterwards. There was a characteristically Lawsonian touch also in the 'note to editors' on the copies of the speech supplied in advance to the British press. It confidently declared, 'The Financial Secretary will speak to a *large audience* [my italics] of businessmen, politicians, academics and industrialists . . . The Prime Minister spoke to a meeting of the same Society when Leader of the Opposition in 1977.'

The speech was delivered against the background not only of the local Treasury difficulty over Lawson's 'non-promotion', but also of Professor Walters's arrival at Number 10 Downing Street, and his strong views about where the exchange rate ought to be, and which monetary indicators were the most important – not Lawson's M3. It was entitled, 'Thatcherism in Practice: A Progress Report'; it was a rationalisation of the MTFS and his general approach, and was designed with the Prime Minister as much in mind as the Zurich audience.

The Zurich speech underlined the Government's abandonment of Keynesianism. Lawson said that previous governments had regarded their prime duty as 'to promote full employment by the use of appropriately expansionary fiscal and monetary policies', with 'inflation a distinct and separate problem, to be solved by direct action on wages and prices, ranging from exhortation, through voluntary and quasi-voluntary guidelines, to statutory controls.'

He took pride in stating that this approach had been dropped:

> Broadly speaking we set as the overriding objective of macro-economic policy the conquest of inflation; while at the same time we embarked on a micro-economic policy of removing wherever possible major market distortions from the economy so as to improve the performance of the supply side of the economy, thus laying the only true foundation for wealth creation and the only hope of increased employment in the long term.[1]

There was a certain rewriting of history in these broad claims. Successive governments had many times used macroeconomic policy against inflation: indeed, it was often to counter inflation that governments indulged in the 'stop' phase of the 'stop–go' policies which Lawson had many times criticised as an economic commentator in the past.

True, as inflation became more endemic, a variety of approaches under the general head of 'incomes policy' was added. But the belief that there was some kind of choice, or 'trade-off', between the degree of unemployment and the rate of inflation was very much a part of the approach to economic policy before 1979. What was new under Lawson's MTFS approach was the *all-pervading* importance given to the fight against inflation, and the chosen means. There was now allegedly no trade-off (employment could not be 'bought' through expansion of demand – that would mainly show up in higher prices): the fight against inflation was the 'overriding' objective, with control of the money supply the means. Unemployment was not a serious subject of Government concern, but should come down spontaneously once inflation was conquered, the public sector reined back, and entrepreneurs were inspired by the weakness of the unions, and the freedom of deregulation, to 'supply'.

When Lawson delivered his Zurich speech, the measured rate of inflation shown by the RPI figures was over 15 per cent, compared with about 10 per cent (but rising) at the time the Government took over. By taking the recent run of statistics and 'annualising' them, and comparing them with similarly adjusted figures for the period immediately before the Conservatives came into office, Lawson managed to claim that the inflation picture had improved since mid-1979. He made no reference to the peak annual figures of 21.9 per cent which had been reached in May 1980.

Of course, the truth was that inflation had for a period got much worse under a Government that had dedicated itself to the conquest of inflation above all else, and under a policy – supreme concentration on control of the money supply, with interest rates being 'left to the market' – of which Lawson had been the political architect. And, even as Lawson spoke, an argument was still raging in London between monetarist advisers who considered that policy was too tight and those who – looking at the rapid growth of M3 – maintained it was still lax.[2]

But not only had inflation worsened markedly: so had the 'real economy': total output (gross domestic product); manufacturing production; manufacturing investment . . . all had dropped sharply; unemployment was mounting fast, from 1.3 million in mid-1979 to over 2 million during the winter when Lawson made his Zurich speech.

Lawson's remarks about the 'supply-side' of the economy were somewhat disingenuous: the 'true foundation' for wealth creation is technological progress, which enables a modern economy to grow on average by around 2 to 3 per cent (compound) a year, thus offering a doubling of living standards every twenty-five years or so. The debate in Britain for many years had been how to make the economy grow even faster; and measures designed to improve the 'supply side' were nothing new: they were a constant preoccupation of both Conservative and Labour Governments from the late 1950s.

If, in Lawson's Zurich phrase, 'market distortions' are essentially factors which impede the performance of the supply side of the economy, then the deflation and high exchange rate which were the effect of the policies embodied in the MTFS were about as big a distortion as one could imagine, and were manifestly dwarfing the beneficial effects; these latter appeared in the Zurich speech as 'a marked improvement in industrial relations, with many fewer man-hours lost in strikes . . . managers now actively managing again . . . British companies throughout the length and breadth of the country . . . becoming more efficient, leaner, tauter, fitter and more productive.' The rhetoric of this sounded splendid but the reality was a 15 per cent drop in manufacturing output between 1979 and 1981, and a plunge of one-third in the level of manufacturing investment, to well below anything recorded since the early 1960s; and rising oil revenues were disguising a very sharp deterioration in the manufacturing trade balance.

It was an awkward time for Lawson to choose to defend the MTFS strategy which he told his audience was the 'heart of our economic policy . . . the core of which is a steady deceleration in the rate of monetary growth over a four-year period, buttressed by a gradual reduction in the size of the underlying budget deficit, which in turn is to be achieved by a steady reduction in the real level of total government spending.'

He had to admit: 'On the crucial monetary front, the picture is somewhat obscure and decidedly patchy.' Speaking a good eighteen months after the 1979 General Election, he managed to blame the poor performance of his chosen criterion, the monetary statistic M3, on the previous Government. They had imposed penalties on the banks for 'excessive' growth of lending; but this 'artificial constraint' merely led companies to borrow more outside the banking system. When the Conservatives removed the 'corset' during 1980, there was a return to more normal bank lending, and an 'unwinding' process. Hence M3, or 'broad money', had ended up growing at an annual rate of 16 per cent in the eighteen months of Conservative rule, almost exactly the same rate as under the last eighteen months of Labour, but compared with a target of 7 to 11 per cent. On the other hand, much narrower definitions of the money supply had grown more slowly.

It was the slow growth of the narrowly defined money supply, along with the strength of the exchange rate, that had convinced Professor Walters that policy was too tight. Lesser mortals were content with the evidence all around them of the worst slump since the war – if not the century. In Zurich Lawson asked: 'Does this mean that monetary policy, in the sense that matters for the conquest of inflation, has been tight, as the Government manifestly intended – and indeed still intends – or has it been alarmingly lax?'

His answer owed more to the cautionary notes that Treasury and Bank of England advisers had urged upon him than he would originally have liked:

> We have made it clear all along . . . that to assess underlying monetary conditions properly it is necessary to take account of the evidence of all the various monetary indicators. And certainly the evidence of the main financial indicators which generally speaking reflect monetary conditions – the strong exchange rate, high interest rates, the tight corporate liquidity position, and decelerating inflation – would appear to confirm the message of the narrow money figures: namely that monetary policy has indeed been tight.

This sounded much more like the old pragmatic Treasury talking than the Financial Secretary who had espoused a simple rule. But then, in a passage which might have produced some belly laughs if it had been delivered to an audience closer to home, Lawson stated: 'Unfortunately it is not quite as simple as that. For the purpose of setting the annual target for monetary growth – and indeed for the 4-year path set out in the Medium Term Financial Strategy – we have . . . chosen broad money as the most useful guide.'

But that was not all. He continued: 'I believe we were and remain right to do so. Narrow money has the advantage of being easier to control, but it suffers from being almost too easy to control.' This was because 'narrow money', M1, contained what were then non-interest-bearing current accounts, or 'sight deposits', which were likely to be switched into interest-bearing deposits, part of M3, if interest rates went up a lot, as indeed they had done. This made both measures unreliable – and broad money was likely to be further distorted by the fact that companies wanting to borrow in the market for a long period might defer their plans while interest rates were high, but meanwhile borrow from banks, at prevailing high interest rates, for a short period.

Lawson managed therefore in this speech to concede that all measures of the money supply were unreliable and subject to distortions, adding, 'It is scarcely surprising that in the sophisticated modern world, and in particular for a country as financially advanced as the UK, monetary control is a highly complex matter.' (Many an adviser was to mutter privately after this speech, 'That's what we told him originally, but he wouldn't listen.') He then went on to say, 'But that is no reason for getting it wrong, still less for abandoning the task altogether.'

With Professor Walters back home in London arguing that narrow money was the most important guide, ridiculing the Financial Secretary's obsession with broad money, and about to have a significant impact on the coming Budget, Lawson breezily stated:

> The conclusion I draw from all this is that monetary conditions in the UK have not been inflationary so far, but that it is essential from now on to secure a lower rate of growth of broad money, and indeed, over the three remaining years of the medium term financial strategy, it might well be prudent to claw back at least some of the excess growth that has already occurred.

This could have been paraphrased: 'We were wrong about monetarism providing us with a simple rule, and, not to put too fine a point upon it, monetary policy in the UK is now all over the place. But it would be far too humiliating politically to admit this.'

The *Financial Times* greeted the speech as 'an honest appraisal' and 'remarkably frank and intelligent'. It saw Lawson's basic plea as that the Government 'should be judged by results, not by numbers'. Nevertheless, in reaction to Lawson's claim that M3 was still 'the most useful measure' the *Financial Times* commented, 'This is an odd explanation of why it is misleading.' Elsewhere the *Financial Times* noted that the market in Government stocks had fallen in reaction to the admission of the effects of the recession on the PSBR, adding 'Experience has taught the market to place more faith in admissions of failure than in promises of future good behaviour.' But the Prime Minister was pleased.

The then Leader of the Opposition, Michael Foot, teased Mrs Thatcher about Lawson's 'candid admissions' about economic policy in the speech. She replied that the speech had been 'remarkably intelligent and persuasive' and privately promised Lawson 'better things next time' in the promotion stakes. Adam Raphael, the *Observer*'s political editor, wrote, 'So perhaps, after all, he need not abandon those dreams of standing some day in Sir Geoffrey Howe's shoes.'

What Lawson did not say in his 'honest appraisal' was that, in adopting monetarism and his 'medium-term plan', he had done very little research on monetary policy. One official commented: 'It is incredible how little he had learnt from US experience: deregulation is incompatible with stable, consistent, measurable monetary aggregates.' Monetary control was not just 'a highly complex matter' because of the 'sophisticated modern world'. The other arm of financial policy – deregulation, and the general encouragement of competition to lend – was a truly eccentric accompaniment to the central attempt at monetary control. And deregulation itself encouraged greater sophistication among the public, and less inclination to hold non-interest-bearing accounts – especially in periods when interest rates were attractively high as part of the attempt to tighten monetary policy. In such circumstances, control of 'narrow', non-interest-bearing money was hardly a major achievement.

Lawson concluded what he regarded as his seminal Zurich speech with some remarks about the exchange rate which were odd at the time, and were going to look even odder in the light of his subsequent exchange rate policy as Chancellor:

> Then there is the exchange rate. The continuing strength of the £, despite the abolition of exchange controls, is a phenomenon which has surprised many if not most observers. No doubt it has a lot to do with the UK's new-found self-sufficiency in oil; but whatever the precise mix of reasons – which in any event can never be objectively determined – the one thing that is clear is that it is the product of the free play of market forces.

The 'free play of market forces' during the 1979–80 period was influenced, however, first by the remarkably high level of nominal interest rates available in the UK and second by the fact that the market perceived that the rise in the pound was not being seriously resisted. This gave international investors the double incentive of high interest rates and large capital gains on their deposits in sterling. The foreign exchange market tends to test the resolve of a country's monetary authorities to the limit; and the limit, before an alliance of Professor Walters and the Bank of England led to a change of policy, was very high indeed. (Having been considered 'about right' by the International Monetary Fund when it was worth $1.70 in late 1976, the pound was over $2.40 in January 1981. Against the D-Mark the pound had been worth just under DM 4.00 both in the closing months of 1976 and around the time when the Conservatives were elected in May 1979, but its average value was over DM 4.81 in the first quarter of 1981, an upward revaluation of 20 per cent.)

The 'free play of market forces' was a concept very close to Lawson's heart. He had been the most prominent advocate after the May 1979 Election victory of the abolition of exchange controls, which took place in November 1979. The Bank of England had been pressing for this for some time; and, quite apart from wanting to make life easier financially for companies, Lawson himself was a passionate believer in the freedom of the individual to conduct his own financial transactions with the minimum of interference from the Government.

Brought up, as they had been, on a diet of regular balance-of-payments crises, the permanent officials in the Treasury were by no means unanimous in supporting Lawson on this. Some envisaged a situation when the oil would not be so plentiful, and a British economy that might not respond to the Lawson treatment in the way he hoped, and would be in need of the protection afforded by exchange controls. The legislation enabling the Government to reintroduce them in an emergency was retained until much later in the decade (notwithstanding the advent of North Sea oil, Treasury officials were expressing private concern about the balance of payments trend during 1981).

One aspect of the abolition of exchange controls that did appeal to the more wary Treasury officials, however, was the thought that a subsequent exodus of funds from London might be just what the economic doctor ordered from the point of view of keeping the pound down. This was also a view that Lawson himself had put forward for several years, including when he was in Opposition. But while eventually there certainly were to be large outflows of investment capital, the British financial institutions proved sluggish in the use of their new financial freedom. And, meanwhile, the 'hot money' attracted by high interest rates continued to pour in from overseas.

People who adopted monetarism tended also to be strong believers in the free market and 'non-intervention', although there was not a necessary connection between the two. We have already seen the odd conjunction of deregulation and the attempt at monetary control – the logical thing would surely have been not to deregulate. In the case of the exchange rate, the 'free market' aspect also dominated at this stage, when Lawson was described by a number of his colleagues as 'a free floater'. This was very much in accord with Mrs Thatcher's instincts – she has nearly always abhorred intervening in the exchange markets by selling foreign currency, or even taking it into the reserves.

Lawson had bluntly told his Zurich audience:

> The present Government has no exchange rate policy as such – for the simple reason, as Switzerland among others has experienced, that the attempt to have such a policy greatly complicates (if it does not actually make it impossible) the difficult enough task of pursuing a sound monetary policy, without at the end of the day having any significant effect on the real exchange rate, whatever may happen to nominal rates.

One does not know what the Swiss audience made of this attempt simultaneously to have it all ways. But it is important to note that, as Chancellor, Lawson was not only to attempt an exchange rate policy, but to make it, for a time, one of the central planks of his policy: indeed, his exchange rate policy was to subsume his monetary policy.

The 'real exchange rate' is the exchange rate adjusted for inflation: thus in the period under review, not only did the pound rise sharply, but British industrialists' costs per unit of output rose far faster than in most of our competitor countries; between 1978 and 1981 the real exchange rate rose by nearly 40 per cent, whereas those for West Germany and France hardly changed at all. The former President of the West German Bundesbank, Dr Otmar Emminger, described this as 'by far the most excessive overvaluation which any major currency has experienced in recent monetary history'.[3]

To Emminger and many others, it was absurd that Britain simply washed its hands at this stage of an exchange rate policy. Lawson rationalised the situation by maintaining that the strength of the pound 'has undoubtedly been one of the main channels through which the crucial and marked change in trend from rising to falling inflation has been effected'. He maintained that 'British exports have so far held up pretty well and the current account of the balance of payments is in sizeable surplus' – but made no reference to the fact that there had been a sharp erosion of Britain's share of world trade in manufactures, and the balance of payments surplus in the early 1980s was more than accounted for by the huge, but temporary, earnings from North Sea oil.

Another fashionable rationalisation at the time, which Lawson seized on, was that the pound was a 'petro-currency', whose rise was the inevitable consequence of North Sea oil. Professor Walters questioned this, as well as the assumptions that M3 was the appropriate indicator for measuring policy, and that nothing could be done to lower the exchange rate.

Walters had stated during the IMF meeting in Washington at the end of September 1980 that he thought the pound was much too high at around $2.40; on purchasing power parity grounds – that is, according to measurements of what it costs to buy an identical basket of goods and services in different countries – he thought $1.70 was a more appropriate rate. Before he took up his Downing Street post in January 1981, he was one of the instigators of an independent study, 'The Appreciation of Sterling – Causes, Effects and Policies'[4] by a Swiss economist, Dr Jürg Niehans, which was ready in January 1981.

Walters had made the point that other oil-producing countries did not seem to enjoy 'petro-currency' status. Niehans also took issue with the 'petro-currency' argument, suggesting that this might account for 20 per cent at most of the pound's previous rise, and that monetary policy had indeed been too tight. He himself was perfectly prepared to recommend a more active exchange rate policy, pointing out that some of Lawson's audience in Zurich, members of the Swiss National Bank, had successfully intervened in the exchange markets to reduce the overvaluation of the Swiss franc in 1978 (in contrast to what Lawson had implied in his reference to the Swiss experience in his speech).

Professor Walters's intervention in seeking a more active exchange rate policy was a turning point. The most significant impact on the March 1981 Budget was made by him and his colleagues in the Number 10 Downing Street Policy Unit. Backed by the Niehans study, they argued that the important thing was to relax monetary policy and reduce the attractions of sterling as an investment currency by lowering interest rates. This was quite the reverse of what was theoretically implied by Lawson's MTFS, with its concentration on progressively reducing the growth of M3. The latter indicator had grown much faster than allowed by the Plan presented in the 1980 Budget; and, according to the Zurich speech, such 'excessive' growth should be 'clawed back'. In fact the new MTFS monetary target for M3 was 'rebased' at a higher level, M3 having expanded in the previous year at well above its target of 7 to 11 per cent.

The March 1981 Budget, when Lawson as Financial Secretary was still 'quasi-Chancellor', is an important reference point. Lawson himself has many times harked back to it as the episode which proved critics of monetarism and the MTFS wrong, and himself resoundingly right. He is especially fond of pouring scorn on the group of 364 economists who wrote a critical letter about the Budget to *The Times* shortly afterwards.

Many a politician might have felt somewhat humiliated by the episode during which the trustworthiness of the Government's attachment to M3 had been so severely shaken. But from Lawson's point of view, despite the failure to achieve both the monetary and public sector borrowing targets during 1980–81, the 1981 Budget still came across as a triumph for the spirit of his MTFS. What did it matter if other people were more influential than he in shaping it?

The beauty of the MTFS was that it had its monetary and its fiscal sides (related, of course), and if things were not going entirely according to plan on one front, it was only natural to capitalise on better developments on the other.

At this point it is worth emphasising something which is taken for granted within Whitehall but not always appreciated outside: the way policy often *evolves* towards a conclusion which the main participants come to accept, even though they may disagree en route, not to say start from different sides, and have to yield considerably before the final decision. On the other hand, just as outside observers are vulnerable to the accusation that they overdramatise 'clashes', politicians and officials are often adept at pretending they have always held the view which has emerged as the consensus, but with which they disagreed earlier.

In the case of the March 1981 Budget, as we have seen, policy was influenced heavily by Professor Walters and his colleagues, including Sir John Hoskyns, in the Number 10 Policy Unit. Having won the argument that Lawson's M3 should be ignored, *and* the exchange rate encouraged to come down – which meant lowering interest rates – Walters and his colleagues then advocated 'an unthinkably low PSBR' for 1981/82, as a means of regaining credibility with the financial markets, so that it would be easier to effect an orderly reduction in interest rates and the pound. Lawson, whose 'hands off' attitude towards the exchange rate was also effectively being overruled, was quite happy to go along with a low PSBR target, which would boost the 'virility' of his MTFS and divert attention from the fact that monetary policy was deliberately being relaxed. There were several 'rough' discussions with permanent Treasury officials, but what finally emerged by mid-March was before long being described as 'a consensus' of Number 10 and Treasury views.

Sir Geoffrey Howe, the Chancellor who actually introduced the March 1981 Budget, was perfectly happy with a low PSBR. 'I'm just an old-fashioned Welsh fundamentalist' he used to say: he shared Mrs Thatcher's opinion that it was thoroughly virtuous to reduce public sector borrowing; and he accepted the Walters/Hoskyns/Lawson 'consensus' view.

According to Lawson, the 1981 Budget was actually a turning point for the economy, to which the subsequent recovery in output was attributable. This is debatable, as we shall see in later chapters. In any case, the 364 economists based their concerns on what was implied by the policies ruling at the time, or which appeared to be ruling.

They stated that, 'Present policies will deepen the depression, erode the industrial base of our economy and threaten its social and political stability.' They pointed out: 'There is no basis in economic theory, or supporting evidence for the Government's belief that by deflating demand they will bring inflation permanently under control and thereby induce an automatic recovery in output and employment.'[5]

There was little doubt at the time that *previous* policies had deepened the depression. And subsequent evidence certainly demonstrated that the industrial base had been eroded. The recovery in unemployment did not begin until five years after the 1981 Budget. The case for Lawson's scorn for the economists rests largely on the fact that output did stop falling during 1981; employment (mainly of part-timers) began to rise in 1982; and a long, slow process of recovery in output began, although it was many years before it returned to the level from which it had declined.

This happened in spite of the fact that the Chancellor, Sir Geoffrey Howe, had opted for his 'unthinkable' Budget – one which deliberately sought to lower the PSBR although the economy was in recession and unemployment was growing. But for several years the degree of recovery was slight; and there are a number of factors which suggest that Lawson's attack on the economists was disingenuous.

The important point is that monetary policy was loosened, and an exchange rate policy was introduced. This counteracted the deflation implied by the reduction in the PSBR.

Lawson had dismissed the idea of an exchange rate policy in his Zurich speech; Professor Walters and his colleagues in the Number 10 Policy Unit, along with the Bank of England, were responsible for an attempt to achieve a more competitive exchange rate. Although there was to be the occasional panic when the pound threatened to fall too fast – as in the summer of 1981 when interest rates were suddenly raised again – the 1981 Budget included a 2 per cent drop in interest rates, deliberately aimed at lowering the exchange rate. The move away from a policy of 'leaving the exchange rate to the market' to one of deliberately encouraging the exchange rate to fall was itself a reflationary move, and a change from the policy the 364 economists had criticised. But it was not announced; nor was the true strategy immediately apparent.

A corollary of this is that the monetary policy outlined in the March 1981

Financial Statement and Budget Report (presented, once again, by Nigel Lawson) was much more restrictive and daunting than what subsequently occurred. The ranges laid down for monetary growth in the FSBR were for growth of 6 to 10 per cent in 1981–82, 5 to 9 per cent in 1982–83 and 4 to 8 per cent in 1983–84. The corresponding growth subsequently recorded was 14½ per cent in 1981–82, 10 per cent in 1982–83, and 9¾ per cent in 1983–84. But it took time for the effective U-turn of monetary policy to be observed.[6]

Thus, in all three of the subsequent financial years monetary growth was significantly above the top limit of the range ordained in March 1981. The growth of M3 was respectively 81 per cent, 42 per cent and 62 per cent above the 1981 plan – and of course, in the two latter years, from a higher base than envisaged. This made pretty good nonsense of the monetary side of Lawson's medium-term plan.

The prospect on the fiscal side also looked disturbing at the time – but that was the whole point. Professor Walters subsequently wrote:

> The point was that, notwithstanding the condition of the real economy in 1980, anything but a tight fiscal squeeze would have destroyed credibility in the feasibility of the Thatcher programme. Scepticism about the political will would have quickly ensued. In my judgement, there would have followed a financial crisis as the markets passed speedy judgement on the borrowing and the implications. Interest rates would have soared instead of sinking.[7]

The fiscal picture early in 1981 partly reflected the fact that the PSBR had been much higher during 1980–81 than envisaged in the original MTFS, at 6 per cent of GDP, compared with the intended 3¾ per cent. From that point of view it could be argued that Lawson's 'concession' was operating – the point made in the *Financial Times* Conference speech of January 1980 and developed in the Zurich speech, that allowance could be made for the fact that the recession had proved deeper than expected, thereby raising outgoings on unemployment benefit and lowering tax receipts. But given that the outturn looked like being 6 per cent (or £13.5 billion) in 1980–81, the Lawson 'concession' was certainly not operating for 1981–82. On 'unchanged policies' the forecast for the PSBR in 1981–82 was £14.5 billion; the outcome of the 'unthinkable' 1981 Budget strategy was a target of £10.5 billion (or 4¼ per cent of GDP). The agreed Walters/Lawson/Howe strategy was more in keeping with Lawson's original concept of a 'firm plan' than with the flexibility that had crept into some of the speeches.

The apparent 'blitzkrieg' strategy for the PSBR understandably disturbed the 364 economists who signed *The Times* letter. Lawson in his Zurich speech had specifically ruled out 'discretionary action to boost the Budget deficit over and above the natural increase brought about by recession'. But within the eighteen months or so that he had been Financial Secretary, Lawson had stood in turn first, for a firm, inflexible plan to reduce the PSBR come what might (the outcome of his weekend deliberations in the summer of 1979); second, for tolerance of cyclical rises in the PSBR, within a general strategy for continuing on a downward path; and, now, third, having seen that cyclical rise in the course of 1980–81, and having claimed credit for flexibility, he supported the Walters plan for dramatically reducing the PSBR in the March 1981 Budget. And there was no doubt whatsoever that this involved reductions from 'the natural increase brought about by recession'.

As an earnest of his dedication to sound finance, the Financial Secretary had almost boasted in his Zurich speech of the fact that, despite their avowed intentions, the burden of taxation had in fact risen under the Conservative Government. He also offered a hostage to fortune, contradicting some of the reasoning behind his later tax-cutting Budgets, when he said, 'The convenient theory so popular in some circles across the Atlantic – that cuts in tax rates produce increased tax revenue – is, alas, as a general proposition, simply too good to be true.'

The section of Lawson's Medium Term Financial Strategy in the 1981 Financial Statement and Budget Report contained some interesting qualifications of the policy from which, a year earlier, it had been stated 'there can be no departure' – some departures, in fact. The money supply, it appeared, had been swollen by companies borrowing from banks to preserve their liquidity in the face of the recession and accompanying squeeze on their profits. But the high personal saving ratio had also been reflected in a build-up of the 'liquid balances' of private individuals, and these had also served to swell the M3 measure of money supply. Among the factors – favourites of Sir Alan Walters, the Bank of England and the official Treasury – cited in the FSBR as indicating that monetary conditions in 1980–81 were 'tight', were: the high exchange rate; high real interest rates; M1 and M0 (the wide monetary base); Private Sector Liquidity (an even broader measure than M3); and 'the absence of any marked upward movement in the price of houses or other real assets'.

It was quite a list – a long way from the pristine simplicity of M3.

This brought the fairly breathtaking admission, from a politician who had only a year earlier sought to gear economic policy to the belief that there was a causal connection between the growth of M3 and subsequent inflation: 'Some of the factors that have been identified as contributing to the rapid growth of M3 in 1980–81 mean that it should not have the implications for future inflation which generally follow an increase in money supply.'

In his Zurich speech Lawson had said the Government had intended 'and still intends' that monetary policy should be tight. The 364 economists, and indeed many other observers, took his statements and intentions at face value. Looking back on these events some years later, Sir Alan Walters commented: 'What many believe to have been the main ingredient in disinflation, the exchange rates, peaked in the first quarter of 1981 and then sterling steadily depreciated *as monetary policy was eased.*' [My italics.][8] Walters also notes that the 364 economists had written against a background in which 'more moderation, if not outright recantation of the MTFS, had been expected'.

Walters maintains that outside observers missed the relaxation of monetary policy. But then this relaxation was not apparent from the MTFS – although the Budget interest rate reduction should perhaps have alerted those 'outside observers'. He also offers the thought that: 'The 1981 Budget was seen to lay the foundations for subsequent expansionary fiscal policy. And it was the *anticipation* of future budget relaxation that sparked the recovery in the latter half of 1981.'

Walters is here teasing Keynesian economists, because one could not actually pin-point fiscal expansion until 1982–83. But the point remains that the U-turn over monetary and exchange rate policy was not emphasised at the time, largely because it would have been too embarrassing for the Government in general, and individuals such as the quasi-Chancellor in particular, to concede that they had 'got it wrong', and policy had been tighter than intended.

The Number 10 Policy Unit felt the credibility of the whole Thatcher Government was at stake in the spring of 1981. Hoskyns and Walters thought that, if the Government was seen to lose its nerve by relaxing fiscal policy so soon after the publication of the MTFS, they would not only have lost political ground to those who wanted policy formally relaxed, such as James Prior, Peter Walker, Sir Ian Gilmour and Francis Pym: they would have lost the confidence of the financial markets too.

What actually was in process was a kind of confidence trick: not only the 364 economists, but also the financial markets, were taken in by the emphasis on tightness in fiscal policy, and by the nominally strict targets for monetary growth.

One writer has noted: 'The shift in policy taking place had not been picked up, even by the professionals. The fiscal tightening of 1981 was accompanied by a relaxation of monetary policy . . . the austere 1981 Budget was essentially a smokescreen for a relaxation of monetary policy.'[9]

The 1981 Budget was to change the course of subsequent Cabinet procedures. Until then, the Cabinet did not learn about the strategy, let alone the detailed contents of the Budget, until just before Budget Day itself. The Budget was a shock to the rest of the Cabinet: some – Lord Carrington, Willie

Whitelaw, Sir Ian Gilmour and Peter Walker decided, after various meetings, that resignation would only be damaging; but they insisted that, from then on, there should be a strategic discussion of the Budget in Cabinet, well in advance. This has been the practice since, although it is still debatable whether this is more than a formality.

The 1981 Budget also marked the beginning of the end of the strict monetarism embodied in the MTFS. As already noted, monetary growth continued to exceed target and no serious attempt was made, à la Zurich speech, to 'recoup' excessive growth from the 1980–81 period. Mr Lawson had been the leading proponent of monetarism among the politicians, and of the need to follow Professor Milton Friedman, and operate the economy in accordance with a 'simple rule' for bringing down the rate of growth of the money supply. In fact a table published in the 1982 MTFS showed that monetary growth under four years of the 'inflationary' Labour Government had averaged 10½ per cent (end 1974 to end 1978), whereas from end 1978 to end 1981 the average rate of growth had been 15½ per cent.

By departing from the strict canons of the MTFS, and encouraging interest rates and the exchange rate to fall, the Government not only disabused industry and the financial markets of the (up to that time, correct) impression that it did not mind how high the pound rose, and even welcomed such 'strength': it also achieved a 10 per cent devaluation between the March Budget and September 1981. Indeed, it achieved too much of a good thing. It is always difficult for a central bank to acquiesce publicly in a fall in the exchange rate, and the classic day-by-day behaviour of officials in such circumstances is to give the impression that it is the 'market' which is leading the way. (The fact that the market may have been tacitly encouraged is not emphasised.) But during such episodes the Treasury and the Bank of England always like to think things are under reasonable control: the two institutions are constantly worried that the currency might go into a 'free fall'.

In justifying two successive increases of two percentage points in interest rates in September and October 1981, back to 16 per cent, the Bank of England put the emphasis on the inflationary implications of a further fall in the pound. It also cited M3, monetary conditions and so on: but the behaviour of the money supply was no worse on these occasions than in the previous autumn, and in Budget week, when, notwithstanding 'excessive' expansion of M3, interest rates had been deliberately lowered. However, strict adherence to the 'simple rule' of monetarism would just have required reference to the money supply. In the early days of Mr Lawson's monetary plan, the world had been told that the exchange rate was to be determined by 'market forces'.

* * *

Nigel Lawson left the Treasury in September 1981 to become Secretary for Energy. This was part of a Cabinet reshuffle during which some of the leading dissenters from his kind of economic policies were either sacked (as in the case of Sir Ian Gilmour) or snubbed (as with James Prior, who was exiled to the post of Secretary for Northern Ireland).

The job of Energy Secretary represented genuine promotion. Lawson was now in the Cabinet. The move also made up for his having been passed over that January.

One organisation which would not have been unanimously pleased to learn that in less than two years Lawson would be back at the Treasury was the Bank of England.

Gordon Richardson, the Governor of the Bank, was far from being an admirer. Having flirted with monetarism, Richardson soon saw what the application of the doctrinaire approach to the money supply and exchange rate was doing to British industry. He opposed Lawson's attempt to have one firm figure for the monetary target in the 1980 MTFS, successfully advocating a more flexible 'range' of targets. Six months before Lawson's Zurich speech, and well before the intervention of Professor Walters, Richardson was convinced that monetary policy was tight, whatever the M3 statistics might show.

But although Richardson was successful in opposing the rigidity of Lawson's MTFS, he failed to prevent one aspect of the 1981 Budget: the imposition of a levy on the profits of the clearing banks. This levy had been pushed relentlessly by none other than the Financial Secretary. There was a political feeling that the banks had perhaps profited a bit too much out of the high interest rates which had hurt others in what was already an abortive monetarist experiment. Mrs Thatcher and Lawson were in alliance on this issue: Lawson wanted to 'do something' about the banks; Mrs Thatcher, from her occasional forays into the City of London, had convinced herself that clearing bankers were an idle lot, and deserved to be punished. The banks were easy political targets.

During his journalistic days Lawson had admired the Bank of England's technical expertise, but strongly opposed the habit of governors speaking out on what he regarded as strictly political issues, such as the level of public expenditure. The Bank, he thought, should not try to influence the political debate, but should handle, as best possible, the technical requirements dictated by the political process.

As Financial Secretary he had to work very closely with the Bank – or perhaps one should say the Bank had to work very closely with him. He now thought he knew better than the Bank on many technical issues, and was obsessed by the subject of the 'funding techniques' by which the Bank satisfied the Government's borrowing requirement. He won a long battle against Richardson for the introduction of index-linked gilts in the 1981 Budget; forced through other technical innovations; and seemed to believe that better funding techniques would have a major benefit in lower interest rates. On one occasion the *Financial Times* commented rather acidly: 'Mr Lawson seems to have been misled by his long struggles with the Bank of England into believing that [funding technique] is the whole problem. It is not. One strong lesson of 1980 is that official funding cannot offset excessive private borrowing.'[10]

Lawson however established a cordial working relationship with the executive director in charge of the Bank's gilt-market operations, Eddie George, which was to stand both institutions in good stead when Lawson returned to the Treasury as Chancellor in 1983. Eddie George was also important in smoothing Treasury/Bank/Number 10 relations in 1981 in regular meetings on monetary policy of 'the triumvirate' of George, Walters and Peter Middleton, then the senior Treasury monetary policy official.

Relations between Lawson and the Bank's then deputy governor, Kit (later Sir Kit) McMahon, were better than those between Lawson and Richardson, but hardly warm. On one occasion in 1980, the US Government approached McMahon (Richardson being away at the time) to ask the Bank's help in unfreezing Iranian assets in the West which had been seized after the taking of American hostages in Tehran. McMahon received the request on a day when he was due to go to the Treasury for a meeting, and asked Sir Geoffrey Howe afterwards if he could have a word privately. Lawson heard, and included himself in the privacy. When McMahon asked Howe if it was all right politically for the Bank to go ahead, Lawson intervened, to ask first why the USA was not using the Bank for International Settlements in Basle, and second, how much money the Bank would make out of it. Howe merely suggested that McMahon talk to the Foreign Office, and the financial negotiations were duly conducted by McMahon himself, with considerable success.

In Opposition the Conservatives had wanted to make the Bank of England more independent, on the lines of the US Federal Reserve, or the West German Bundesbank. Lawson's encounters with the Bank during his period as Financial Secretary led him to the position where, in the words of one close observer, 'He wanted to neuter the Bank.' His relationship with Richardson has been described as 'tempestuous' and certainly did not help Lawson to modify his attitude.

As he left for the Department of Energy, Lawson knew he had gained credit within the closest Government circles for his energy, single-mindedness and general economic beliefs. Even though he was forceful and aggressive, Lawson is credited with having been able to bring out the best in his Civil Servants. 'He knew how to hold an enjoyable meeting, with jokes, which encouraged ideas – and he did listen to the qualifications people had about his own plans, which was a great strength,' one official recalled. 'He could be jolly good company – but also ungracious, bitter and unforgiving.'

His dominant personality was going to come into conflict with an even more dominant personality, that of his next-door neighbour at Number 10 Downing Street, when he returned as Chancellor. Meanwhile, it was Sir Geoffrey Howe, the then Chancellor, and Mrs Thatcher herself, who shouldered most of the blame for the damage brought by the 1979–81 monetarist policies.

FIVE

Energy Secretary and the 1983 'Inheritance'

September 1981 – June 1983

'Bright, industrious, pugnacious. Different people who know him well would put the emphasis on different adjectives, but together they summon up a recognisable picture of Nigel Lawson, the new Energy Secretary.' That was the way the *Financial Times*, his old employer, described him on September 15th, 1981, after Lawson moved into a Cabinet post for the first time, adding 'those who know him well stress that he is really an enthusiast rather than a doctrinaire or an ideologist. Although he may initially give the opposite impression, he is in fact a good listener'.

Some might think that Lawson listened a bit too much to his monetarist friends in the 1970s. But by now Lawson had seen the damage done to British industry by the policies of 1979–81; and, while few politicians are able to admit that they got it wrong (even slightly), those who worked with him felt that by the time the transition from the Treasury took place, he was already beginning to rethink his monetarist position in the light of experience. Although he might ridicule his critics in his rumbustious way, and question the validity of statistics which showed that the UK had fared far worse than other industrial countries during the general world recession of 1980–81, his natural pragmatism was slowly reasserting itself. This did not prevent him from making dubious points such as the common one at the time, the rationalisation that British industry had had to get rid of a lot of dead wood anyway. (There had been *some* dead wood, but during the struggle for survival in 1980–81, many first-class companies had to dispose of a lot of live wood too.) But in reasserting his long-held beliefs in the virtues of the market-place – nothing particularly monetarist about that – he sometimes trod on the toes of industrialists who felt a little short of Government sympathy. As the *Financial Times* noted: 'An energetic speaker, he has been a popular figure at commercial gatherings. This has not always been an easy task as he has maintained a strong stance in defence of free trade and the need for foreign competition.'[1] What many industrialists knew at the time was that the 'non-exchange-rate policy' espoused by Lawson for so long had stacked the competition rules against them.

The esteem in which Lawson was held by the Prime Minister at the time was well illustrated by a report in one newspaper which read as though it had been dictated by Mrs Thatcher's Press Secretary Bernard Ingham: headlined 'Backing with Gusto for Monetarism', it said, 'Mr Nigel Lawson, like Mr Norman Tebbit, a member of Mrs Thatcher's old "Gang of Four", is a man after the Prime Minister's own heart . . . he subscribes to her brand of "dry" conservatism with gusto and enthusiasm. A vigorous and often pugnacious advocate of the Government's monetarist policies, he has been instrumental within the Treasury of (*sic*) keeping many frail spirits in line on public spending cuts and on a commitment to tight control of the money supply.'[2]

Subsequent events were to show that Lawson's monetarist days were over. Meanwhile, he was to have a stint of just over eighteen months at the Department of Energy. One of Lawson's tasks as Financial Secretary had been to meet delegations from the oil industry who wanted their tax bill reduced. On his appointment to Energy the director general of the UK Offshore Operators' Association said Lawson had been 'sympathetic' to their position in the past. Since from the oil industry's point of view he was now a gamekeeper turned poacher, this implied they were expecting great things from him. But at the start Lawson seemed more concerned about the poor physical surroundings of his new office, and showed more interest in acquiring new furniture than in taking up an invitation, accepted by his predecessor David Howell, to attend the Offshore Europe Technology exhibition.

The message that came from the industry was that the existing tax system for the North Sea, 'which has become less and less based on profit, will discourage exploration and development . . . we are concerned with the offshore tax system which is now, at the top end, over 90 per cent of profits.'[3] Taxation would wait until the Spring 1983 Budget when, on Lawson's urging, Sir Geoffrey Howe introduced what he described as 'a substantially more favourable regime to assist the companies as they go on to develop new fields, and, in order to help finance new activity, a package of relief on current fields'. Once the new Energy Secretary had sorted out his office furniture, he devoted himself immediately to an energy issue which fitted in both with his desire to roll back the frontiers of the State (in a way which broadened share ownership up to a point) and with his Medium Term Financial Strategy: this issue was a massive privatisation of State assets in the North Sea – initially estimated at between £1.5 billion and £2 billion in the case of the British National Oil Corporation (BNOC), and over £1 billion in the case of British Gas.

These were what City analysts like referring to as 'big numbers'. It was becoming apparent that, while the MTFS was looking fairly tattered as a strategy for monetary control, it was a potentially effective instrument for the Treasury in fighting departmental 'spending ministers'. Lawson had been able to argue as Financial Secretary that excess spending would raise public sector borrowing and threaten the entire credibility of the Government's policies. Even so, it was always a struggle, particularly in the light of the Government's commitments to increase spending on defence and law and order, at a time when, as Lawson's speeches had recognised, the recession was also adding to public sector borrowing. Public spending bids by ministers the previous July had amounted, for the coming 1982–83 fiscal year, to some £5.5 billion above what had been assumed in Lawson's March Financial Statement and Budget Report. Was the Cabinet to abandon any pretence that the PSBR side of the MTFS was under control, and make a virtue of higher public spending? Or was it to put the best face on things, and fudge the figures through a massive programme of asset sales?

The fact that 'Wets' were sacked in the reshuffle which brought Lawson into the Cabinet was one indication that there was to be no formal U-turn. The privatisation programme that Lawson immediately embarked on had the advantage of being doctrinally sound and pleasing the faithful – at a time when unemployment was still mounting and there were many doubts about the existence of an 'economic recovery'; but it was also to be the first of a series of major contributions to reducing the PSBR and maintaining the fiscal spirit of the MTFS, even if critics could reasonably maintain that through the inclusion of receipts from privatisation and sales of council houses, the PSBR figures were being 'fudged'.

Lawson gained considerable political credit within the Conservative ranks for the speed with which he embarked on the privatisation programme – his dramatic announcement came within a month of his arrival at his new Department; and, although much preliminary work had been done under his predecessor David Howell, there was little doubt among officials that the scale and speed of what followed was attributable to Lawson's dynamism. He had acquired a new enthusiasm. As Adrian Hamilton put it at the time: 'If the new Energy Secretary is now pressing ahead with the sales where his predecessor, Mr David Howell, stepped back from it . . . it is largely because the Government's funding needs have become so overwhelming.'[4]

Thus for Lawson his time at Energy became a kind of excursion from the

Treasury where he could carry on the good work of reducing State expenditure and raising revenue to cut the Government's borrowing requirement – or, in the first instance, stop it from rising. As he openly stated when announcing the privatisation plans: 'The Government's central economic objectives must constitute the framework into which the policies for individual sectors are fitted . . . it would be self-defeating if economic and energy policies were at odds.'[5]

As for the gamekeeper turned poacher, the question arose: was he in fact still a gamekeeper? He warned the oil companies operating in the North Sea they 'must accept their share of the necessary improvements to the tax base' as their contribution to controlling Government borrowing.[6] A depletion policy which considered stretching out the years during which future generations could draw oil from the North Sea? That would delay the flow of tax revenues to assist the MTFS. The emphasis was to be on rapid exploitation, and this in turn would aggravate the problems for the balance of payments in the late 1980s and 1990s, when the physical flow of oil was bound to slow down, on the basis of all known forecasts. On the other hand the real price of oil subsequently weakened, and history may show that he was exploiting North Sea resources at the right price.

Apart from the boost he gave to privatisation, Lawson's spell at Energy was also going to lead him to be credited with having wisely built up stocks of coal, so that when Arthur Scargill delivered his challenge to the Government in 1984, Mrs Thatcher and her colleagues were well placed to hold out. It is therefore worth recording that in a speech to the CBI conference on Energy shortly after his appointment, he actually criticised the high level of stocks held by the National Coal Board at the time, warning Sir Derek Ezra, the NCB's then chairman, that it must find a way of squaring its record output and high stocks with the low level of demand then ruling.[7]

The build-up of coal stocks was, in fact, the result of a Cabinet decision taken after the Government and the National Coal Board had caved in to threats from the National Union of Mineworkers in February 1981. Coal stocks were then low, and the Cabinet did not dare risk a prolonged strike. But as a result of this retreat, the Cabinet had collectively decided that this must never be allowed to happen again, and a decision was taken to build up stocks for the next confrontation with Arthur Scargill, the NUM leader.

In addition to the privatisation moves, Lawson also ended the British Gas monopoly of the right to buy all gas produced in the North Sea. They were selling it at below world market prices, and Lawson argued that this was holding up further investment in, and exploitation of, gas in the North Sea. The hurry he was in to unveil his new measures led even the usually well-disposed *Sunday Telegraph* to record that this normally diligent Minister 'did not appear to be as well briefed as he might have been on the details of what will by his own admission be the largest denationalisation operation in British history.'[8]

There was criticism at the time about the Government's relinquishing ownership of such important national assets as the operations in the North Sea. No other country outside the USA and Australia allowed development of oil resources to be conducted solely by the private sector. Lawson replied with his usual forcefulness, saying talk about Britain losing control of its oil as a result of privatisation was 'nonsense'. He said: 'The North Sea oil fields are British and will remain British. All oil from the North Sea must continue to be landed in the United Kingdom unless I permit otherwise. Secondly, the trading arm of the British National Oil Corporation will remain wholly owned by Her Majesty's Government and through this the right under participation agreements to buy up to 51 per cent of all oil produced in the North Sea will continue unimpaired.' (There was a certain ministerial licence in these remarks: in fact, of course, large sections of the North Sea oil fields are in Norwegian waters.) The oil-producing business of BNOC would go to a British private company (eventually named Britoil) with 'a wide spread of ownership among the public'.[9]

In the end, the privatisation of the Government's North Sea oil interests a year later in November 1982 caused Lawson some embarrassment. There were many headlines on the lines of 'Britoil flop', as 51 per cent of the new company was sold in the face of stock and oil markets that were much weaker than when the original idea had been conceived. The issue was undersubscribed. Nevertheless, Lawson pressed ahead. By the time of the Election campaign in May 1983 he was to be dropping the first hints of eventual plans to privatise the electricity industry.

The last six months of his time as Energy Secretary were dominated by embarrassments over Britain's ambivalent role as both a leading oil producer and a member of the Group of Seven (G7) Industrial Countries* and the Organisation for Economic Co-operation and Development (OECD): from the point of view of the consuming nations, the 1982–83 fall in the world oil price was good for inflation and growth, and therefore welcome – provided it did not aggravate the Third World debt problem too much by bankrupting any members of the Oil Producing Exporting Countries (OPEC) and thereby causing a banking crisis. While OPEC members were cutting back production in order to try to protect their cartel, and to stabilise the price in their long-term

* United States, Japan, West Germany, France, United Kingdom, Italy and Canada.

interests, Britain was pumping oil out of the North Sea as fast as it could.

Lawson came under pressure from OPEC to cut production or at least do something to stabilise prices. But his undertakings with the oil companies were to encourage rapid exploitation of the North Sea, and he had always argued that the best depletion policy was the verdict of market forces. Nevertheless, after much toing and froing, he eventually offered an olive branch to OPEC, and intervened in April 1983 to tell the oil companies not to push North Sea prices down too far.

Having spent so long hiding behind the virtues of non-intervention and the wisdom of market forces, the Energy Secretary proceeded with no obvious sense of shame or embarrassment to give a speech in which he claimed credit for having taken action to avoid a third oil shock. Was this perhaps a harbinger for interference in other markets, such as the foreign exchange market?

'We have sufficient experience of the effects of oil shocks,' he told an energy conference, 'and of the cost of economic adjustment to recognise the desirability of doing what we can to avoid unnecessary fluctuations and to achieve equilibrium by the smoothest possible route.' We see here a minister who is beginning to acquire a taste for intervention, rather than a desire to stand back and let the market rule at all times.[10]

From the start of his period as Energy Secretary, Lawson kept his hand in with general economic policy, and continued to be a standard-bearer. There is little doubt that his eye had been focused for some time on the Chancellorship, and continued to be so while he was at Energy. There had been a series of criticisms of the Government's economic strategy from the former Prime Minister Edward Heath and ministers sacked from Mrs Thatcher's Cabinet, such as Sir Ian Gilmour, including calls for reflationary tax cuts and full membership of the European Monetary System.

In a speech to the right-wing Selsdon Group Lawson said the critics' proposals were 'close to bribery dressed up as statesmanship'. There was no scope for tax cuts – these could only take place by departing from the MTFS, and cheating either borrowers or future generations. Apart from anything else, a U-turn would be 'wrong electorally'. They had been elected on policies to reduce public spending, borrowing and monetary growth. The current adjustment to low inflation was painful but necessary. The only levers in a free society were monetary levers . . .[11]

His reaction to calls for full entry to the EMS was more circumspect. He first resumed thinking seriously about exchange rate policy when he was at the Department of Energy. He said the EMS was continually under review, there were arguments for and against, etc. – but he did devote more time in the Selsdon Group speech to this proposal than to anything else. As far as he was concerned, the EMS was also a form of financial discipline, albeit external rather than internal, and would have similar consequences for interest rates as the MTFS. He said it was wrong to think of joining the EMS exchange rate mechanism as a route to lower interest rates. (His thinking in this respect was going to develop considerably.)

As far as his Treasury colleagues were concerned when he arrived back in the top job in June 1983, Lawson was 'still a floater' – that is to say, he had not yet given any outward sign of change in his attitude to the exchange rate since the Zurich speech. As one of his colleagues commented: 'As Financial Secretary he was so focused on the monetary indicators that he resisted any suggestion of looking at the exchange rate'. But it is interesting to note that even in late 1981, he was at least thinking of the EMS as an alternative financial discipline, should he finally lose faith in his own MTFS and the monetary statistics.

The Energy Secretary also gave a Treasury-style speech in January 1982. His opening sentences are Lawsonian gems (he was addressing the Association of [Overseas] Economic Representatives in London – that is to say, the economic experts from overseas stationed in London embassies):

> When you originally invited me to address this distinguished gathering, and I gladly accepted, I was a Treasury Minister; and you wanted me to make some comments on the economic scene. Despite my new ministerial responsibilities, I have assumed that you would still wish me to do this. One thing you will be spared, however, as a result of my translation, is a discussion of the minutiae of monetary control. Instead, I shall seek today to paint with rather a broader brush.

Lawson addressed the question of why the world economy was experiencing, at one and the same time, the worst inflation and the worst unemployment since the Second World War. This involved identifying the formula on which the unprecedented prosperity of the past hundred years had been based. 'The lesson of history is clear. That formula has been the development of *free markets* – both national and international – within the framework of an over-arching *financial discipline*.' Financial discipline was the economic counterpart of the wider framework of social order that it was the inescapable duty of the State to provide. Financial discipline 'received its classical expression in adherence to the gold standard and the doctrine of the balanced budget.'[12]

We have already seen Lawson harking back to a golden age in the August 1980 lecture reprinted as a Centre for Policy Studies pamphlet. There was also a reference in a speech to the Institute for Fiscal Studies in 1981 when he said, 'If neo-Keynesian demand management were the necessary condition of economic growth, we would all still be living in caves and wearing woad, instead of listening to lectures at the centrally-heated Charing Cross Hotel.'[13]

Given the choice, there are no doubt some who would prefer living in caves. But the point is that Lawson, in saying Keynesian demand management is not a necessary condition of economic progress, and that things were fine under the Gold Standard, is setting up another man of straw. Keynesian demand managers did not claim to have invented economic growth; they did claim however that given the appropriate policies, growth could be more rapid, and more even, than under the 'classical' model, with less cyclical cost in unemployment and so on. Indeed, Lawson himself argued thus in the 1960s.

However, this time the argument is more interesting, and invokes the great traditional Conservative hero Edmund Burke.

> Burke's celebrated political dictum about the dependence of liberty on order applies with equal force in the economic sphere. Thus it is that our individual political and economic freedoms have been traditionally sustained by a framework of political order and financial discipline. And thus it is that the fundamental error of the post-war world has been to seek to turn this on its head, both politically and economically. In short, what we have seen in the economic sphere has been the growing restriction of the freedom of individual economic agents, coupled with a steady erosion of overall financial discipline.[14]

This was all very neat, but he then went on to say that 'prevailing opinion in the Western world began first to take for granted, then to forget, the essential precondition of that success.' This was rather strange: he was referring to the breakdown of the Bretton Woods exchange rate system – which he had lauded as the great discipline in his earlier lecture: what actually happened was that 'prevailing opinion' resisted its breakdown until the last; it had, in fact, been the likes of Lawson and new converts to monetarism who hailed floating exchange rates as 'the new freedom'.

Lawson's period in ministerial office can be seen as a search for an anchor. He had enthusiastically seized on floating exchange rates as a means to faster economic growth earlier, but was to discover that they were the obverse of 'financial discipline'. He now harked back to the Bretton Woods 'dollar standard'; the Medium Term Financial Strategy was his disciplinary substitute.

'The Medium Term Financial Strategy, with its commitment to declining monetary growth and Government borrowing, represents a conscious return to that over-arching financial discipline which history has shown to be one of the key preconditions of economic success and whose abandonment has led directly to the inflationary excesses of recent years,' he stated. 'Just as the classical formula for financial discipline – the Gold Standard and the balanced budget – had both a monetary/exchange rate and a fiscal component, so does the Medium Term Financial Strategy.'[15]

This speech to overseas economic representatives in London was the precursor to Lawson's practice, for a time, when Chancellor, of telling the rest of the world, through the medium of speeches and press conferences at meetings of the International Monetary Fund, that it should adopt a medium-term financial strategy. The fact that the monetary side of the MTFS had long since fallen apart is just one of those things. But there was another clue to future developments in the speech: 'There is scope for differences of opinion as to how the necessary discipline is best applied . . . Even after the final collapse of the Bretton Woods system, there has been a continuing role for the exchange rate as a medium of financial discipline, first in the form of the European snake and since 1979 in the form of the EMS.'

Lawson did not keep his opening promise to eschew the minutiae of monetary control. He went on to say:

> It is a grotesque caricature of the present Government's economic policy to pretend that it consists of leaving everything to an automatic pilot known as sterling M3. It is very nearly two years now since we published our Green Paper on Monetary Control, in which we explicitly stated that to assess underlying monetary conditions properly it is necessary to take account of the evidence of *all* the various monetary indicators.

A grotesque caricature? Perhaps in January 1982, given the way the MTFS was evolving, but we have seen how Lawson went out on a limb to save his 'automatic pilot' of M3 in the Zurich speech of January 1981. As for the reference to other indicators in the March 1980 Green Paper, they were there at the insistence of the Bank of England and some Treasury officials, and hardly highlighted by the Financial Secretary at the time.

Lawson had told the building societies that if they competed more aggressively for deposits with banks, more emphasis would have to be placed on 'broader' monetary indicators. But banks themselves were by now competing aggressively for mortgage business, and both these developments were going to have a sizeable impact on monetary control, or lack of it, during Lawson's Chancellorship. He chose this occasion to make a point that was unexceptionable on the surface, but none the less cavalier in the light of what was really happening underneath, when he said: 'It is clear, to take a topical example, that to the extent that the sharp increase in bank lending for housing has simply replaced lending by the building societies, the consequent inflation of this year's sterling M3 growth figures has no necessary monetary significance whatever.' (The 'extent' proved to be not very great.)

We then see the experience of office, as opposed to the eager espousal of new and interesting theories in Opposition, when Lawson tells the economic representatives: 'In general . . . in a world in which the monetary system is in a constant state of evolution, the exercise of judgement and discretion is inescapable. The real question seems to me to be who is exercising that judgement and that discretion.'

Again, this would seem, on the face of it, to be an unexceptionable statement. It is just that when Lawson and his colleagues first introduced their simple monetary rule, they had been consciously reacting against those boring old Keynesian managers of demand, who were always exercising judgment. Just as the Lawson view was that businessmen knew better than 'the man in Whitehall' about industry, so the financial markets were supposed to be better judges of financial matters than pragmatic, 'judgmental' officials. This remark by Lawson amounts to a tacit admission that his days of 'naïve' monetarism were now over. The feeling that things are best decided by the market had actually led to the abolition of the Bank of England's official minimum lending rate (MLR) on August 20th, 1981. But something had to take its place, and the Bank continued to operate in the financial markets to influence interest rates. Indeed, we were to reach the point later in the decade when Lawson told the Commons Expenditure Committee that interest rates changed when he said so – a far cry from the Financial Secretary who believed in leaving these things to the market.

The speech to the economic representatives carried a classic, though indirect, dig at certain officials at the Bank of England. Lawson said, on the subject of judgment and discretion, 'if it is being exercised by those who don't really believe in the policy in the first place – and there are central bankers, as well as politicians, who fall within this category – then any departure from predetermined rules and guidelines will understandably be regarded with the gravest misgivings, since it will as likely as not represent a backsliding from financial discipline as such.' (Backsliding by those who 'believe' in a policy is all right . . .)

There was an ironic pointer to the future when Lawson added: 'The plain fact is that the true objective of those who urge the Government to abandon its medium-term financial strategy is the abandonment of financial discipline altogether.' This was just the charge that was going to be thrown at Lawson himself in 1988–89.

There were other indications of Lawson's retreat from monetarist rhetoric in this speech. There was an open reference to the connection between wage increases and inflation – 'Costs are being contained across the whole economy. Pay increases last year were at half the rate of the previous round . . . the combination of moderation in pay and higher productivity has led to a dramatically small increase in manufacturers' unit labour costs.' This was not the kind of language and reasoning of the early monetarist.

Lawson had suggested years earlier that the UK might need some traumatic shock of the kind that Japan, West Germany and, in a different way, France had suffered. He now used a wartime analogy to excuse the high and rising level of unemployment. 'It is a war against inflation that we are fighting. In war, casualties are inescapable. They are neither intended, nor are they unexpected. They are a sign neither of wickedness nor incompetence. The object is quite simply to win the war while minimising the casualties incurred.'

This is a very revealing analogy. The Prime Minister had christened those who opposed monetarist policies 'the Wets'; and the counterpart of the Wets in Westminster parlance became 'the Drys'. The introduction by Lawson of the wartime metaphor suggests that perhaps one should have recourse to the terminology of defence, and refer to those who at this stage opposed formal expansionary measures as 'the hawks'.

Lawson was in fact speaking on the eve of a January Cabinet meeting to discuss the 1982 Budget strategy (the first under the new procedure insisted on by the 'Wets' after the shock of hearing about the 1981 Budget); and, despite the purge of the previous September, there were still Cabinet members such as Peter Walker and Michael Heseltine who thought more should be done to check unemployment, by now over 3 million and rising. There was a growing Tory minority who thought that measures to expand public sector investment would be sensible in themselves, and create employment. The 'hawks' might by this stage be losing their faith in pure monetarism but, with inflation at 12 per cent, they did not want to relax fiscal policy. (Inflation had peaked at 21.9 per cent in the spring of 1980, come down to 13 per cent by the end of that year, but stuck at around 12 per cent for the following twelve months.)

Lawson's speech was seen as a way of rallying the troops, on behalf of Mrs Thatcher and the Chancellor Sir Geoffrey Howe. The whole tone of this particular speech was hawkish; at this stage one can see the failure to achieve the monetary targets as unforeseen and unintended, and the refusal to countenance overt expansionary measures as consistent with Lawson's being relaxed about inflation of up to 5 per cent, but more concerned about 'double-digit' price increases. When inflation was indeed down to below 5 per cent, at the time Lawson assumed the Chancellorship in June 1983, it becomes a more interesting question whether missing the monetary targets was intended or not.

On the other hand, right from the start, officials in both the Treasury and Bank of England had been horrified by the attempt at rigidity and fixed rules.

A number of them – even those regarded by ministers as 'more monetarist than most', thought they would have been failing in their duty if the targets *had* been achieved in the early days. There were some interesting occasions when officials tried to explain to ministers what a good thing it was that the MTFS was not working too well.

The beauty of the MTFS's focus on the money supply *and* public sector borrowing was that occasionally the Government managed to hit one of these targets, and could therefore boast that they were on course – while explaining the other one away as the result of distortions, special factors and so on.

In his speech to the economic representatives, Lawson said that the Government was indeed 'on track' for the 'unthinkable' PSBR figure of £10.5 billion projected for the 1981–82 financial year. In the 1982 Financial Statement – published with the Budget on March 9th – it fell to the new Financial Secretary, Nicholas Ridley, to explain away the monetary figures and introduce new targets. Lawson had, after his Zurich speech, stuck gamely – or perhaps stubbornly – to the M3 indicator in the 1981 FSBR when projecting targets for the following year, although several other indicators had been cited to explain that monetary conditions had been 'tight' in 1980–81 despite the failure to control M3.

It turned out once again that M3 had grown far faster than intended – by 14½ per cent instead of 6 to 10 per cent. A target range of 8 to 12 per cent was now presented for 1982–83 (higher than the stated intention in 1981 for 1982–83, which was 5 to 9 per cent, *and* from a higher base); but this time the Government openly took itself off the sole hook of M3, and the target was expressed in terms of 'narrow money' (M1), 'broad money' (M3) and even broader money, including building society deposits, 'public sector liquidity'. What was more, it was acknowledged that the projections for the following two years (showing a downward path) 'will be reconsidered nearer the time, and will take account of structural and institutional changes which may affect the economic significance of the different aggregates'.

It was interesting that, from a position where, in the high monetarist period of 1979–80, all the emphasis was put on M3, which was given a declining target path *which would be achieved*, equal emphasis was now given to M1 and M3 – 'both broad and narrow measures of money convey useful information about financial conditions' – and:

> the exchange rate can help in the interpretation of monetary conditions, particularly when the different aggregates are known to be distorted. The exchange rate is a route through which changes in the money supply affect inflation. It can also be an important influence on financial conditions. External or domestic developments that change the relationship between the domestic money supply

> and the exchange rate may therefore disturb the link between money and prices, at least for a time. Such changes cannot readily be taken into account in setting monetary targets. But they are a reason why the Government considers it appropriate to look at the exchange rate in monitoring domestic monetary conditions and in taking decisions about policy.

Sir Leo Pliatzky, a former Treasury official, has commented: 'By 1982 the targeted aggregates were increasingly seen and described as *indicators* of monetary conditions and a guide to the need for a change in interest rates, to be taken into account along with other indicators'[16] – such as the exchange rate. One minor piece of the history of Conservative flirtations with monetarism is that the Financial Secretary who actually presented the FSBR which demoted M3 in 1982, Nicholas Ridley, was a passionate monetarist in the late 1960s and early 1970s, well before the conversion of Lawson himself.

The 1982 FSBR also gave hints of a burgeoning interest in 'money GDP' as a target. 'Money GDP' is simply the total value of output of goods and services at current prices, the problem being that it is a 'lagging' indicator, and, even then, does not warn about excess demand which might be spilling over into imports. However, in the sense that economic policy during both Keynesian and monetarist regimes is essentially a trade off between the growth of output and prices, the concept of aiming at a certain result for money GDP has long been with us. The 1982 FSBR cited it, along with M1, as a reason why financial conditions had been 'moderately restrictive' in 1981–82 despite the rapid growth of the target indicator, M3. In due course, money GDP was to achieve more prominence, *faute de mieux.*

The general approach of the 1982 presentation of the MTFS was much more flexible than had been conceived by Lawson in 1980. 'Control of the money supply will over a period of years reduce the rate of inflation' (1980) becomes, 'Sustained progress against inflation will require a further deceleration in the underlying rate of monetary growth in later years' (1982). The revised target ranges reflect changes in savings behaviour, and 'institutional developments'; subsequent ranges will be 'reconsidered nearer the time' and 'will take account of structural and institutional changes which may affect the economic significance of the different aggregates.'

In other words, 'The world is a much more complex place than we, in our innocence, believed.'

The FSBR conceded: 'In the last year all the broad measures of money have continued to grow more strongly, relative to money GDP, than might have been expected given the high level of interest rates and the past upward trend in velocity,' that is to say, the velocity of circulation of the money stock. An upward trend in velocity (the speed at which money circulates) implies that correspondingly less monetary growth is needed to fuel economic transactions. But if velocity is falling, then a larger rise in the money stock may not have alarming inflationary implications. It may simply compensate for the fall in velocity. The basis of monetarism was that there was a stable and predictable relationship between the money supply and increases in total spending (i.e., velocity was predictable), and that excess growth in the money stock would, after a time-lag, spill over into inflation. Professor Walters's belief in the purity of the time-lags led him to attribute the fall in inflation in 1980 and 1981 not to anything the Conservative Government had done, but to 'the monetary contraction of 1978–79 – roughly a two-year lag' – and largely under the Labour Government.[17]

The FSBR was in effect stating that the 'stability' and the 'predictability' of the monetarist diagnosis of Lawson's original MTFS were questionable. It explained:

> The demand for liquid balances as a medium for saving, rather than spending, seems to have increased significantly in the last three years, implying a shift in velocity. The growth in the wider monetary aggregates has been part of a marked rise in the private sector's total holdings of financial assets relative to income. This may reflect in part the expanding role of the banks as financial intermediaries. It may also be the result of the private sector's attempt to restore the real value of financial assets eroded by past inflation.

(Sir Alan Walters has criticised the Government for having adopted as its target, M3 – 'about 60 per cent of which is interest-bearing credit instruments which are not used for transaction purposes.')[18]

The 'institutional developments' included 'the removal of artificial constraints on money and credit markets', notably exchange controls and the 'corset' restriction on bank lending. 'The most obvious example is in the area of mortgage lending. To the extent that this lending is not additional, but reflects a transfer of business from other financial institutions [the point Lawson made in his speech to the economic representatives] it will raise the growth of M3 relative to other measures of money.' Given these distortions, 'wider aggregates, which include deposits with other financial institutions as well as banks, may be a valuable guide to the growth of broad money.' But 'these aggregates may also at times be affected by institutional changes . . .'

We can see from these agonised admissions that the kind of briefs with which Lawson would be presented by his officials when he returned to the Treasury as Chancellor were likely to give him every excuse to get off his monetary hooks. It is all a far cry from the primitive belief that increases in the money supply portend a corresponding increase in inflation in due course. The growth in M3 had been 20 per cent during 1980, implying a similar rate of inflation in 1982, according to the original monetarist view. But already the Government could see the rate of increase in the RPI coming down to 9 per cent in 1982; and it was to be below 5 per cent by the time of the June 1983 General Election. However, the fall in inflation could be explained more easily by the effects of lower commodity prices abroad, and a deceleration in wage increases as a result of the 1980–81 recession – in other words, by a conventional Keynesian approach, not by monetarist equations.

With Lawson, who had shown no interest in exchange rate policy, temporarily absent from the Treasury, from the autumn of 1981 to the summer of 1982 there was, in fact, a dry run for the policy of aiming at an exchange rate target that Lawson himself was to adopt when Chancellor. The crucial difference was that the policy did not at the time become widely known, and it was conducted in a more flexible way – the top Treasury, Number 10 Downing Street and Bank of England officials most concerned with monetary policy were aiming at holding the pound stable, give or take 2 per cent or so, against the index which measured its value against an average of all the major currencies, not just the West German mark. One official commented in January 1982: 'People have not noticed the degree of shift from M3 to the exchange rate.' Another said, 'We are very worried about the downside risk for the exchange rate.'

In July an official commented: 'There is a kind of circularity: the Governor [of the Bank of England] complained about M3, and we moved to a wider range of monetary indicators. He now wants us hooked on a sterling index of 90 [average value of sterling in 1975 = 100] which gives similar rigidity.'

The following month a senior monetary official said: 'There hasn't been quite the change people talk about. The numbers are different and there is more pragmatism, but there is still great emphasis on monetary targets, and interest rates would probably not now be falling but for the good money figures.'

Given the fact that unemployment was still rising during 1982, and the increase in output was exceedingly slow, there was a growing feeling in the Treasury in summer 1982 that interest rates had to be brought down again, and that British industry could do with another boost to competitiveness from a lower exchange rate. The feeling was that they should try to keep inflation under control without hitting output and employment too much. Thus with inflation now below 10 per cent and falling, there was a change of emphasis in the priorities of policy of a kind we were to see with more force later on when inflation fell below 5 per cent in Lawson's Chancellorship.

The first manifestation of this was the complete abolition of all official controls on hire purchase arrangements in July 1982. The second was a deliberate lowering of interest rates in order to engineer a devaluation of the pound. Between the autumn of 1982 and spring 1983 the devaluation reached 15 per cent at one stage; but as policy switched to stabilising the exchange markets and raising interest rates, the pound rose again to a level where the devaluation since the autumn amounted to 7½ per cent – within the range of what the Treasury had originally been trying to achieve. The emphasis was now once again on exchange rate stability.

The principal change in the 1983 Financial Statement which preceded Lawson's return to the Treasury was in its size – bigger – and presentation – more readable. The principal surprise was that, for once, the monetary aggregates – M1, M3 and private sector liquidity – for which there were now targets, had all kept within their target range for the previous year. But they had all been calculated from a new base, and were, therefore, not in accordance with the original MTFS. The general tone was the more flexible one that had evolved since Lawson had left; the basic UK cost-push mechanism of inflation was acknowledged with: 'Lower domestic costs will enable British industry to compete more effectively, at home and abroad, without adding to inflationary pressures'.

What kind of economy was Lawson inheriting? Basically a very sluggish one. Despite his great protestation that the 1981 Budget was a turning point, growth had in fact been exceedingly slow. Real incomes actually fell between 1981 and 1982; and, although a recovery in consumer spending began during the second half of 1982, this was largely precipitated by rising consumer credit and lower saving. Real incomes began to rise during 1983, assisted by some pre-Election tax cuts in the Budget. The 1981 Budget was far from being the success story that Lawson repeatedly claimed.

The return of the Conservatives with a large majority in June 1983 was hardly attributable to a general sense of economic well-being. Mrs Thatcher had been carried along on the crest of a South Atlantic wave known as the 'Falklands Factor', after the eventual fight-back, with considerable US logistical support, against an Argentinian invasion of the Falklands which took place because the British Government had given the impression it did not care about the islands. Lawson himself was disgusted by the Falklands affair, and the Treasury he inherited was saddled with a public spending bill for the new airport and garrison costs running into billions of pounds.

The Opposition continued to be mortally divided, so that under the British electoral system, it did not matter that their combined shares of the vote added up to far more than that achieved by the Government. Moreover, the Labour

Party was undoubtedly handicapped by what was widely regarded as the weak leadership of Michael Foot.

The economic record itself was abysmal. The years 1979 to 1983 had been the slowest period of economic growth since the Second World War, in spite of the contribution made by North Sea oil. The *National Institute Economic Review** for May 1983 gives a sombre picture of how things appeared at the time: gross domestic product had plunged 5 per cent between 1979 and 1981, and only made up 1 per cent of this during 1982. Unemployment had risen from 1.3 million in May 1979 to 2 million in 1981 and over 3 million (12.7 per cent) in spring 1983.

The NIESR commented:

> There is not much doubt that total output stopped falling around the middle of 1981 and that there has been some increase since. But it is not easy to see how large the increase has been . . . the current recovery has been exceedingly slow so far . . . there must in fact be some doubt as to whether the upturn in output during 1982 has been sufficiently clear and large enough to warrant description as a cyclical recovery at all.

The Central Statistical Office's *Economic Trends* shows that the common measure of improvements in living standards, 'real personal disposable income', grew barely 2¾ per cent between 1979 and 1983, compared with a 10 per cent rise in the preceding four years, 1975–79. There had in fact been a marked fall in 1981, virtual stagnation during 1982, and a small recovery in 1983.

It had also been a very depressed period for consumer spending, although a fall in the savings ratio produced a pre-Election 'boomlet', with consumer spending rising 3 per cent in real terms between the fourth quarters of 1981 and 1982, and continuing the momentum during the first half of 1983. Even so, the rise in consumer spending between 1979 and 1983 as a whole proved to be a mere 5 per cent.

The fall in the savings ratio was associated with the abolition of Government controls on hire purchase arrangements in July 1982, and what the NIESR referred to coolly as 'easy bank credit'. Indeed, the NIESR noted that, within consumers' expenditure, purchases of durable goods such as washing machines, televisions, videos and the like had shot up by 20 per cent between the first quarters of 1982 and 1983. Lower interest rates, and the fact that after the depths of the recession existing stocks of durables were 'ripe for replacement' were also cited by the NIESR as an influence on spending.

* A quarterly review produced by the National Institute of Economic and Social Research (NIESR).

Then there was the reduction in inflation itself. The effects of inflation on consumers had been a subject for much debate among economists since the mid-1970s, earlier feelings that inflationary expectations caused 'a flight from money and into goods' giving way to the diagnosis that people liked to protect the real (inflation-adjusted) value of their liquid assets, and to build them up during a burst of inflation. Thus the NIESR said that, with the fall in inflation since the peak of the early 1980s, the 'inflation loss' on liquid assets was estimated to have fallen from over 10 per cent of disposable income in 1980 to 4 per cent in 1982.

We have seen that the rate of inflation as measured by the annual change in the retail price index was around 10 per cent (10.3 per cent) when the Conservatives won the May 1979 General Election, and rose to a peak of 21.9 per cent in May 1980. Under the influence of the severe recession of 1980–81, and a worldwide fall (of nearly 20 per cent) in commodity prices, the rate of increase in the RPI had fallen to 11.7 per cent (May 1980 to May 1981), 9.5 (May 1981 to May 1982) and a low point, for the 1980s, of 3.7 per cent from May 1982 to May 1983. This was the rate of inflation Nigel Lawson inherited in June 1983.

Superficially, it was almost a golden inheritance for Lawson. The low rate of inflation spoke for itself: nothing like this had been recorded since the 1960s. Defeating inflation in order to lay the foundations for economic growth had been a constant theme of the Thatcher Government so far. The defeat appeared to be within sight, so that inflation as a constraint on expansion was hardly the factor it had been in the early 1980s – even allowing for the fact that the devaluation of the pound between 1982 and 1983 had still to feed through fully into prices.

The sheer scale of the recession the economy had been through, and the evident paucity.of the recovery so far, indicated that there was considerable scope for expansion from now on. If one assumes that the normal growth of the economy made possible by technological progress is some 2½ to 3 per cent, and one allows for the 4 per cent or so drop in output between 1979 and 1981, a gap of some 9 per cent had opened up, and, as the NIESR pointed out, the recovery from this had hardly begun in mid-1983.

The classic causes of the 'stop' phase in the British economy over the years had been accelerating inflation (usually manifested in excessive wage earnings – that is to say, a situation where average earnings were accelerating away from what could be afforded with gains in productivity) and balance of payments crisis. The 'crisis' need not have occurred immediately the balance of payments went into deficit, but at some point where the financial markets lost confidence in the Government's ability to finance the deficit without resorting to corrective measures (usually restrictions in fiscal and/or monetary policy, and, eventually, devaluation of the pound).

I have described elsewhere my belief that the availability of North Sea oil during the early 1980s gave the United Kingdom the unique opportunity to transform its industrial structure without running into balance of payments constraints.[19] A joint Trade and Industry, Treasury and Foreign Office memorandum pointed out: 'The direct contribution of North Sea oil output to the balance of payments, taking into account both the reduction in oil imports and the current level of net oil exports, can be gauged from the total value of continental shelf oil sales, which in 1983 amounted to £17 billion.'[20]

But the contribution of the North Sea was disguising a dramatic deterioration in the country's non-oil trade, which was in turn associated with the reduction in the industrial base under the policies stemming from 1979–80.

John Harvey-Jones, then chairman of ICI, Britain's most important industrial company, told the House of Lords Select Committee on Overseas Trade that 'in 1980, as a result of that period of very high exchange rate, 20 per cent of our customer base in the United Kingdom disappeared.' The early 1980s saw balance of payments surpluses, and Lawson and his colleagues encouraged the investment of such funds overseas, to provide income for when the oil should run out.

But domestic investment in the UK suffered badly. We have already seen that there was a fall of a third in manufacturing investment between 1979 and 1981. The shrinkage of the old industrial base, and the contraction of new investment, led Britain to a point where its traditional historical surplus in manufactured goods disappeared entirely in 1983, when there was a deficit of £2.1 billion.

There had been a current balance of payments surplus of £2.9 billion in 1980, £6.3 billion in 1981, and £4 billion in 1982. Even in 1983, when the surplus in manufactured goods disappeared completely, there was a current surplus of £3.4 billion after allowances for oil and 'invisibles' (which includes trade in services such as insurance and other 'City' activities, as well as income on overseas investments).

But the surplus was disappearing fast. The ratio of exports of manufactures to imports of manufactures had come down from 119 per cent in 1980 to 95 per cent in 1983. (In their joint memorandum to the House of Lords, the DTI, Treasury and Foreign Office rather quaintly, and no doubt in wish fulfilment, misprinted one phrase as 'imports of *manufacturers*'.) A typical example was provided by Ford Motor Company, which was a net exporter from the UK every year, between 1965 and 1980, but whose imports of vehicles and materials began to exceed its exports from the UK in 1981, and by 1983 was exporting goods to the value of £834 million but importing £1.5 billion.

Among the rationalisations given by the Government for not worrying about the trend was the view that 'invisibles' or 'services' could somehow fill the gap. But the UK's share of world 'invisibles' trade was also falling. Manufactures remained very important to Britain's overall trade: the share of 'services' in UK exports in 1982 and 1983 (average) was only 24 per cent, of fuels (mainly oil) 15.9 per cent, and manufactures and other visible trade (including food and tobacco) 60 per cent.[21]

By including oil in their figures for exports, ministers managed to maintain during this period that Britain was holding on to its share of world trade. It was not: comparative statistics from the Organisation for Economic Co-operation and Development showed a loss of share in the world market for manufactures, and a build up in the penetration of imports of manufactures into the UK. Considering the size of the contribution from the North Sea, the interesting thing about the balance of payments surpluses recorded by the UK in the early Eighties is that they were so low – especially in the light of the fact that the country had gone through a heavy recession, which dampened the demand for imports anyway. At the end of 1981 a Treasury official commented privately: 'The balance of payments forecasts are really quite terrible, considering we have oil and the price has been rising. I dread to think what the balance of payments position would be at full employment.'

The balance of payments' forecast presented in the March 1983 MTFS had been for a fall from a surplus of £4 billion to £1 billion between 1982 and 1983, notwithstanding a still rapidly rising contribution from North Sea oil exports.

Imports were continuing to rise far faster than exports, although it was hoped that the 1982/83 devaluation would lead to an improvement by 1984 – and the North Sea would still be increasing its contribution.

The new Chancellor thus inherited an inflation rate – 3.7 per cent – of the sort that in his .earlier writings he did not regard as a serious constraint on growth; indeed, as we have seen, he thought modest inflation was a positive benefit to an atmosphere of economic growth. He might make ritual declarations about the need to achieve an inflation rate of zero, but he did not feel strongly about this. But the balance of payments was already a problem on the horizon. And from the point of view of developments that were to affect his future conduct of economic policy, Lawson appears to have made no attempt, either as Financial Secretary or at Energy, to alter the profile which indicated that the British balance of payments would begin to lose the hitherto massive, and rising, contribution from North Sea oil after the mid-1980s.

SIX

The Floating Chancellor

June 1983 – January 1985

Nigel Lawson's first Chancellorship was the star turn of Mrs Thatcher's second Government. Many political observers, not to say the participants themselves, felt that Thatcher's 'second term' was a period of drift. Whereas she and her colleagues had woken the country up with the drastic nature of their treatment for the economy during the first term, and the third term saw a radical assault on all manner of established institutions – from health to education and the law – there is a sense in which the Thatcherite ideologues feel 1983–87 were somehow 'wasted years'.

This is odd, because the Thatcher Government undoubtedly gained in stature through successfully resisting the prolonged strike in 1984 called, without so much as a democratic vote, by the miners' leader Arthur Scargill. It may be that the sheer effort of that fight – in which Lawson, and his 'Wet' successor at Energy, Peter Walker, were as hawkish as Mrs Thatcher herself – drained some of the ideological fervour; certainly, the Government rested for a time on its laurels, and the aftermath of the miners' strike was something of an anticlimax.

But Lawson's first Chancellorship was an undoubted political success. This difficult, private man, with a reputation for arrogance of which he was conscious but admitted to friends he had made no effort to shed, seemed an unlikely candidate to be fêted by Conservative backbenchers four years later as the man who won them the 1987 General Election. This seemed unlikely not only because it would seem that he had gone out of his way to antagonise many of his colleagues; but also because, even though it was Sir Geoffrey Howe, the retiring Chancellor, who carried the can for the deflationary first term, Lawson had certainly managed to acquire the reputation of a deflationist. Few of the

1983 intake of Conservative MPs would have read or remembered his Keynes-ian and expansionist writings of the 1960s and early 1970s. And those that did had long since given him up for lost as an unrepentant monetarist.

Lawson, the disbeliever in economic forecasts that did not suit him, had himself lost credibility in the matter of his own forecasts. From the Budget of 1981 onwards, he had been predicting recovery for the British economy, via 'a slowing down in the rate of destocking, as inventories approach the desired level, by a fall in the savings ratio, as inflation and inflationary expectations fall, and by some upturn in the world economy.'[1] There was in fact a slowing down in the rate of destocking from 1981 onwards, and what was later to become a dramatic fall in the proportion of incomes saved was under way. But, rather than an upturn, there had been a downturn in the world economy, and, as we saw at the end of the last chapter, the 'recovery' in the British economy so far was a parlous one. Moreover, whether the decline in savings was attributable to greater confidence about the inflationary prospect, or to the beginning of what was to become a credit boom, is an open question.

There was, therefore, as Lawson assumed the Chancellorship in June 1983, a lot of room for improvement in the economy. Lawson himself had given a characteristically risky forecast during the campaign, suggesting that unemploy-ment was about to fall. This was greeted with some derision in the Treasury itself, where a number of officials were hoping that the new Chancellor would face facts and give the Medium Term Financial Strategy a decent burial. The Bank of England had been reluctant to acknowledge even the existence of the MTFS in its public pronouncements.

The gloomy atmosphere about the economy in general and unemployment in particular was not alleviated by the tone of Lawson's 'rhetoric' in the early days of his Chancellorship. It all sounded deflationary, with an emphasis on sticking to the MTFS objectives for lower public sector borrowing, and on marching down from 3.7 per cent inflation towards zero. Yet four years later we were to find that real incomes and consumers' expenditure had grown by some 25 per cent since 1979, four-fifths of which took place during Lawson's 1983–87 Chancellorship; and that, in practice, Lawson was to be far more expansion-minded than his monetarist slogans suggested, and to do almost everything to avoid applying the brakes to the economy.

So great was the damage done to the industrial base in the early years, however, and so sluggish the revival of manufacturing investment that was supposed to follow from a strategy of lower public sector borrowing, leading to lower interest rates, that the economy was going to be in poor shape to cope with the demands put upon it by the credit boom and the abandonment of monetarism. By not acknowledging his expansionist aims publicly, and by emphasising the 'party line' that retrenchment would lead to recovery, Lawson failed to fire the animal spirits of businessmen. His distaste for altering the 'deflationary plan' of the MTFS into an open growth strategy – it would sound too much like governments run by Labour or by Edward Heath – meant that British industry tended on the whole to believe what he said, rather than interpret what he wanted. When the consumer boom came, industrialists were not sufficiently prepared. But the inflationary and balance of payments implications were not going to show up until after the 1987 General Election.

One of the routes to the eventual balance of payments crisis was going to be the development of competition between banks and building societies to a point where the country, by 1988, was awash with mortgage finance, much of which was being spent on imported goods rather than houses. It is interesting therefore that one of the first things Treasury officials pointed out to him when he arrived back in mid-June 1983 was that a mortgage 'famine' was developing. Building society deposit rates were out of line with bank interest rates, because they had been set in November 1982 before base rates rose from 9 to 10 per cent. And the Prime Minister would not welcome an increase in mortgage rates in her hour of electoral glory.

The mortgage rate was not at this point at the centre of the monetary stage. That point was going to be reached in 1988, when influencing the mortgage rate seemed to become the principal aim of monetary policy. The Bank of England noted the sharp rise in mortgage lending in the early 1980s, and calculated that nearly half the annual flow of mortgage lending of £15 billion a year amounted to 'equity withdrawal' – that is to say, it was not used to finance extra housing, but devoted to other ends, including personal consumption. Equity withdrawal had doubled between the late 1970s and 1982, to a level where it was equivalent to 4 per cent of total consumer spending. Personal sector debt was high by British standards, but not as high as in the USA. Senior Treasury and Bank of England officials were relaxed at this stage about higher consumer borrowing, regarding it as a natural consequence of deregulation in the financial markets – a reaction to the earlier period of mortgage and credit rationing. Nevertheless, the Bank of England warned in its September 1983 *Quarterly Bulletin*: 'A credit-financed expansion could be a cause for concern if it exceeded due limits . . . credit-financed spending may be concentrated in particular areas where it risks raising prices . . . this could have implications for expectations and price inflation more generally.'

Mortgages were not the primary focus of monetary discussion in Treasury and Bank. A general review of monetary policy under the chairmanship of the Chief Economic Adviser to the Treasury Sir Terence Burns was sparked off by a letter from the deputy governor of the Bank, Kit McMahon, to Lawson almost as soon as the new Chancellor arrived at the Treasury.

The Bank's letter asked the $64,000 question: what did the newly arrived Chancellor of the Exchequer wish to do about monetary policy? It pointed out that inflation was much lower than when the MTFS had been conceived, and unemployment much higher. Did this make any difference? Was there a bigger role for the exchange rate to play in the setting of monetary policy?

The letter caused a furore. It had not been discussed with the Treasury in advance. The Bank got off on the wrong foot with the man they had found difficult enough as Financial Secretary. But the letter did precipitate a big exercise within the Treasury on monetary policy, with the principal result that the exchange rate, from the summer of 1983 onwards, loomed a little larger in official, if not Chancellorial thinking behind monetary policy.

Indeed, the exchange rate – a relatively high pound, from the point of view of the competitiveness of British industry implying tightness of monetary conditions, and hence a presumption to lower interest rates – was in effect granted a sizeable 'weight' in the balance of factors which lay behind monetary policy advice to the Chancellor. So, too, as a result of the Treasury review, was 'narrow money'. In Lawson's case now, the narrower the monetary target the better. He began to pay particular attention to 'non-interest-bearing M1' and from summer 1983 'narrow money' was given a much bigger weight in decision-making. But Lawson was less convinced than the Treasury and Bank about the exchange rate, and retained his 'floating' instincts rather longer.

Official policy had been evolving during the changeover period between Howe and Lawson. The Treasury and Bank of England had no difficulty in agreeing on massive intervention in the exchange markets to stop the pound rising further during the fever of Election week. Officials were divided between those who merely did not want the pound to rise, and those who, looking at the latest gloomy forecasts for the economy, believed the currency needed to be encouraged downwards again to improve industry's competitiveness. After the devaluation of the last quarter of 1982 and the first quarter of 1983, the pound had strengthened in anticipation of the Thatcher victory that was never seriously in question. On the Friday of the General Election result – a 144 majority to the Conservatives – the Bank of England intervened heavily to hold the pound down; and on the Monday its money market operations were geared to edging interest rates downwards, in the hope that this would take the buying pressure off the pound.

Mrs Thatcher herself was keen on a reduction in interest rates, and Lawson was able to start his Chancellorship with a reduction of a half per cent in base rates in his first week, from 10 to 9½ per cent. This was a popular move politically, but totally inconsistent with the letter and spirit of the MTFS. The monetary aggregates generally were growing at above the target rates. The episode underscored the feeling that a re-examination of monetary policy was necessary, and was to prove the first of many pragmatic moves under Lawson where the bias was to cut interest rates – or resist raising them – if at all possible, whatever the money supply measure (or measures) of the year was doing.

Since the fall in base rates was manipulated by officials among whom the preponderance of opinion was that the pound was already too high, it is interesting to note the diplomatic way in which the event was recorded several months later in the Bank of England *Quarterly Bulletin*:

> The market pressure was heavy enough, however, that the authorities could have had to take strong action in the money market to resist it. To do that would inevitably have created the impression, both in the real economy, where the recovery did not yet seem to be firmly established, and in the financial markets, that the authorities were not prepared to contemplate even a modest fall in short-term interest rates, which was a harsher attitude than the overall situation seemed to justify.

The interest rate cut was insufficient to help the building societies, whose rates were still out of line, and were subsequently raised anyway. In fact the 'famine' reflected the fact that the societies could not attract enough deposits, at interest rates then ruling, to satisfy a fast-growing demand for mortgage finance, at a time when the banks were making a huge bid to increase their 'deregulated' presence in the mortgage market. The building societies' problem actually reflected the buoyancy of the mortgage market, a market in which Mrs Thatcher always took a particular interest. Indeed, it was at her wish that the mortgage limit for interest relief had been raised from £25,000 to £30,000 in the March 1983 Budget. (The Treasury had managed to dissuade her from raising it to £40,000 or £50,000.) The rise in mortgage rates so soon after the Election was a little unfortunate – but not as unfortunate as it would have been before the Election.

For one who later tried to be known as a 'tax reforming Chancellor', Lawson at first showed surprisingly little early enthusiasm for tax reform. 'It was when he later discovered he had scope for tax *cuts* that he began to show a real interest in the subject of tax reform,' said one Treasury colleague. Also, and notwithstanding a speech he was to make to rally the troops on the subject that autumn, Lawson did not give officials the impression he was seriously interested in the mechanics of getting inflation down to zero.

From the public point of view, Lawson got off to an abrasive start by announcing a package of public spending cuts in July. This annoyed fellow Cabinet Ministers, and served to strengthen suspicions that the public spending assumptions in the spring Budget and the MTFS had been 'doctored' with an unusually low contingency reserve, and convenient assumptions about how departments would 'underspend' during the 1983–84 financial year.

This was the first step in a big review that summer of strategy for public spending over the next four years. His initial aim was to hold the level of public spending in real terms, so that, as the economy grew, its share of GDP would fall, producing scope for a constant stream of tax reductions within the framework of the MTFS. So far from wanting to drop the MTFS because of the manifest problems on the monetary side, he was keen to renew it as a central element in keeping the lid on public spending.

The first package of 'cuts' early in July was misleadingly reported by some newspapers as £1 billion, whereas it comprised £500 million of actual reductions (concentrating on defence) and £500 million from a proposed sale of part of the Government's shareholding in British Petroleum. The proposal was leaked in advance, and provoked an outburst from the less hawkish Cabinet Ministers, with Lord Hailsham, then Lord Chancellor, saying: 'This is no way to run the country.'

Lawson told a subsequent Cabinet meeting that July that extra departmental spending bids totalling £5 billion for the 1984–85 financial year would have to be withdrawn, or he would be forced to raise taxes in his Budget.

He was abrasive with many of his Cabinet colleagues, particularly upsetting those who felt their departments had behaved themselves by observing the cash limits imposed on them, and which were threatened with being penalised for extra 'demand led' expenditure elsewhere – notably from higher unemployment.

Despite promises during the Election campaign that the Welfare State was safe, Lawson in his first year as Chancellor showed particular interest in proposals for cutting back spending on health and social security. Originally when the Thatcher Government had come into office in 1979, it had wanted to cut public spending. Its commitments to defence, law and order and so on were for sharp increases however; and the sheer scale of the recession meant that social security costs were much bigger than expected. Even so, it had contained the rise in public spending over four years to 6 per cent, low by post-war standards. It was against this background that Lawson now aimed to freeze the real level of public spending, to make room for one of his ambitions: a succession of reductions in the basic rate of tax, to encourage 'incentives'. Tax 'cuts' then, enthused him more than tax reform.

Mrs Thatcher and her Chancellor agreed that tax cuts would be better timed politically if they came later in the Parliament, and that the priority was to stabilise public spending. Hence the early threats to the Cabinet of tax increases if agreement could not be secured. There was to be no question of a bargain of trading tax cuts for further public spending reductions in the 1984 Budget; both Thatcher and Lawson recognised that the rest of the Cabinet would draw the line at that. Indeed, the climate in the Cabinet was such that Lawson ended up in October with only about half the spending cutbacks he had originally demanded, and settled for a higher outturn for the PSBR in 1983–84 than originally planned. They both backtracked on a plan, originally put forward by Sir Alan Walters, for derating changes in the level of unemployment benefit from the retail price index. Walters had argued such a change would encourage people to search for work; but even Treasury officials who were looking for cuts had to concede that, with unemployment still rising, the argument on which the Walters proposal was based was a thin one.

Apart from the dramatic reductions in the top rates of taxation in the June 1979 Budget, and the cut from thirty-three to thirty pence in the basic rate (itself financed by the inflationary VAT move) the Government had made little headway with its promises to reduce the burden of taxation by the time Lawson became Chancellor. Indeed, the average burden had risen – National Insurance contributions, for example, had gone up. Sir Geoffrey Howe had taken refuge in the view that what mattered was not what people paid, but their perceptions of what they paid; by this criterion he felt the lower top marginal rates under his Chancellorship had achieved something.

There had, in the year before the 1983 Election, been an internal Whitehall review of the prospects for public expenditure and taxation over the rest of the decade, and this had produced a sombre result: on one (more favourable) assumption of economic growth, spending would remain at 45 per cent of GDP and tax rates would have to stay where they were; on less favourable assumptions, tax increases would be required unless there were appreciable cuts in spending. As Sir Leo Pliatzki has pointed out:

> A Paper . . . was circulated to Cabinet, setting out a number of drastic options affecting the welfare state and defence. The Chancellor did not argue for decisions on these options there and then but . . . Cabinet declined to consider the . . . paper on options, and the Chancellor did not get his remit. In effect, therefore, the Cabinet made a macro choice in favour of maintaining existing programmes, even at the cost of maintaining existing tax rates. The threat of tax increases was perhaps not taken too seriously. From that point the Treasury gave up, for practical purposes, the attempt to cut total public expenditure, but adopted a new strategy of stabilising it in real terms.[2]

Lawson, as Energy Secretary, had been a member of that Cabinet. He knew that, because of the tendency of some public spending programmes to go on rising – unemployment, for instance, was costing more and more as the figures went on up – he would have to threaten some cuts elsewhere simply in order to make the overall total stand still. One thing which was soon going to help him was that the Nato commitment to increase defence spending by 3 per cent a year in real terms ended in 1984–85.

It was in the autumn of 1983, when the public spending review for 1984–85 was well under way, that the old Keynesian 'growthman', whom one had come to know as a 'born-again monetarist', replied, when I asked how he would wish to be remembered, that he would like to be seen as 'the British Erhard' – a reference to the man credited with the West German 'growth miracle' after the war.[3]

September 1983 saw the beginning of Nigel Lawson's career on the international stage as a Finance Minister. It was early days, however, from the recognition point of view. On the British Airways aeroplane which took the Chancellor and his team, plus a number of the British financial press, to Trinidad for the Commonwealth Finance Ministers' meeting, a stewardess asked me whether I had seen 'the celebrity on the plane'. 'You mean Nigel Lawson?' I asked. 'No, David Gower.'

Lawson had never been much of a 'Commonwealth man', and showed little sympathy in Trinidad for the problems of the hard-pressed debtor countries of Africa. On this occasion the hero of the oppressed debtors was the unlikely right-wing figure of Robert Muldoon, then Prime Minister and Finance Minister of New Zealand. Few would have laid a bet in September 1983 that Lawson would, a few years later, emerge as the champion of the debtor nations of sub-Saharan Africa.

Lawson made no secret that he did not enjoy travelling very much, and at first seemed unhappy with the international stage generally. But as he grew into the job he was to show obvious signs of enjoyment with International Monetary Fund meetings, and to regard each occasion as the opportunity to present some initiative or other to the rest of the world. At the September 1983 IMF meeting in Washington, however, he was playing himself in, opening his key speech with the words, 'It is 22 years since I first had the privilege of attending the annual meetings of the Bank and Fund – although on that occasion, in Vienna, I had the very different responsibility of a financial journalist.'

Almost the first substantive concern the 'free floater' of the early 1980s showed was for the 'unsettled' course of exchange rates and interest rates. 'Present levels, particularly interest rate levels, cannot be regarded as satisfactory,' he said. 'Impatient voices are heard demanding new approaches, new systems, new institutions.' But, 'It was inflationary domestic policies that precipitated the breakdown of the original Bretton Woods arrangements, not the other way about. When things go wrong, there is a temptation to blame the system. This is a temptation to assume that all problems that are not cyclical must be systemic, and can be solved only by changes to the international financial system.'

We then see the first signs of Lawson's crusade to preach his own Medium Term Financial Strategy to the rest of the world.

> None of us can in fact duck responsibility for the way we conduct our domestic economic and financial policies. That in the end is still what this discussion is really all about . . . it was for this reason that I began my remarks today with an account of our recent experience in the United Kingdom, and suggested some conclusions about the roots of our current recovery which might have wider relevance and applicability . . .[4]

To his distinguished overseas audience, Lawson placed the emphasis on three elements in the recovery (and a lot of emphasis on what, as we have seen, was a fairly exiguous recovery so far, with unemployment still rising fast): the first factor was monetary control, but, instead of preaching monetarism, the relatively new Chancellor discreetly referred to the exercise of 'steady downward pressure on monetary conditions'; second, 'despite the recession, we have reduced our budget deficit significantly as a percentage of GDP'; and third, 'we have introduced reforms to remove structural rigidities in the economy, abolishing a whole raft of controls, on pay, prices, dividends, on industrial development and consumer credit, and perhaps most important of all, on foreign exchange transactions.'

What he did not say was that the removal of 'structural rigidities' on the growth of consumer credit was the beginning of a dramatic 'reflation'. Nor did Lawson address the question of why, when the general view at the time was that the vast US budget deficit was exerting an expansionary influence on both the USA and world economies, the fall in the British budget deficit should also be expansionary. He told his audience: 'The more firmly engaged any country is on a sound financial strategy, the better it will be able to withstand external shocks and weaknesses.' He also might be thought to have offered a few hostages to fortune in asserting: 'I am convinced of the need to have monetary and fiscal policy operating in harmony' and, 'The factors which are most likely to damage recovery would be an excessive expansion of demand by mistaken monetary and fiscal policies.'

It is also ironic that Lawson, in citing an example of a 'mistaken' fiscal policy, on this occasion (and many others) mentioned 'an unsustainable budget deficit that puts damaging pressure on interest rates'. The idea that there might be damaging pressure on interest rates at the same time as a budget surplus had not at this stage entered his philosophy.

One concern he wished to allay was the fact that there had been a slight rise in the inflation figure since he assumed office, from 3.7 to nearly 5 per cent. This largely reflected the delayed reaction to the earlier fall in the exchange rate, but we see Lawson sounding a theme he was to echo in later years – namely, that there was no change in the trend if the 'volatile' element of housing costs were stripped out of the index.

Nevertheless, the edging up in the inflation rate was of sufficient concern for him to tell the Conservative Party Conference in Blackpool early in October that he was aiming for zero inflation. This was by way of reassuring the troops and those who continued to be more monetarist than he now was. Meanwhile he had taken advantage of one good month's set of monetary statistics to push interest rates down a further half per cent on October 4th – itself nicely timed for the Conservative Conference.

Although he went through a phase of telling journalists in briefings that he *was* serious about aiming for zero inflation, the evidence suggests that he was more serious about getting across the *message* that he was serious, rather than actively aiming in this direction. The fact was that, in the autumn of 1983, Lawson was boasting about 'economic recovery' without having seen much evidence of it. True, helped by a resumption of the normal rise in real incomes, and by the growth of bank and building society credit, he was able to point to a growth rate for the economy as a whole of 3 per cent in the November Autumn Statement – both for 1983 and 1984. But at the existing exchange rate, the foreign trade sector was not contributing much. After the recession the economy had been through, a period of above-average growth was required to arrest the growth rate of unemployment, let alone to bring it down. And, to the extent that productivity – output per person – in the economy was improving, an even more rapid recovery was required to assist employment.

In the USA, economists regarded a 'recovery' as a situation where output had regained its previous cyclical peak. The position was nowhere near like that in the UK. Even Lawson's old friend the economics commentator Samuel Brittan had called (in the *Financial Times*) for a £5 billion expansion package during 1983. And Tim Congdon, one of the most prominent of the monetarist economists in the City, had pronounced that there was scope for unemployment to fall by 1 million without upsetting his monetarist beliefs.

It was against this background that interest rates had been brought down the further half per cent to 9 per cent on October 4th. Official pronouncements talked of encouraging money-supply figures, but in the words of one official,

'The monetary figures were OK, but not as healthy as they might have been.' The plain fact was that, worried about the sluggishness of the 'recovery', the Chancellor wanted interest rates down, and the Bank of England was happy to go along with this. There was an increasing feeling that interest rates should be encouraged down whenever possible, provided the exchange rate was not falling too fast.

The monetary review in the Treasury set off by the Bank of England's letter saw its public fruition in Nigel Lawson's first major domestic speech as Chancellor, the Mansion House speech, at the traditional Lord Mayor's Banquet. The review was to show that, although the exchange rate was looming large in the minds of some officials, and being 'taken into consideration' by the Chancellor, it had not yet achieved total prominence in monetary policy. Some of the most senior officials in the Treasury were anxious that, as the Government got off the M3 hook, it did not impale itself on the exchange rate. By rebasing the monetary targets, altering them, and chopping and changing them, the Government had managed to fool many observers into believing it was as monetarist in practice as it had been in theory. But it was easier to fudge missing a monetary target than it could ever be with a formal exchange rate target.

If the Treasury was not yet ready for a public exchange rate target, however, the Chancellor himself was still searching for another hook on which to impale himself, and foreshadowed the 1984 MTFS with a proclamation of the virtues of M0 – the 'wider' monetary base, which, in addition to bank cash-balances with the Bank of England (narrow monetary base), embraced notes and coins in circulation (and consisted principally of the latter).

Lawson also stated at the Mansion House: 'Within the context of the Medium Term Financial Strategy, what happens on the supply side will in the long run be the main determinant of our national economic success.' Although he could quote striking productivity gains, these at this stage were the result of *less* being supplied – but by markedly fewer workers. He said productivity gains and lower unit cost increases were 'quantifiable' but 'the dramatic change in expectations which has accompanied our strategy is not.' There was now a climate of 'realism and commonsense' in industrial bargaining; perhaps – but the principal dramatic change in expectations was shown by manufacturing industry's investment, which was running at only two-thirds the levels of the late 1970s. And the evidence to be given to the House of Lords Select Committee on Overseas Trade two years later was going to bear out how dramatic the change in expectations *for the worse* had actually been.

He then unveiled the results of his review of monetary policy, saying immediately that this had *not* been done 'with the intention of changing policy objectives'. The 'overall strategy . . . [had] produced a sharp fall in inflation and a recovery in output without destabilising changes of policy.' But he had thought it 'worthwhile to re-examine some of the technical aspects of the operation of policy, and in particular to examine the balance between rules and discretion; and between monetary and fiscal policy; and whether we are taking account of the most useful indicators, with the appropriate weights, in judging monetary conditions.' There would be 'some changes of emphasis' representing 'a continuing evolution of a well-tried strategy. The MTFS is alive and well.'

The claims made for monetary policy now were rather different from in earlier Lawson years. 'Monetary targets have provided an indispensable financial discipline. They have not been, nor have they ever been intended to be, a form of automatic pilot.' Originally, of course, when they were introduced under the Labour Government, this was true. But the whole point of the way they had been incorporated into the MTFS by Lawson as Financial Secretary was that, against the advice of the Bank of England and Treasury officials who considered them more as a help to the complex business of running economic policy, they *were* regarded as an automatic pilot. Lawson added: 'Over the years we have adjusted the targets themselves; and we have always sought to take account of shifts in the demand for money, whether due to financial innovation or to institutional change.'

This was an intriguing justification: it amounted to saying that 'because we have altered our originally rigid approach, therefore our original approach was not rigid.'

The Chancellor unashamedly passed over the phase when 'broad money' (M3) was the only target. 'It gave the sharpest possible focus to policy and played a crucial role in reversing expectations about future inflation.' Expectations about future inflation had indeed been reversed by the recession and the fall in world commodity prices; but 20 per cent growth of M3 had coincided with, rather than led to, inflation of 20 per cent. 'There never was a time when it was thought that one monetary indicator said all that there was to be said about monetary conditions,' the Chancellor went on. That is certainly what he had been advised when he arrived at the Treasury. But the kind of advice he had listened to in the 1970s, from, for example, *The Times* newspaper, during the crucial 'conversion' period, had been different: 'the money supply . . . is like water flowing from a tap attached to a hosepipe which is about two years in length. Once you have turned the tap on nothing will stop the water coming out of the other end of the hosepipe in the form of price increases.'[5]

The Chancellor now went on to sound almost like the very unmonetarist Radcliffe Report (of 1959) – actual policy decisions had to be taken with an eye to 'the growth of liquidity in the economy' – but then injected his own latest enthusiasm 'and to the amount of money immediately available for current transactions – as shown by the narrower aggregates.' As he had done before, he cited in evidence of 'continuity' the March 1980 Green Paper on Monetary Control, which contained safeguard clauses he had been none too keen on at the time, such as 'no single statistical measure of the money supply can be expected fully to encapsulate monetary conditions' and, 'in assessing monetary conditions, the authorities have to have regard to a range [of indicators].'

Lawson went on: 'The interpretation of M3 has been complicated by the far-reaching effects of structural changes resulting from the removal of exchange controls and direct controls on bank lending, which left our financial markets fully exposed to the forces of competition, both international and domestic.' (He had said earlier in the speech, 'The need for change on the supply side is not confined to industry. It applies also to financial services.')

Another way of putting this would be to have said: 'Whatever the importance of the money supply before we came in, and whatever its relationship to inflation, through financial deregulation, which we believed in, we created conditions which guaranteed that control of the money supply, which we also believed in, would be impossible.'

Lawson's enthusiasms and searches for panaceas were often to puzzle his officials, let alone the wider public. In this speech, while policy was going through the gradual dethronement of M3, he managed to say in passing that M3 had 'remained an important indicator – perhaps the most important', in a speech which was in effect introducing Mo as his new favourite.

Let down by the M3 relationships, the Chancellor had had his officials looking at possible associations between the narrower aggregates and subsequent inflation: 'Moreover, it was the surge in the narrow aggregates in 1977 which was followed by the surge in inflation in 1979. And the deceleration in the growth of narrow money in 1979 and 1980 preceded the recent decline in inflation.' (In favouring 'narrow' money, Lawson was now moving in Professor Walters's direction.)

'Preceded' – but did it cause? *Post hoc, ergo propter hoc?* Back to the Rees-Mogg hosepipe? Leaving such considerations aside, the officials had warned him that, even if there had been some kind of predictive value to these relationships, M1 now had 'a large interest-bearing component – currently over 25 per cent of the total.' It had 'thus acquired some of the characteristics of broad money, and is becoming less and less like a measure of transactions-related balances.' On the other hand, the Chancellor said, 'The wide monetary base, Mo, and its predominant component, notes and coins with the public –

have not been subject to the same distortions as M1.' He said, 'M0 could have a more important part to play as a key indicator of the growth of narrow money.'

He then said there would be different target ranges for different indicators, particularly since the 'trend velocity of non-interest-bearing money is quite different from that of broad money.' And, bearing the scars of experience, the Chancellor humbly added: 'It will not always be possible to ensure that all target aggregates are held always within their ranges.'

The exchange rate? It had been Gordon Richardson, as Governor, who had been keen on targets for the exchange rate, and his deputy Kit McMahon had raised the subject of giving greater attention to the exchange rate in his June letter to the new Chancellor. (Richardson's second term ended in the summer of 1983.)

Some Treasury officials had been thinking for some time that the exchange rate was too high; efforts had certainly been made to stop it rising further around Election time; and it had been edged down during the summer. But although Lawson had from time to time showed an interest in the exchange rate, he was not yet ready to promote his judgment above that of market forces. Indeed, people close to him at the time regarded him as 'a free floater' until 1985.

For the moment, as far as Lawson was concerned, the focus was still to be on the monetary aggregates; but officials had persuaded him that when the exchange rate affected these aggregates, it had to be taken into account. As he said at the Mansion House:

> I need say only a brief word about the exchange rate. Of course it is important to the economy, not least as one of the most obvious transmission mechanisms in the inflationary process. And by providing information about financial pressures at home and overseas, it is of key importance to the interpretation of monetary conditions. In particular its movements can throw light on whether there have been unexpected shifts in the demand for money.

He then demonstrated that he was still in one of the cold phases of the hot and cold relationship he had had with the exchange rate over the years:

> But equally, the exchange rate can change for many reasons, some quite unconnected with fundamental developments here or abroad: its signals as to the tightness of monetary policy can therefore be misleading. So while we shall continue to take the exchange rate into account in interpreting monetary conditions, there will, as before, be no target for it, nor, contrary to some ill-informed speculation, any complicated mechanical formula linking it with other indicators.

He was not at this stage interested in putting the pound into the exchange rate mechanism of the European Monetary System.

Summing up, Lawson asserted that 'the rules by which we have operated policy have been an unequivocal guide to expectations.' Many, within and without Government circles, must have smiled wryly at the word 'unequivocal'. But what Lawson was in effect saying was that some officials had questioned whether the MTFS should continue, others had wondered about a greater role for exchange rate policy, but 'the twin pillars of our policy remain the Medium Term Financial Strategy and the encouragement of enterprise in the market-place.' Yet in another passage there were echoes of what every other Government had been trying to do before him: 'The objectives of policy implied that the growth of money GDP should gradually decline, and that within that growth an increasing share should be accounted for by output growth and a decreasing share by inflation.' (One takes it that, also implied, is the acceptance that the objective of a gradual decline in money GDP would change in the remote eventuality of Britain achieving a sustained period of zero inflation.)

At the time the Chancellor was speaking, it so happened that his old favourite M3 had just come back within its target range – the rise in building society rates earlier in the summer had attracted deposits away from banks. But more relative interest rate changes were expected, and the Chancellor could not rely on M3. In going for Mo he seemed to be following Mrs Thatcher herself, who had a year earlier waxed happily on television, no doubt to the bemusement of many of the viewers of LWT's *Weekend World*, about Mo. Professor Walters, always a believer in the 'narrower' monetary aggregates, had drawn to her attention the fact that Mo hardly rose at all during 1982. But several officials recalled that Lawson had shown some interest in Mo during his closing months as Financial Secretary in 1981.

The introduction of Mo to higher status was to take place formally in the March 1984 Budget. It really was yet another example of Lawson's propensity for getting himself needlessly on 'hooks'. The presumption, explicit in the Mansion House speech, was that Mo would be an operational guide to the movement of interest rates. But the Bank of England had already examined Mo – which, as we have seen, is broadly cash in circulation – and come to the conclusion that 'movements in cash are unlikely to be helpful as a guide to general economic or financial conditions' and, 'it has not proved possible to find a stable econometric relationship between interest rates and cash balances in this country.'[6]

When Paul Volcker, then head of the US Federal Reserve, heard about the Chancellor's plan to give Mo equal status with M3 in assessing monetary conditions he laughed heartily in the presence of British officials and said, 'It's meaningless.'

Christopher Johnson, of Lloyds Bank, commented at the time: 'Using interest rates to crack Mo could be using a sledgehammer to crack a nut. It would mean a heavy price in terms of further deflation of the real economy.' On the other hand, Johnson showed a healthy sense of realism and foresight when adding: 'If Mo comes within the target, the Chancellor will claim the credit, for what it is worth. If it overruns, there will be plenty of plausible explanations.'[7]

In the Financial Statement for March 1984 there were two monetary targets, for M3 and Mo. Not only was the MTFS continued, the scale was extended to cover five financial years, instead of four when it was originally unveiled in 1980, with Mo allowed a target range of 4 to 8 per cent growth in 1984–85, reducing to an 'objective' of 0 to 4 per cent in 1988–89. The previous year's Financial Statement had given a target range for M1, M3 and private sector liquidity. A cynic might be tempted to say that M1 and private sector liquidity were dropped in 1983 because they had risen faster than the target range; M3 was retained because it had kept within the range; and Mo added because it looked promisingly subject to good behaviour.

In general the juggling with indicators and new targets from the date of Lawson's return to the Treasury onwards suggests a kind of schizoid approach: a desire to be seen to be impaled on hooks; yet a continual search for hooks that would not cause too much trouble, and would justify a policy bias in favour of lower interest rates wherever possible.

Lawson's ideal option would have been non-interest-bearing M1. But this, in the words of one official, had been 'wildly distorted' by the increased use of credit cards, the introduction of cash machines, and interest-bearing bank current accounts. With broad money – M3 – also distorted by the deregulation of the credit system, Mo was 'the best available'. But the same senior official acknowledged: 'The truth though was that he did not really have *any* satisfactory indicator.'

Mo was seen as telling officials 'something' about the current behaviour of consumption. This was a long way from the original monetarist conception of the money supply – its alleged predictive value for subsequent inflation. Mo was merely a 'concurrent indicator'. It was also subject to the criticism that the move towards a 'cashless' society would tend over time to restrict its growth – but that, of course, might be what the increasingly unmonetarist doctor ordered for a Chancellor who wanted targets he could hit easily.

From the point of view of the Bank of England Mo was certainly a target that ought to be easy to hit, although such success would not mean very much.

There was another unexpected advantage. For years the extreme 'narrow monetarists', or 'monetary basists' had argued that the only real way to control the money supply was by controlling the supply of reserves from the central bank to the commercial banking system, 'narrow monetary base'. Indeed, Mrs Thatcher herself had shown an interest in this, under guidance from the Swiss, during the monetary control debate of 1980–81 – until she was told that the implication was chaos for interest rates. But by announcing that M0 was now one of the two monetary targets, the Treasury and Bank seemed to please the monetary base lobby, even though at no stage did they attempt to control the *supply* of 'base money'. M0, like M3, simply became an indicator which guided the monetary decision-makers in their decisions to change interest rates, with one official joking some years later: 'Eddie George [the Bank's top monetary official] was perpetually in favour of putting interest rates up, and the Chancellor either of lowering them or of not putting them up.'

The Treasury's summer 1983 monetary review, the October Mansion House speech, and the unveiling of the new, five-year MTFS with M3 and M0 in parallel in the March 1984 Budget served, paradoxically for those who had urged the review, to delay the process by which greater emphasis was put on the exchange rate. Spotting this, the chairman of the Commons Select Committee on the Treasury, Terence Higgins, said when Lawson was giving evidence before the Committee on December 19th, 1983:

> In recent weeks or months one has got the impression that there has been some reversion to the previous position (before the autumn of 1981 and 1982, when changes in interest rates seemed to be determined by exchange rate considerations), namely the exchange rate is taken as an indicator of monetary stance, but of comparatively little importance in its own right.

Lawson, who of course had not been at the Treasury during the period when officials, with the 'free floater' absent, had indeed elevated the status of the exchange rate, said no, they had decided right at the beginning to have monetary targets, not an exchange rate target, but they had always taken the exchange rate into account. He added, significantly, 'I may say that I do not believe, and I have thought a fair amount about this, that there is in practice any halfway house between the sort of approach to the exchange rate which we pursue and a fixed exchange rate. I think these are alternatives and I do not believe there is any viable halfway house between them.'[8]

When reminded by one member of the Committee that he had been an advocate of devaluation in the 1960s, Lawson neatly squared his belief in 1983 that the market should determine the exchange rate with his earlier position, arguing that the Labour Government 'was seeking to maintain a wholly artificial exchange rate . . . the market forces at that time would indeed have led to a lower exchange rate – and eventually did.' Yet later in the same session with the Committee he was asked a prescient question by John Browne, MP: 'How long do you see yourself able to abide by the free market in allowing sterling to drop against the US dollar?' The question was going to arise dramatically just over a year later, when in January 1985 the pound fell almost to one dollar. On this occasion the pound was falling towards $1.40. Lawson merely acknowledged that massive capital flows across the exchanges, aggravated by the US budget deficit, did 'tend to produce a system of exchange rates which is affected much more by capital flows than is altogether healthy'. Nevertheless, 'I believe that the best way of coping with the difficult and often turbulent conditions in foreign exchange markets is through a policy of allowing market forces to work, intervening in order to smooth movements of currency but not basically for any other reason.' This had been done with success: the 'effective' rate for the pound – its average value against the other leading currencies – had changed little during the year, despite the fall against the dollar.

The Committee followed up the Chancellor's views on exchange rates in a session with Sir Terence Burns in January 1984.

'I think what he had in mind,' said Sir Terence, 'was that it is very difficult, once one moves away from the fixed exchange rate world, to be at all precise about hitting any particular exchange rate target range. Whereas one thought that there might be some broad influence from things like monetary and fiscal policy, it was very difficult to know precisely how they would work. Therefore, whereas he is very happy to take the exchange rate into account in judging the overall state of monetary and fiscal conditions, he is very unhappy with the idea of having a moving exchange rate target or band of some kind . . . it is virtually a market rate . . . in general the movement of the exchange rate we observed has been the exchange rate which has been determined by the market place.'[9]

Questioned further, Sir Terence came out with a prophetic remark about subsequent problems with economic policy: 'The distinction . . . which the Chancellor was attempting to draw was with the idea that there was some way in between the floating exchange rate and the fixed rate whereby you could pick some particular target and could ensure that you could hit that target over a period of time . . . even the process of attempting to hit any particular exchange rate may well produce gyrations in interest rates and tax rates which would be destabilising to financial conditions.'

So Lawson went ahead in the March 1984 Budget with his two monetary targets M3 and Mo. He was becoming more enthusiastic about tax reform, and introduced changes in corporate taxation, which included a progressive lowering in the rate of corporation tax from 50 to 35 per cent, offset by the phasing out of certain investment allowances, including those which benefited the leasing business of banks. He said:

> With unemployment as high as it is today, it is particularly difficult to justify a tax system which encourages low-yielding or even loss-making investment at the expense of jobs . . . it is doubtful whether it was ever really sensible to subsidise capital investment irrespective of the true rate of return. Certainly, with over three million unemployed it cannot make sense to subsidise capital so heavily at the expense of labour.

This justification struck a popular chord, even in some sections of the serious press. With unemployment over 3 million and rising, there was a recrudescence of the old 'automation' scares about machines putting people out of work. The truth was that the level of demand in the economy was not high enough, and that, in the long run, investment creates more jobs anyway. One would hardly have thought from the Chancellor's remarks that capital investment had actually fallen so much after 1979. And the idea of favouring 'labour intensive' investment did not sit too easily with Lawson's long-professed aim of raising the productivity of the British economy. There seemed to be a confusion between the process by which capital is 'deepened' in relation to the labour force and the growth process by which capital investment widens the industrial base of the economy, and creates more jobs.

A more direct route to altering the unemployment trend would have been to raise public spending. But he repeated the decision already taken in the earlier public expenditure survey: public spending was to be kept 'broadly level' over the following three years in real terms. And, although there was a 12 per cent increase in the basic personal tax thresholds (compared with 5 per cent if they had merely been indexed for inflation) the general effect of the Budget was designed to be 'revenue neutral', with the PSBR falling from £10 billion in 1983–84 to £7 billion in 1984–85, and from 3¼ to 2¼ per cent of GDP.

By halving stamp duty, abolishing tax relief on life assurance premiums and removing the previous surcharge on investment incomes, Lawson said he would 'remove biases which have discouraged the individual saver from investing directly in industry'. This was very much in accordance with one of his long-held beliefs in encouraging the spread of share ownership, although subsequent studies suggested that the *proportion* of shares held by private individuals continued its long-term decline, *vis-à-vis* investment through financial institutions, during the 1980s. Lawson also put the taxation of interest on bank deposits on the same basis, or 'composite rate', as building societies;

all of these changes, he said, would 'reinforce the Government's policy of encouraging competition in the financial sector.'

Apart from some dismay in the popular papers about the extension of VAT to take-away meals – the Chancellor himself was said to be a great eater of take-away fish and chips in his constituency village of Stoney Stanton in Leicestershire – the Budget was initially popular with both press and Conservative backbenchers, and accompanied by a fall in base rates, to the 8½–8¾ per cent range.

The basic fact that the Budget had done nothing to address the unemployment problem became more widely apparent later in the year. Andrew Britton, a former Treasury official who had become director of the independent National Institute of Economic and Social Research, commented early on: 'I have read at least one newspaper article suggesting that the economy is being reflated by stealth, that the Chancellor is practising demand management although he is preaching monetarism. That is quite untrue; demand is not being managed at all.'[10]

In spite of the fact that the saving ratio was falling, because of the increase in consumer borrowing resulting from financial deregulation, this trend had not yet assumed such proportions as to make up for what the Chancellor was not doing on the demand management side. Yet, small though its impact was at this stage, the growth in consumer credit was already causing damage to the balance of payments, which, because it was not yet in deficit, was hardly 'news'; the current surplus fell from nearly £4 billion in 1983 to £2 billion in 1984, despite a still rising contribution from North Sea oil. As the deputy governor of the Bank of England pointed out: 'In response to an increase in domestic demand of 9 per cent from the low point of the recession, UK manufacturing output has increased by less than 4 per cent, while imports of finished manufactures have risen by as much as a third.'[11]

The 1984 Budget was notable for several other reasons. One was that the measures were leaked in the *Guardian* with a degree of precision that was unprecedented in newspaper pre-Budget speculation. Lawson, the former journalist, displayed all the wrath of the poacher turned gamekeeper. His opportunity to make a big splash in his first Budget had been circumscribed by his own MTFS objectives, and by the fact that in any case political wisdom dictated that 'goodies' should be preserved until nearer the Election. From a detailed point of view he was also learning that Mrs Thatcher herself might have put her name to 'tax reform' in principle, but had strong objections, despite her name for radicalism, to many of the individual elements required to make up 'root and branch' changes. There was also the perennial issue of computer problems at Inland Revenue – either they had not got one, or, when they had, it could not cope with major reforms, or do the required thing at the right time.

He had thus been in the position of wanting to make his name in his first official Budget (the 1980 Budget in which the MTFS had been launched was surely his in all but name) without having that much to offer. He therefore decided to make the most of what he had got.

In order to achieve the maximum impact of surprise on the public, he made an even bigger play of pre-Budget secrecy in 1984 than had been customary. He had also worked harder, he told close friends, than at any time in his life. He was furious at the *Guardian* leak (through Hamish McRae and Victor Keegan) and even banned McRae from a subsequent Treasury briefing.

Yet the leak had the useful effect of helping diffuse some of the expected protests from vested interests affected by his changes (an effect which was supplemented by some vigorous selective lobbying by Number 11 Downing Street of individual Conservative backbenchers with links with City interests affected). On Budget Day itself, the speech was still a minor triumph, and he was credited with rather more of a 'reforming instinct' than he perhaps deserved.

Whereas it is said of some senior ministers that they make a point of not reading the newspapers, Lawson seemed obsessed by them, and occasionally summoned editors in to argue a point with them, or, in the case of the *Financial Times* on one occasion later in his Chancellorship, pulled out a sheaf of cuttings from his pocket at the beginning of lunch and took issue with the staff. (The story goes that the editor of the *Financial Times*, conscious that the paper had been going through a phase of being critical of the Government – by no means always the case – had asked his staff to be exceptionally courteous on this occasion. But, from the moment Lawson produced the cuttings, 'all bets were off' in the words of one present.)

Despite the embarrassment over the *Guardian* leak, and the irritability shown by the Chancellor, he gained considerable respect among his staff for his mastery of the detail of the Budget process. He reminded some of them of the archetypal 'City editor' that he once was – manifesting a close interest in everything from the macroeconomic conjuncture to the most minor 'down page' City story. But, while prepared to listen and discuss the issues he raised, or the tax reform options thrown up by the Treasury and Inland Revenue machine, he was at this stage none too keen on discussing such 'off balance-sheet' items as a conscious attempt to reflate the economy. Nor, until later, was he interested, following the monetary review, in a more active exchange rate policy. Yet his own forecasts showed a slowing down in the growth rate of the economy from 3 to 2 per cent in the course of 1984.

Lawson published a 'discussion document' in March 1984 on public expenditure trends over the next ten years, pointing out that there were many pressures for higher spending, but arguing that bowing to such pressures would be reminiscent of the bad old days, pre-1979. 'It would, of course, always be open to the government to decide, once the virtuous circle of lower taxes and higher growth had been established, to devote some of these resources to improved public services rather than reduced taxation,' the document conceded. But the emphasis was on the need to contain public expenditure over the following ten years – even 1 per cent a year real growth in public spending would result in the tax burden being 'only a little below what it was in 1978–79'. A general review of social security was taking place at the time, with the Chancellor arguing that social security and defence – two of the largest elements in public expenditure – had to be the subject of a special attempt at 'freezing' if the total was to come under control. (Under the Nato commitment defence spending did in fact peak during this 1984–85 financial year, and actually fell, in real terms, later.)[12]

With his hostile approach to public spending, and a refusal even to show interest in how to reverse the unemployment trend, Lawson had a difficult time with his Cabinet colleagues during the spring and summer of 1984. Characteristically, he seemed to take a positive delight in this. One of the remaining 'Wets' in the Cabinet commented during that period, no doubt with his tongue in his cheek: 'Things are not agreed in advance. Too many Treasury proposals are overturned in Cabinet. It is not healthy for a Chancellor to be treated like this . . .'

Lawson made a practice of inviting a group of outside monetarist economists in to see him from time to time, as a counterweight to official advice. In the spring of 1984 he commissioned some forecasts from the monetarist City University Business School, in the hope that they would show a different prospect for unemployment, with which he could then confront both Cabinet colleagues and Treasury officials. They did not, and the results were not widely circulated.

He made several important speeches in the spring and early summer of 1984. In April he addressed the question, 'What are we going to do when the oil runs out?' He noted that the UK had moved from producing 'virtually no oil' in 1975 to self-sufficiency by the end of 1980 – 'a matter of only five years' – and that 'by 1983, 3 years later, the real level of production was almost 60 per cent higher than the level of consumption.' A peak would be reached in 1984–85, but the good news was that the decline would take place over a much longer period and that 'even at the peak, it accounts for only 7 per cent of total Government revenues and an even smaller proportion of GDP.' Yet he conceded that this amounted to £9 billion a year and 'enabled us to reduce Government borrowing without having to increase other forms of taxation anything like as much as would otherwise have been necessary.' He did not spell out that at the time North Sea oil was accounting for as much as a fifth of the UK's foreign earnings from visible trade.

As Adrian Hamilton, commenting on the speech at the time, pointed out: 'Off-shore production may not decline as rapidly as it built up, but the *dynamic* provided by the North Sea to national economic growth will fade very quickly . . . as imports rise and exports of oil decline, so that the balance of payments will deteriorate . . . the North Sea has eased decline, not reversed it. The urgent question now is how to face years of dwindling oil revenues with a better formula for growth.'[13]

Lawson himself noted that declining oil production 'will probably require a real exchange rate lower than it is today'. This did not necessarily mean that the actual, or nominal exchange rate would have to fall – 'the real exchange rate can also adjust by better productivity performance and greater restraint on pay. Policy will need to be conducted to make it more likely that the adjustment will occur in that way.' This implied, if not an incomes policy, then a permanent reduction in the rate of wage increases to the level of competitor countries, *plus* an increase in the rate of productivity growth to their levels. Earnings growth was in fact to revert in the direction of 9 per cent per annum; and, while productivity undoubtedly increased in much of manufacturing industry, it was from a narrower manufacturing base so that it soon became obvious that an exchange rate adjustment was needed – indeed, this became a policy decision in 1986, as we shall see.

Lawson was on firmer ground in predicting that the reduction of tax revenue from the North Sea would be offset elsewhere in the accounts than he was in assuming that the balance of payments would be able to cope. It was up to the market to provide – 'which industries and services they will be, I do not know.' He also, no doubt reflecting Cabinet pressures of the time, changed his tune slightly from an assumed 'freeze' on public spending to saying 'even some modest growth of public spending might be possible. But expenditure must fall as a percentage of output' – rather as, in Financial Secretary days, he had shifted the emphasis from absolute falls in the PSBR to reductions as a percentage of output, or GDP.

While he was still seemingly impervious to growing public concern about the rise in unemployment – his 1983 Election campaign prediction looked increasingly dubious – he boasted that, with the help of North Sea oil, the UK had made 'the vital and long overdue transition from a high inflation to a low inflation economy'. This theme was developed at the Confederation of British

Industry dinner on May 23rd. Recent CBI surveys had pointed to rising unemployment and considerable concern about the state of the 'real economy'. Lawson told them that 'to all intents and purposes' the Government had now defeated inflation, as well as having abolished controls and cut various taxes. 'Now it us up to you' he told the captains of industry. His audience had been somewhat upset by the reversal of the Budget interest rate cuts early in May, which was officially justified by the fact that the differential between London and New York had widened because of a sharp rise of 1½ per cent in US interest rates, rather than because the monetary aggregates were misbehaving. If the Chancellor had developed a serious concern about unemployment by now, he could have simply tolerated the interest rate differential and let the pound slide. That moment had not yet arrived.

The pound did begin to slide in July, however, and the Treasury and Bank made no bones about the fact that they were raising interest rates to protect sterling – base rates rose from 9¼ per cent on June 27th to 10 per cent on July 10th and 12 per cent on July 12th. This was pretty embarrassing for a Chancellor who had justified a 'neutral' Budget on the grounds that it brought interest rates down half a per cent to 8/8¾ per cent. Those who had praised the great tax-reforming measures of March 15th were beginning to have second thoughts.

There was a certain amount of recrimination in the air. The Treasury Select Committee had aired the subject of whether the exchange rate needed to come down. Mrs Thatcher had rashly said inflation was under control and the money supply did not matter. The Bank of England had gone out of its way in June to get across two messages: first that there was no need, in its view, to raise interest rates for domestic reasons; second, it said, the structure of Exchequer receipts as a result of the Budget meant that the official statistics might look worse than they were – 'almost all the forecast PSBR of £7¼ billion is likely to occur in the first half of the financial year, with the major offsets from the acceleration of VAT payments on imports and from asset sales due in the autumn and beyond . . . the pace of growth of broad money is likely to be faster in the early part of the current target period than is to be expected over the period as a whole.'[14]

The financial markets panicked over the bad June M3 figures, despite this warning. And, ironically, the sharp rise in interest rates took place despite the emphasis the Chancellor was now putting on Mo as a guide to interest rate changes; as the Bank pointed out in September, 'Mo has remained comfortably within its 4 to 8 per cent target range since March.'

There were other background factors. The miners' strike had been going on since the beginning of 1984, so it could hardly be blamed on its own for a lack of confidence in sterling. But there was a brief summer dock strike – an uncomfortable reminder of the 'bad old days' which Thatcherism had been supposed to banish.

It was a pretty bleak prospect for the economy as the summer holidays approached, and this was underlined by the National Institute of Economic and Social Research in its August review. Unemployment was still rising, and might continue to go up in 1985; and the balance of payments surplus had disappeared, even allowing for the distortions of the miners' strike.

The exiguous recovery would have been even less but for the rise in consumer borrowing that was associated with the continuing decline in the saving ratio: 'From 1980 to the end of 1983 hire purchase debt rose more than twice as fast as disposable income, building society mortgages over two and a half times as fast, and personal bank loans almost one and half times as fast.'[15]

It was against this depressed background that the Chancellor delivered a talk, the Mais Lecture, to an audience at the City University on June 18th, 1984. The lecture was remarkable both for its apparent complacency, and for its attempt to turn conventional economics on its head. The preparation of the lecture was kept to a very small group within the Treasury, and was regarded by some officials as 'an aberration, written in a hurry'.

Lawson addressed the question being asked 'in many quarters' about Government policy: 'Has the emphasis of policy changed from the defeat of inflation to the promotion of growth and employment? And, even if it hasn't, given the present low level of inflation and high level of unemployment, isn't it high time it did?' The very question, he said, was based upon 'a fundamental fallacy'. The conventional post-war wisdom was that unemployment was a consequence of inadequate economic growth, and economic growth was to be secured by *macro*economic policy; inflation, by contrast, was increasingly seen as a matter to be dealt with by *micro*economic policy – 'the panoply of controls and subsidies associated with the era of incomes policy'.

But the present Government's policy took it that 'the proper role of each is precisely the opposite of that assigned to it by the conventional post-war wisdom. It is the conquest of inflation, and not the pursuit of growth and employment, which is or should be the objective of macroeconomic policy.' And, 'It is the creation of conditions conducive to growth and employment, and not the suppression of price rises, which is or should be the objective of microeconomic policy.'

We have seen that this theme had precursors. Lawson had over the years been developing the view that the elements of growth lay with better productivity, and it was up to Governments to remove the impediments to growth. But the 'conventional wisdom' had grown up precisely because the crude business cycle, left to itself, could be an impediment to growth. Excessive downswings by the private sector could be tempered, ideally avoided altogether, through the use of what had come to be known as 'stabilisation policy' – broadly, the use of macroeconomic policy to manage demand.

The belief that successful demand management was a chimera was common to monetarists of all shades. But even Samuel Brittan of the *Financial Times* was prepared to say Lawson's role reversal for macro and micro policy was 'at most 70 per cent right'. Brittan wrote: 'It is pretty clear that demand management policies do have a major *short-term* impact on output and employment as well as prices and money wages.'[16]

Lawson in fact set up a false dichotomy, appealingly neat though his 'role reversal' seemed. Macroeconomic policy had in fact been used for years in the battle against inflation, as well as to encourage employment and growth. It is moreover questionable whether a national 'norm' for incomes is really a 'micro' policy anyway. Similarly, during the 1960s and 1970s governments had tried to supplement the growth effort with 'micro' intervention policies of one sort or another. It was also increasingly recognised that exchange rate policy was an important tool of macroeconomic management – but Lawson, in his Mais Lecture, was still in his phase of being dismissive of exchange rate policy, and laughed off the recession of 1980–81 as having owed more to 'the unwarranted cost increases in 1979–80 than to the rise in the exchange rate'. Perhaps: the rise in the real exchange rate had reflected the cost increases *and* the rise in the nominal exchange rate. The point was that conventional macroeconomic management would have required the exchange rate to *fall* to bring UK costs into line with those elsewhere – a view Lawson was going to have to recognise tacitly in later years.

The Chancellor cited the rise in employment in the USA over the previous ten years as an example of what can happen in an enlightened, dynamic labour market, with the appropriate 'micro' policies. He passed over the fact that in the middle of the period US unemployment had risen to over 11 per cent in 1982, and fallen to 7.5 per cent in 1984 after a massive fiscal stimulus and a relaxation of monetary policy, both very 'macro' measures.

At various stages in the previous twelve months Lawson had referred to the ultimate 'manifesto' objective of stable prices – he had even gone through a fanciful stage of thinking it would be nice to have one year when prices did not rise at all, as in the late 1950s. He returned to the theme of 'onward to stable prices' in the Mais Lecture; and, taken with his apparent disavowal of the use of macroeconomic management – tax cuts and/or increases in public spending – to achieve growth and employment, the lecture was read as a very gloomy one indeed by 'conventional' commentators.

On the other hand, there was a certain 'desire to shock' about the lecture, and Lawson himself might not have begun with the question of a change of emphasis if he had not been thinking about that very possibility himself, now that inflation was around 5 per cent but unemployment was still rising. He might have been protesting too much.

There was an element of St Augustine about his attitude to zero inflation – 'God give me stable prices, but not yet.' Such was his desire to hold back public spending, however, that his expansionist tendencies were going to manifest themselves mainly in lower interest rates, wherever possible, and tax cuts. He would have to make ritual noises about zero inflation, but his actions were not to suggest that he was in a great hurry towards it.

One of the great problems his own officials had in interpreting Lawson was not only his sudden enthusiasms, but also his equally sudden bouts of boredom. He showed intermittent interest in the goal of a 'balanced budget', and eventually, with the aid of the Treasury's strange way of mixing up capital and current transitions, was to achieve it through sales of assets. But he was also to be heard in the spring of 1984 telling the Treasury Select Committee that he had no long-term policy to achieve a balanced budget – it was not necessary.[17] He also propagated from time to time the idea that the route to fuller employment lay in cuts in real wages, although the subsequent Lawson consumer boom was built on rising, not falling real wages.

The Mais Lecture was entitled 'The British Experiment' and concluded: 'The true British Experiment is a political experiment. It is the demonstration that trade union power *can* be curbed within a free society, and that *inflation* can be eradicated within a democracy.' Events were already suggesting, however, that whatever had happened to the unions, employers in Britain had not lost the old habits of granting inflationary wage increases.

One of the problems the Treasury had during 1984 was that the miners' strike was making the underlying economic picture look even worse than it was, although they could point out that much of the output lost then would be made up later. Lawson himself at the end of July told Parliament: 'It is unlikely that the rate of growth for this year will quite reach the 3 per cent that was envisaged at the time of the Budget'; and, given the latest interest rate rises, and the effect on mortgages, the Budget forecast of a 4½ per cent rate of inflation in the fourth quarter 'may not be reached until next year. But the inflationary trend remains firmly downward. Our commitment to the objective of stable prices is neither diminished nor deferred'.

He then caused a parliamentary furore, by saying, as only he could, that the extra public expenditure incurred as a result of the miners' strike (£300 million to £350 million, mainly from 'burning large quantities of oil in the power stations so as to eke out for a very long time the massive coal stockpile') was 'even in narrow financial terms . . . a worthwhile investment for the nation.'[18] History does not record whether the theft of £90 from the Chancellor's wallet in Number 11 Downing Street during August was by a miner claiming some of the investment back.

It was a difficult autumn for Lawson and the credibility of his policies. This did not stop him lecturing the US Government at the Washington IMF meeting in September about its budget deficit – the deficit that was giving an uplift to both the USA and world economies. In general, however, he was preaching the virtues of US economic flexibility, seeing hope in the growth of 'labour-intensive service industries which are not so much low-tech as no-tech', and arguing for slower growth of real wages in the UK.[19]

This marked a reversion to the curiously negligent attitude Lawson had had earlier in the decade towards manufacturing industry, and which had been remarked upon by James Prior. It brought a sharp rejoinder from Robbie Gilbert, former adviser to Prior at the Department of Employment, but now head of research at the Institute of Economics and Statistics, Oxford. Gilbert pointed out that the evidence for private sector services taking up the slack in employment from manufacturing in the UK was negligible – a proliferation of part-time barmaids was not enough. The main growth of employment in services in the past had been in the public sector – prime target for *cuts* under Lawson. 'Whatever the cause, the trend is clear enough,' wrote Gilbert. 'Rather than pay people to do a service, we buy machines that let us do it for ourselves. We even buy the goods themselves from retailers who adopt the same philosophy – hypermarkets, discount houses, superstores – so that all this additional business for shops has been accompanied by a drop in the numbers employed there.'[20]

Both at the IMF meeting, and at the subsequent Conservative Party Conference in Brighton, Lawson had a gloomy message about unemployment. In keeping with a practice that was to develop, he had taxed his officials for some weeks before the IMF meeting for some kind of international 'initiative' he could unveil in Washington. They came up with a relaxation of the normal rules about suspending export credit cover to countries which had rescheduled their debts, and Lawson hoped this idea would spread. He was displeased to find that the great initiative received negligible coverage in the British press, which was much more concerned with the statement that 'I see little prospect of reversing the trend of unemployment unless we can decisively moderate the growth of real wages.'[21]

The admission about unemployment led to some speculation that a softening of policy was to be expected, and that in turn led Lawson to say in a series of speeches, including the Mansion House one in October, shortly after the Conservative Conference, that he was resolutely sticking to his current policy. His reception had been decidedly lukewarm at the Conservative Conference, although the political wrath against him was diverted for a time by the bombing of the Grand Hotel, Brighton, where the Prime Minister was staying, the following night.

The nearest Lawson got to a public change of policy that autumn was in a public change of face, when both in the Commons and in television interviews he attempted to show, in contrast to his normal reputation in these matters, that he actually 'cared' about unemployment. In a classic Lawsonism, however, he said that unemployment was not an economic problem, only a social one. And shortly afterwards he managed to tell a visiting US journalist that, 'economically and politically, Britain can get along with double digit unemployment'.[22] Despite the public protestations there was considerable worry in Whitehall behind the scenes. While not normally 'Wet' Tories were saying at the Brighton Conference and elsewhere that 'something must be done' about unemployment, officials in Whitehall was quietly dusting down from the shelves a variety of possible public spending projects on roads, sewers and the Channel Tunnel. These were seen not so much as contingency plans for 'reflation', however, as a cushion for the economy if, with unemployment now 3¼ million and rising, there should suddenly be a downturn in the world economy the following year.

The general concern about the real economy produced an attitude of 'benign neglect' on the part of officials to the exchange rate. The principal force in currency markets during 1984 was the strength of the US dollar, which of course adversely affected all the other major currencies; but in the second half of 1984, with the miners' strike prolonged, and threatening at times to get worse (as with the Falklands in 1982, there was much more panic in the Government ranks during these struggles than one might have deduced from the subsequent victory celebrations) the pound came under pressure independently of its relationship with the dollar. After the panic of July, the Government had taken the opportunity to edge interest rates down again whenever possible, and they were reduced in successive stages from 12 per cent in July to 11½, 11 and 10½ per cent in August, and from 10 to 9½/9¾ per cent in November.

The decline in the pound provoked by the strength of the dollar suited a number of Lawson's Treasury advisers who wanted the pound down, and by November it had been devalued by some 10 per cent from its value a year earlier. (By contrast the German D-Mark, also affected by the dollar's strength, fell by about 3 per cent during that period.) There was a happy coincidence between the views of officials on tactics and the Chancellor's basic belief in 'free floating' for much of this period. But we have seen that the Government became worried when the pound fell too fast in July. And there were flurries of concern in the autumn as well.

There was a difference between allowing the market to take the pound down in 1984, and the more active exchange-rate policy Lawson was to adopt in later years, when the Bank of England would be instructed to intervene in the markets to try to hold the pound at a particular level. And if Lawson himself saw the situation as allowing market forces to operate, he was being seen increasingly as a man in a hurry to get interest rates down, against the world trend at the time, and found himself having to reassure the financial markets from time to time about his underlying financial rectitude.

But after eighteen months as Chancellor, he was also beginning to think he knew better than the markets. In the Mansion House speech of October 18th he referred back to the way the Government had in 1981 abolished regular use of the Bank of England's minimum lending rate in order to give the markets greater influence on interest rates. 'We felt that over time this should bring about a quicker and smoother adjustment of rates than would be achieved if the authorities were administering them along the lines of the earlier regime for minimum lending rate.'

He now added: 'But for this to work well it is important that there is no misunderstanding in the markets about the guidelines of Government policy. The sharp rise in interest rates last July occurred at a time when there were some anxieties about whether our monetary policy was on track. These anxieties, as I think is now recognised, were without foundation, [Lawson was speaking, of course, amid more anxieties . . .] but they combined with industrial disputes and a misplaced preoccupation with the sterling/dollar exchange rate to put massive upward pressure on interest rates in the money markets . . . I pointed out at the time that it is characteristic of financial markets to overshoot, and that that was what had occurred.'[23]

He attributed the fact that interest rates, though they had to come down, were still above their pre-July levels due to the continuing miners' strike, and pointed out that they had remained 'relatively steady during another period when the dollar had "surged ahead".' He said the monetary aggregates were on course, and that he was not going to raise interest rates now simply for exchange rate reasons (the pound had been falling both against the dollar and the D-Mark that week). So there was a reaffirmation of basic policy.

> We take the exchange rate into account when its behaviour suggests that the domestic monetary indicators are giving a false reading, which they are not. Provided monetary conditions are kept under firm control, excessive movements, whether in the money or exchange markets in response to outside influences, will tend to correct themselves relatively quickly. The position is underpinned by the fact that monetary growth over the past 12 months is well within the target ranges.

By December, however, the Bank of England was once again unveiling embarrassingly bad figures for M3, still given equal weight with M0; official protestations that the monetary figures were distorted, by the effect on bank deposits of a massive oversubscription of the privatisation issue for British Telecom, were only accepted up to a point.

The Autumn Statement, which gives the basic background to the spring Budget, indicated that economic growth was likely to turn out at 2½ per cent between 1983 and 1984, and 3½ per cent between 1984 and 1985, of which 1 per cent would be recovery from the distortions of the coal strike. The coal strike meant that the PSBR would be some £1¼ billion above target for 1984–85, but 'latest forecasts suggest that there would be scope for tax cuts of about £1½ billion if the PSBR were to be the £7 billion, or 2 per cent of GDP, assumed in the last MTFS.'

Stories that the Chancellor had not always got his way in Cabinet over spending cuts – the Prime Minister, for instance, refused to support him over further reductions in the housing budget that autumn for the 1985–86 spending round, and plans for cuts in student grants were reversed after an unexpected 'middle class' revolt – proved to be only straws grasped at by those who wanted a change in policy. The spending plans for 1985–86 as a whole were frozen at the 1984–85 level, and increases in, for example, defence were offset by real reductions in the budgets for education and science, and transport.

The general pressure from backbenchers, and from the Prime Minister herself, who was also growing concerned about the unemployment trend, was that the coming Budget should be presented as a 'budget for jobs'. Lawson himself took this line in interviews at the turn of the year, and, against a background where hawkish ministers used to argue that 'if anyone is unemployed it is basically their own fault', actually went so far as to say, 'There are still far too many people genuinely looking for work, and unable to find it', and that he would reduce taxes and reform the tax system.[24]

The Budget was due to be discussed at a weekend meeting of Treasury ministers and officials at Chevening, in Kent, the Foreign Secretary's official residence. (The Chancellor was later allocated, for a time, his own country residence at Dorneywood, in Buckinghamshire.) But the Chevening weekend was overshadowed by a sterling crisis which led to the final demise of Lawson's belief that, when it came to the value of the pound, the market knew best.

SEVEN

The Sterling Crisis of January 1985 and its Aftermath

January–July 1985

The January 1985 sterling crisis was both a low point for Nigel Lawson's reputation and a turning point in his attitude towards the exchange rate. The unspoken alliance between the Chancellor, who wanted interest rates down, and Treasury officials concerned that the pound was still too high, had resulted in a 10 per cent devaluation of the pound during 1984 while the official policy was one of 'free floating' with occasional intervention – spending foreign exchange from the reserves, or taking it in – to 'smooth' the workings of the market.

The desperate underlying state of British industry – beneath the rhetoric of 'recovery', 'three years of steady growth since the brilliant Budget of 1981', etc. – had been brought out by the National Institute of Economic and Social Research. 'Even in the first half of this year, manufacturing output was running some 15 p.c. below its peak in 1973 . . . production is now more than 40 p.c. lower than in the late 1970s for motor-vehicles and man-made fibres, over 30 p.c. for textiles, and over 20 p.c. for metals, metal goods, mechanical engineering, clothing and "other manufacturing".' And the new 'small businesses' in which the Government had put so much faith? These 'cannot as yet have had more than a small impact on the total picture.'[1]

It was no wonder that Treasury officials looked at the underlying trends and worried about the exchange rate. At certain stages during 1984 the official line had been to concentrate on the 'effective' (average) rate for the exchange rate, or the rate against the European currencies. Indeed, reporters and analysts were discouraged from looking at the dollar/sterling rate because this largely reflected the strength of the dollar – largely, but not entirely. During the IMF Meeting in Washington in September, the West German Bundesbank had intervened heavily to prevent the D-Mark itself from weakening against the dollar; and the Bank of England had favoured more concerted international intervention to steady the market, but Lawson had refused.

The Treasury and the Bank were undoubtedly concerned about the continued fall in the pound during December and in the first ten days of January 1985. Even for the 'devaluation camp' there was something unnerving about the speed of decline; and fears arose of 'a free fall'.

Moreover, no matter how much the Government tried to put the emphasis on the 'sterling index', measuring the pound's average movement against all the major currencies, or on the fact that North Sea oil was worth more when the dollar strengthened (because oil is priced in dollars), if the pound were to fall below the level of one dollar this would inevitably be seen as a loss of virility. In the course of 1984 sterling had dropped from over $1.45 to just over $1.15, with most of the reduction taking place in the second half of the year – speeding up in November and December.

As January opened, Lawson's policy of concentrating on the monetary aggregates and letting the pound find its market level, implied, to the innocent beholder, that, if the market took it forcefully towards one dollar, then that would be that. Mrs Thatcher, too, had many times affirmed her faith in the wisdom of the market's assessment of such matters. On Friday, January 11th, 1984, in his regular briefing to Westminster lobby correspondents, the Prime Minister's press secretary Bernard Ingham faithfully reflected his political mistress's previous views on the matter when the subject was raised by the press. The Government was totally unperturbed by the fall, the correspondents were told; sterling's value was determined by the market; the prospect of a fall even to one pound equals one dollar could be looked upon with equanimity.

There was, in fact, a complete breakdown that day between the tightly knit group of Chancellor, Governor and key officials which decides exchange rate policy (with the Prime Minister involved on key occasions), and the Number 10 press office. That very morning, with the pound under severe pressure, the Bank of England had raised its money market dealing rates in a clear signal that it wanted interest rates up, and base rates were subsequently raised by 1 per cent to 10.5 per cent. The pound still closed at a new low of just under $1.13.

The rise in base rates did not exactly suggest that the Government was still unconcerned about the run on the pound; but a number of Sunday newspapers, and the BBC, ran stories on Sunday, January 13th, reflecting Bernard Ingham's briefing. The Prime Minister and Chancellor were in fact very concerned about the potential humiliation of the prospect of a 'one dollar pound'; it was true that they at this stage did not like using the foreign currency reserves to protect sterling. But raising interest rates was most certainly a form of intervention in the markets.

The incident is partly explained by the way in which Mrs Thatcher and Ingham operated. Ingham seems to have managed press relations from Number 10 partly on the basis of information and conversations with the Prime Minister, and partly by 'reading her mind'. The latter approach inevitably produced the occasional inaccurate reading, and at the subsequent inquest Mrs Thatcher's practice was not to 'tear a strip off' Ingham – in the way she behaved with so many other officials – but to say 'I didn't like the way X or Y came out' (in the newspapers). On this occasion, amid fast-moving financial markets, it was an out-of-date reading. But Ingham had gained his credibility with the parliamentary lobby by speaking with equal, blustering confidence, whether armed with information or with psychic powers. It probably did not help that at this stage the Treasury itself, which ought to be on top of press briefing in such matters, had as its chief information officer an official who was brilliant, but not especially outgoing with the press. If Ingham read his political mistress's mind, Robert Culpin at the Treasury sometimes appeared to assume that the press were stupid if they could not read his. In any event, as Hugo Young has pointed out, Ingham had already received 'absolution' from the Prime Minister before Lawson made his own views known.[2]

The curious thing was that a very similar report, presented less dramatically and with a lot less impact on the financial markets, had appeared in the previous week's *Sunday Times*, on January 6th. It was largely in response to a question about this that a senior official told me on Friday 11th that letting the pound fall to one dollar was certainly not official policy; that the Treasury and the Bank had deliberately engineered the rise in interest rates on the Friday morning. And they would do the same again, or more, on the Monday if the market was still selling sterling. This was duly reported in the *Observer.*

The market was indeed selling sterling on the Monday morning – heavily. Mrs Thatcher had ordered Government information officers to contact the daily press and the BBC and tell them Numbers 10 and 11 Downing Street *were* worried about the falling pound on the Sunday, and to deny reports to the contrary. But the damage was done, and the differing stories merely added to the market's confusion. Meanwhile the second day of the Chancellor's country-house weekend to discuss Budget strategy with officials was taken up with short-term tactics about the exchange rate, and frantic calls from the Prime Minister, and to the Governor and other senior Bank of England officials. The irony was that on the agenda at Chevening was the question of what scope there was for tax cuts in the Budget, given the fact that the

Chancellor had not been too successful in restraining departmental ministers during the autumn expenditure round. The very fact that it was known that tax cuts were being discussed, and public spending targets being missed, was one of the factors worrying the markets. Had the Government's resolve been weakened, it was being asked?

In order to show the seriousness of their desire to protect the pound now, the Treasury and Bank of England disinterred the old minimum lending rate (buried in August 1981 in order to allow greater influence to market forces), reintroducing it at 12 per cent for one day only, to tell the banks to raise their base rates by a further 1½ per cent to a 'crisis' 12 per cent.

The episode was humiliating for Lawson, and a damning reflection on the press relations of both Numbers 10 and 11 Downing Street. But it is always difficult to handle the public relations of exchange rate policy, not least when obfuscation is central to the policy. This time Prime Minister and Chancellor were caught out, on the basis of a briefing by the Government's most senior press officer. But it was certainly not unprecedented for the 10 Downing Street publicity machine to mishandle such a sensitive and difficult area of policy.

The pound had touched a new low of just over $1.10 on the morning of Monday, January 14th, before the Bank of England intervened to steady it, and then raised interest rates. That Thursday Nigel Lawson attended a meeting of the Group of Five Finance Ministers and Central Bank Governors (from the USA, Japan, West Germany, France and the UK), which principally discussed the strength of the dollar and what to do about it. Lawson's interest in this of course was that concerted intervention by the G5 Central Banks to hold the dollar down would help him in his battle to fight off the humiliation of the prospect of a one dollar pound. Lawson had been against concerted intervention at the IMF meeting in September, although a more potent factor was that the USA itself was against such intervention.

There was now an example of the special relationship between President Reagan and Mrs Thatcher at work. Before Lawson arrived in Washington for the G5 meeting, Mrs Thatcher telephoned Reagan and pleaded with him to soften the US stance against co-ordinated intervention in the exchange markets. Since the Williamsburg Summit of 1983, the policy had been only to intervene in 'disorderly markets', which in practice meant almost never. Reagan listened to Mrs Thatcher, and the result was that the Americans changed tack; they agreed, with the other four, 'to undertake co-ordinated intervention in the markets as necessary'; the G5 followed this with a burst of official dollar selling to hold the US currency down.

For the rest of January the Government relied both on high interest rates *and* exchange market intervention to keep the pound above $1.10; there was also an attempt by the Prime Minister on television to 'talk the pound up', saying it had gone down too far and was undervalued. But there was a further panic on Monday, January 28th and the Treasury and the Bank engineered another 2 per cent jump in base rates to 14 per cent.

By now the Government had used every shot in its locker to defend the pound, short of an emergency Budget. In doing so it had changed its policy stance considerably – a matter which Lawson was called upon to explain that very afternoon of Monday, January 28th, in a routine appearance before the Commons Treasury Select Committee.

The episode also revived doubts about the Chancellor's political touch. Edward Pearce, in the *Sunday Telegraph*, suggested that Lawson was a classic example of Mrs Thatcher's penchant for promoting ministers 'without political facility'. It had been noticeable to many officials and journalists who came into contact with Lawson that, for all his intellectual reputation, he could be surprisingly inarticulate. 'Accordingly,' wrote Pearce, 'we had a fatal confluence of two things: Lawson's deep intellectual convictions, which logically disposed him against resistance to the market, and a want of that skill with words and judgment of men's reactions which can at least leave a politician looking like a wise midwife to the inevitable.' Lawson had been in favour of 'free floating' for too long.[3]

In the course of this difficult January the money supply statistics by which the Government had set so much store did not look too bad. Mo was well within its target range, and M3 had come back into its. But these basic criteria were not good enough for the market, because both the interest rate action taken by Lawson, and the exchange market intervention, were prompted solely because of the threat of a one dollar pound. At various stages it was suggested that falling oil prices and disagreements among OPEC countries were affecting sentiment about the pound; but such factors had been around before, and it so happened that the other great North Sea oil-producing country, Norway, actually lowered its interest rates during January in an effort to stem inflows of funds into the country.

The January crisis seems to have been about more deep-seated concerns as to where the British economy, and British economic policy, were headed, of which the bungling of the briefings on exchange rate policy were symptomatic. Although it was partly a question of the strength of the dollar, there was no French franc or D-Mark crisis that month. The financial markets, supposed, at one time, by Lawson to be the supreme judges of these things, had temporarily lost faith; and when they lose faith, they have to be induced, some would say 'bribed', into holding their funds in London, via the medium of higher interest rates. The 'hook' of the MTFS on which Lawson had impaled himself did not help, because, although it was a useful weapon against 'spending ministers', it also fulfilled a prediction by Gordon Richardson that it could be a 'rod' for the Chancellor's back, if he was seen by the markets not to be hitting his self-imposed borrowing targets.

The loss of faith in Lawson's policies at the time seemed almost complete when one foreign exchange dealer was quoted as saying the pound had become 'a one-commodity currency' – oil. Roy Jenkins wrote a letter to *The Times* saying the crisis was due to the fact that 'the rest of the world cannot see how we are going to pay our way when the oil runs out.'[4] Lord Kaldor, the Labour peer and distinguished economist, also wrote to *The Times*, saying:

> Owing to the rapid deterioration in our non-oil balance (chiefly on account of the rapid increase in our *net* imports – in excess of exports – of manufactures) the benefit derived from oil to the balance of payments has now been fully swallowed up by the deterioration in our trade balance in commodities other than oil . . . assuming that the revenue from oil continues at current levels, an old-fashioned balance of payments crisis cannot be more than a year or two ahead.[5]

It is worth emphasising that these, and a number of similar warnings by Professor Wynne Godley, of Cambridge University, were delivered long before the added problems of the excess demand of 1987–89.

Lawson himself admitted, rather candidly, to the Treasury Select Committee that there was 'some feeling in the markets that the Government was no longer giving sufficient priority to maintaining downward pressure on inflation. These doubts about domestic policy were fanned by indications that public expenditure and borrowing were running much higher than intended this year, and by calls for yet further increases in public expenditure.' He added: 'The action we have taken has clearly shown that these uncertainties are unfounded. We have acted domestically and, in concert with other major countries, internationally to calm the turbulence in the exchange markets. We have demonstrated that this Government, while anxious to see unemployment come down, is most emphatically *not* prepared to take any risks with inflation.' He might have added: 'At least, not when we are found out.'[6]

For good measure the Chancellor added that 'our actions have been symmetrical, as well as being consistent. I have in mind particularly the period . . . during the latter part of 1980 and the first part of 1981, when we took the sharp rise in sterling then very much into account; even though the figures for M3 did not seem to indicate any tightness, we felt that policy *was* tight.' The true story of the 1980–81 period was, of course, somewhat more fraught than this easy claim to symmetry and consistency made it seem; but, then, his officials were continually surprised at the facility with which Lawson managed to rationalise almost any action, in the face of a check to progress, as being entirely in keeping with previous plans.

It should be noted at this point that Lawson nearly always put up a good performance at these Treasury Committee sessions. He was usually relaxed, in command of his material and occasionally very funny. On the rare occasions when he seemed stumped he had a disarming way of saying something on the lines of 'I think it's time to give Sir Terence Burns a turn'. He had been a strong believer in the parliamentary select committee system when in Opposition, as a helpful guide to the background to policy decisions, and did his homework before each session.

Lawson spelled out on this occasion that the G5 had omitted any reference to 'disorderly markets', adding, 'We indicated our readiness to intervene whenever we thought it necessary to do so.' Asked whether he agreed with the Prime Minister's statement on television that sterling had gone down too far, he said, 'I think the Prime Minister is absolutely right that sterling is undervalued against the dollar; the dollar is grossly overvalued' (no reference to the relationship with European currencies) adding, 'I think there is confusion in some people's minds about belief in a market system and belief in the market always being right. I believe profoundly that the market system is the best system of all for running an economy. That does not mean to say that the market is always right.'

In this context he showed himself well aware of the kind of pitfall that was later to present itself: 'If the market overshoots, as it frequently does – and it is something inherent in the market when it happens – it can at the end of the day correct itself, whereas if an interventionist government gets committed to a particular policy, or particular figure, it goes on and on and finds it very difficult to correct it.'

Indeed, on this very occasion one MP suggested to him that it looked as though the pound was fluctuating as if it were within the limits of the EMS, to which Lawson replied: 'We are not pursuing a policy of unavowed alignment with the EMS. It is perfectly true, however, that there have not been great fluctuations' and, 'we look at the effective exchange rate index to give us the best single measure of the external value of the pound.' He also stated: 'I do *not* think it makes sense to talk about particular levels of exchange rates at which one might take particular action, nor what action one would take at those levels.'

At this stage Lawson was still expressing public concern about balance of payments deficits. He described the US deficit of over $100 billion as 'absolutely massive – even if you adjust for the size of the American economy as a whole. That, I believe, is a completely unsustainable position.' (The UK deficit in 1988–89 was to be as great a proportion of GDP as the US one then.)

Lawson seemed in his testimony on this occasion to be making the best of a bad job, and emphasising the problems of public expenditure control in a way he hoped would give him greater pull with the Cabinet later in the year. Thus, instead of the usual ministerial line that everything was really all right and the markets were wrong, he actually repeated, 'As I said in my opening statement, I think that there *were* fears, in the market, that policy was too lax, when they could see (and this is something which is a fact) that the public expenditure and borrowing were overrunning this year significantly, for reasons which are, I think, well known to this Committee.' Yet even on this day when he had hoisted interest rates by 2 per cent, his passion for tax cuts overcame him and he said, in the context of the impending Budget, 'It is perfectly possible – and I hope that it will prove the case – that [the fiscal] policy is consistent with reductions in taxation.' (There were those who thought that his obvious enthusiasm for tax cuts had been one of the causes of the collapse of the pound.)

It was around this time that Lawson and his colleagues were beginning to give up hope of keeping public expenditure flat in real terms, and putting the emphasis on at least making it decline as a percentage of GDP. 'We have not achieved as much as we had hoped to achieve, that is absolutely true. However, even if you look at what we *have* achieved, public expenditure under this Government has increased on average by 1½ p.c. a year in real terms. As I said, we would have wished it flat . . . under our predecessors – even including those years when the IMF came in and forced them to cut public expenditure – it was increasing by 3 p.c. on average.' He said the lower 1½ per cent growth rate was still significant because the economy 'during this recovery (which is now nearly 4 years old and still going strong) has been growing as a whole at [a rate of] 3 p.c. a year real, allowing for the temporary effects of the coal strike.' As this ratio continued 'it will give scope for reductions in taxation. The scope will be even greater, of course, if we can maintain public expenditure constant in real terms.'

The Committee asked him about the EMS, and whether membership would not have been a help in this latest crisis. 'I do not think it would have made any difference whatsoever in the present context,' Lawson replied, adding, 'we would have less manoeuvrability and flexibility than we have now in dealing with these sorts of situations.'

Nevertheless, the January 1985 sterling crisis did in fact prompt a review in Whitehall of the option of going into the EMS. The Bank of England had actually wanted to raise interest rates earlier, during December, and Treasury officials subsequently conceded that they had not paid enough attention to the implications of the fast fall in the sterling–dollar rate, and that the interest-rate weapon should have been used in December or early January – certainly before it was forced by the market. One official commented tartly: 'Of course it didn't help that Bernard Ingham was stuck on last year's rhetoric.'

It was not only the state of the economy and the blows to his economic policy that were troubling the Chancellor of the Exchequer in the autumn and winter of 1984–85. He also found himself carrying the political can in the House of Commons for the failure of Johnson Matthey Bankers (JMB) and the manner in which it was rescued by the Bank of England. Unlike most Chancellors, the former City editor of the *Sunday Telegraph* always manifested a particular interest in the minutiae of City matters, often giving the impression he thought he knew better than his technical advisers at the Bank of England. In his early days as Financial Secretary, he had intervened and fussed to such an extent about the fine print of issues of government stock that the Bank man responsible, Eddie George, actually called his bluff by saying that if the Treasury wanted they could take over the responsibility for the whole process.[7]

In the end George won the respect of the Financial Secretary, just as he had done of senior Treasury officials and Professor Walters. George's good relationship with Walters and the top Treasury monetary policy official Peter Middleton in the early 1980s was an important counterweight to the perpetual friction between the then Governor, Gordon Richardson, and Mrs Thatcher, as well as to the tense relationship between Richardson and Lawson. By the time Lawson took over as Chancellor in the summer of 1983, Richardson was about to retire, his readiness to serve a third period as Governor having brought a cool response from the Government.

A close colleague of Richardson's said: 'If Gordon had stayed, it would have been a disaster. Lawson and he could not have handled each other.' But Lawson and George got on reasonably well from 1983 onwards, not least because Numbers 10 and 11 Downing Street admired the latter's technical expertise and knew that he was sympathetic to the basic aims of the counter-inflation policy, if differing frequently on monetary tactics.

Relations between Lawson and the deputy governor Kit McMahon had been edgy in the 1979–81 period, and continued so after Lawson became Chancellor. The Lawson camp never forgave McMahon for making no secret of his intellectual contempt for monetarism. The relationship between the Chancellor and the new Governor, Robin Leigh-Pemberton, was described by a colleague as 'one-sided but good'. Richardson had been originally appointed by the Heath Government, and reappointed by Labour in 1978. Leigh-Pemberton was of course a Thatcher appointment, and a highly controversial one at that. He was a prominent Conservative, albeit in local government, and his appointment was more blatantly political than had been the case with the recent run of governors. It is interesting therefore to note that one of the occasions on which Leigh-Pemberton attracted Mrs Thatcher's attention before his appointment was when he stood up to her in an exchange about the money supply figures in 1980: she blamed banks such as the one of which he was then chairman, National Westminster, and he said she was talking nonsense and the matter had to be seen in perspective.[8] He agreed to bring chapter and verse to her at a Number 10 Downing Street reception he was due to attend shortly. When he arrived and started to explain the figures on a postcard, she apparently snatched the card from him and put it in her handbag.

In July 1984, Lawson had given a speech to the Conservative Bow Group setting out his strategy for reinforcing the City of London as a leading financial centre. He said the Government could 'fairly claim credit for pushing along the pace of change' with regard to competition and innovation within the financial markets, and put his weight behind the general Bank of England/ Government moves to make British financial institutions adequately capitalised, and the need for protection of investors. His speech was so wide-ranging that the *Financial Times* commented, 'The Chancellor's speech was unusual in ranging over issues which are the responsibility of different ministers' – such as the Department of Trade.[9]

One British financial institution that was not adequately capitalised at the time was Johnson Matthey Bankers. While the Government and Bank of England were getting excited about the impending changes in the City, JMB was indulging in the time-honoured banking malpractice of expanding its loan book too fast, and concentrating an excessive proportion of its portfolio on one or two dubious borrowers. Things came to a head in the summer of 1984, and when Lawson returned from the IMF meeting at which he had to admit that the British unemployment outlook was getting no better, he found the Bank recommending that JMB be rescued.

It was the beginning of a saga for Lawson which ran on through the winter and spring of 1984–85, during which as Chancellor he was criticised by Labour MPs such as Brian Sedgemore and Dennis Skinner, and the then SDP's Dr David Owen, and had to face calls for public enquiries, and the resignation of the Governor. Lawson found himself at times reassuring the House on the basis of inadequate information – the Bank did not tell him the full scale of their commitment to JMB, which at one stage involved a £100 million loan, and laid Lawson wide open to Opposition taunts about the misuse of taxpayers' money. One month the Chancellor was telling the Commons there was no evidence of fraud at JMB. The next month the Fraud Squad was called in.

Relations between Government and Bank were widely considered to be at their lowest ebb since the pre-war days of Montagu Norman as Governor, and it took a very long time for the dust to settle. The Bank's reputation undoubtedly suffered; the good relationship between Eddie George and Numbers 10 and 11 Downing Street on monetary policy was sorely tested; and the public and private slanging of each institution by the other was a remarkable episode in a British establishment that normally prides itself on working as a team, and closing ranks when necessary.

The very week before the rescue, Lawson and Leigh-Pemberton had been at the Washington IMF meeting, where one of the subjects had been the Third World debt crisis and the threat to the banking system. The Bank of England were very worried at the time that, if they had allowed JMB to fail, this would have had serious repercussions on other banks, and that the risk was simply not worth taking.

Eventually the Bank recovered all the money it had put into the rescue, but not the interest. It had lost something more intangible. Being criticised by the Chancellor in public was a new experience for the Bank – 'they did to some extent fall down on the job,' said Lawson to the Commons in June 1985. He thought, with considerable justification, that the problems at JMB should have been spotted a lot earlier, and 'on the £100 million loan, I think I should have been told at the time'. With regard to the rescue operation itself, Lawson said, 'I am satisfied that the Governor was acting properly within his discretion.'[10] This was a somewhat Delphic remark. Lawson had been dissatisfied with the deputy governor, and Treasury officials believe that the Chancellor himself, if involved at an earlier stage, might not actually have rescued JMB at all.

The Bank had told the Treasury about the £100m. loan, but nobody told the Chancellor. The eventual enquiry into the system of banking supervision was, however, basically an 'inside' one by Bank and Treasury, with one outside banker. 'Damage limitation' rather than further public embarrassment, became the order of the day, and led to a new Banking Act. The fact was that, even if the rescue of JMB was justified, the system of banking supervision which had allowed the crisis to develop was obviously suspect, and bound to reflect badly on the Bank. But Bank officials thought the Chancellor should have spent more time attacking Sedgemore, and less criticising them in public. 'It was a good example of Lawson's strategy for preservation,' said one, 'which is to attack allies if need be rather than build friendships.' Eventually, Mrs Thatcher ordered Lawson to concentrate his fire on the Opposition.

The Bank fits into the Whitehall economic policy-making machine at many levels, from low-level official contact to regular meetings between Chancellor and Governor, senior Bank and Treasury officials, and occasional – often 'crisis' – meetings at Number 10 Downing Street. The morale of the Bank suffered during 1984–85, and so did the Treasury's trust in it – which had seldom been overwhelming under Lawson anyway. It did not help relations in the course of 1985 that, apparently in recrimination for his personal political embarrassment over JMB, Lawson delayed the announcement of the re-appointment of Kit McMahon, the deputy governor, until the last possible minute, and there were even newspaper reports, apparently inspired by the Treasury, that he might not be reappointed. Even the customary granting of a knighthood to McMahon was delayed until an indignant Leigh-Pemberton intervened personally with the Prime Minister.

In fact, having been reappointed, McMahon only stayed on for 1985, and accepted the offer of the job of chairman and chief executive of the Midland Bank. The new deputy governor was Sir George Blunden, a former director of the Bank brought back from retirement because at that stage the Government could not decide between the two senior candidates within the Bank, Eddie George and David Walker. The latter, a recruit from the Treasury in the 1970s, had played a crucial role in persuading the banks to keep British industry going during the acute financial problems of 1980–81, and was subsequently closely involved with encouraging the changes in the City to which Lawson referred in his July 1984 speech to the Bow Group. (After that, he was asked by the Prime Minister to head the Securities and Investments Board, the supervisory organisation in the City, while retaining a directorship of the Bank.) Sir George Blunden had known Mrs Thatcher for some time, got on well with her and with Lawson, and was the perfect man to iron out some of the many ruffles which had appeared in the relationship between Downing Street and Threadneedle Street.

The period from the January 1985 sterling crisis to the Budget on March 19th was an extremely difficult one in the financial markets, and required close co-operation between the Treasury and the Bank, although the underlying relationship between them was continuously soured by the JMB affair. From the point of view of the development of Lawson's thinking on economic policy, perhaps the most intriguing passage in his Budget speech was where he said:

> There are those who argue that if we stick to sound internal policies the exchange rate can be left to take care of itself. In the long run that may well be true. But

> significant movements in the exchange rate, whatever their cause, can have a short-term impact on the general price level and on inflationary expectations. This process can acquire a momentum of its own, making sound internal policies hard to implement. So benign neglect is not an option.

That was real confirmation of a turning point, although completely overshadowed at the time by the usual attention inevitably given to specific tax changes. Lawson *had* been practising 'benign neglect' – right up to early January. But it was the benign neglect of Bernard Ingham which public attention focused on. Now interest rates had to be kept high, *and* the Bank of England was given more latitude to intervene in the exchange markets. Even so, it was a nervous time: the agreement Lawson thought he had won from the US administration to hold the dollar down proved rather tenuous: European central banks appeared, for a time, to be on their own; the pound fell, during February, below the $1.10 at which the Treasury and Bank had tried to hold it, and touched a low of just under $1.04. President Reagan, his January 'good deed' done for Mrs Thatcher, managed to say a few weeks later: 'The main problem is not the strength of the dollar; it is the weakness of foreign currencies . . .'

The review, that February, of the question of EMS entry for the pound took place at the instigation of the Bank of England, which in turn had picked up strong signals from the Europeans that they would like sterling to join. In particular, the attitude of the West German Bundesbank had altered from lukewarm to enthusiastic. The Bank argued that during the January crisis the pound would have been less vulnerable to speculative pressure within the EMS; it also thought the EMS would provide a credible monetary discipline at a time when there was much scepticism in the financial markets about the Government's monetary policy, and indeed, about the whole MTFS approach.

The searing experience of the January sterling crisis was a major influence on Lawson, who now displayed considerable interest in, and enthusiasm for, the EMS. In fact the speed with which he moved from being virtually a 'free floater' to being seriously interested in joining the EMS caused some amusement among officials, who were witnessing the development of a new Lawsonian passion. Lawson decided that in future he was going to act more promptly in the face of undesirable movements in the exchange rate. In earlier periods when the EMS had briefly come up as a topic, the pound's alleged role as a 'petro-currency' was always seen as a factor inhibiting entry to the exchange rate mechanism. But by 1985 things seemed more evenly balanced; and, with North Sea oil production peaking and due to fall, Lawson and the Treasury were doing their best to play down the importance of oil to the economy. Nevertheless, the Treasury was less enthusiastic about the EMS than the Chancellor and the Bank: it begged to differ on whether interest rates would have been successfully held down in December/January if the pound had been within the EMS; pointed out that Britain would still have had to employ its own foreign currency reserves (not very high at the time); and maintained that oil price changes might still pose a problem for the pound within the EMS. Mrs Thatcher herself was firmly against the EMS; Sir Alan Walters, then living in Washington but still a part-time adviser, reinforced her gut anti-European instincts with technical arguments. The time, in the Government's oft-repeated phrase, was 'not ripe'.

Meanwhile, the pressures on the pound continued, and on one day towards the end of February the Bank of England used $250 million from the reserves as part of a dramatic co-ordinated intervention with the Bundesbank to protect their currencies from a renewed rise in the dollar, and to hold the pound at $1.07. This was in reaction to a statement from President Reagan that the US administration did not want to see the dollar fall. To add to British Government frustrations, this occurred after Mrs Thatcher, on a trip to Washington, had lectured the new US Treasury Secretary James Baker about the dollar being too high.

Given the continuing rise in unemployment, the Chancellor had wanted to make his March 1985 Budget a 'Budget for Jobs'. He had also wanted to press ahead with tax reform, broadening the base of VAT, and removing the tax advantages on pension schemes (having tackled life assurance premium relief the previous year). But what had in fact become a continuing January/February sterling crisis meant that essentially his brief was to keep the markets calm. A change in market sentiment to the dollar early in March helped the pound, and Mrs Thatcher told Lawson and the Bank that she wanted the pound at a respectable level against the dollar, and not to fall from that level. After falling some 13 per cent on average since the beginning of 1984, the sterling index rose sharply during March; and the pound was 'revalued' by 10 per cent against the average, and over 20 per cent against the dollar. Official tactics were evolved to hold the pound in the $1.25–$1.30 range at least, although, with sterling at D-Mark 4.00 against the German mark, a fall against the European currencies would have been welcomed by industrialists.

Mrs Thatcher not only desired peace and quiet on the currency front: she did not show too much enthusiasm for the Chancellor's tax reform plans. Almost as soon as the cheers had died down after his first Budget in 1984 Lawson had been hinting of great tax reforms ahead on the personal taxation front. Whereas the abolition of tax relief on life assurance premiums had saved the Treasury some £600 million a year, mortgage and pensions tax relief amounted to £6 billion or so annually. But Mrs Thatcher was firmly against such proposals – 'Our people won't stand for it.' Then there was the question of his fiscal scope, within the confines of his own financial strategy.

In the 1984 Autumn Statement, Lawson had indicated that he might have £1.5 billion spare for tax cuts, over and above indexation of personal allowances for inflation. It had also become clear that both the Prime Minister and a significant body of ministers and backbenchers wanted any spare tax-cutting revenue to be devoted to raising allowances further, in order to help the lower paid, rather than to cuts in the basic rate of tax. The political logic was, in any case, that basic rate cuts should be saved to nearer the Election. There was also a significant body within the Conservative Party that would have preferred public sector investment projects, rather than tax cuts. Lawson, however, argued that public sector investment was capital-intensive, whereas tax cuts stimulated enterprise, and ought to encourage lower pay settlements, and therefore boost jobs.

In his Budget speech he said: 'The argument over which will have a bigger impact on demand, increased public expenditure or lower taxation, completely misses the point. The case for lower taxation rests on supply-side policy: lower taxes will help to enhance incentives, eliminate distortions, improve the use of resources and heighten the spirit of enterprise.'

It was clear from the atmosphere in the exchange markets that, if he wanted to steady the pound, the Chancellor would have to produce a 'cautious' – not to say boring – Budget, and that was what was basically decided at the January weekend meeting at Chevening, in intervals between telephone calls around the Home Counties about the sterling crisis itself. By the time the Budget came, he had to admit that, because the coal strike had gone on longer than expected, and upward pressures on public spending remained 'intense' ('not least from increased take-up of social security benefits and further local authority overspending'), the scope for tax cuts was less, particularly since he wanted to impress the markets with a low PSBR target (of £7 billion for 1985–86), the coal strike being the main reason why the PSBR had overshot considerably in 1984–85.

The £1.5 billion had become £0.75 billion and was principally devoted to raising personal allowances by twice the rate of inflation. 'This year, a Budget for jobs and for enterprise has to give high priority to raising the tax thresholds.' He also reduced National Insurance contributions for the lower paid, for employees and employers – 'these changes represent substantial reductions in the cost of employing the lower paid. They will significantly improve the flexibility of the labour market and the prospects for jobs.' The main 'reform' was the announcement of an imminent discussion document, which would include proposals for separate personal tax allowances for husband and wife, transferable if desired, later in the decade.

Widening the range of VAT as a way of increasing scope for reductions in direct taxation was one of the reforms that had attracted Lawson, as he had said in various newspaper interviews after his 1984 Budget. But he found himself forced by vested interests and Prime Ministerial pledges, not to put VAT on food and children's clothes, for instance. Apart from extending VAT to cover advertising in newspapers and periodicals, he announced in his March 1985 Budget speech that he was dropping any plans to extend the scope of VAT during the lifetime of the Parliament. (Lawson liked to make up for such restrictions by abolishing at least one tax in each Budget. He had removed the National Insurance Surcharge and the Investment Income Surcharge in the 1984 Budget; he now abolished the Development Land Tax.)

Lawson emphasised in the Budget speech that although his public spending 'stabilisation' policy had got off to an awkward start, he was still aiming to keep public spending 'broadly flat', albeit from a 1½ per cent higher level (in volume terms). 'To achieve even these new figures, future Public Expenditure Surveys will have to be at least as tough as their predecessors; and there can be no let up in the tight control of individual spending programmes . . .' This was the harbinger of many an unpleasant cut in the public sector over the next few years, to balance the effect of any further uncontrollable increases.

The lack-lustre nature of this would-be 'tax reforming' Budget contributed to the sense of 'drift' which was to characterise the 1983–87 Conservative Government. The Treasury had always regarded mortgage interest relief as a gross distortion to the pattern of savings and investment, but Mrs Thatcher was wedded to it as an encouragement to the spread of property ownership.

The pensions lobby was remarkably effective, both on Conservative backbenchers and the Prime Minister. To Lawson's Treasury advisers it was scandalous that the average saver was taxed first on his income and then, say, on his building society interest, whereas subscribers to 'lump sum' pension arrangements were not taxed at any stage on this form of saving. But Mrs Thatcher loved the idea of encouraging provision for old age – no matter that most of the tax concessions favoured those who were already likely to be in a good position to finance their old age anyway.

There had been much speculation about the possibility of the Chancellor's moving on from life assurance to pensions funds for the next target. In his speech, Lawson managed to make the best of things, and displayed his ability to bounce back from set-backs, a Houdini-figure escaping from the latest strait-jacket. A favourite trick in Budget speeches was to lead people up the garden path: 'There is also a case for changing the tax treatment of pension funds, as part of a thorough-going reform of the tax treatment of personal savings generally. Any fundamental reform of this kind would, in the same way as tax treatment of husbands and wives, need to be preceded by the publication of a Green Paper. [Pause] The House will, I am sure, be interested to learn that I have no such Green Paper in mind . . .' He had lost a battle with the Prime Minister, but the sighs of relief from those who had been led to expect the change, and the rhetorical trick, were a minor compensation to the beleaguered Chancellor.

It is, incidentally, interesting to note how clever the Government's publicity was over the matter of taxation. A Party that had promised to lower its burden actually increased it from 34 per cent of GDP in 1978–79 to over 39 per cent by 1981–82 – principally through the near-doubling of VAT. The ratio had come down a little, then increased after Lawson's first Budget – from 38.6 per cent in 1983–84 to 39.2 per cent in 1984–85, and came down to 38.5 per cent during the 1985–86 financial year following this Budget.[11]

In serious macroeconomic terms the March 1985 Budget was not a Budget for jobs at all. The National Institute of Economic and Social Research was forecasting a rise in unemployment in 1985–86, and it was already over 3 million. The purpose of the Budget was to keep the exchange rate up, thereby counteracting the aims of the earlier 'benign neglect', which had been tacitly embarked on because of concern about the real economy. Despite the 'recovery', non-oil output in the economy was barely above the 1979 level even now. The 1985 Budget report said 1985 might be the peak year for oil's contribution to the economy and balance of payments. Between the first half of 1981 and the second half of 1984, domestic demand for manufactures had grown by 20 per cent but UK output of manufactures by only 9 per cent.

On the face of it, given an inflation forecast of 5 per cent, the central target for M3 of 7 per cent for 1985–86 did not allow much scope for real growth in the economy. But, then, it was almost to be M3's last serious policy performance. There were targets for M3 (5 to 9 per cent) and M0 (3 to 7 per cent), but the FSBR noted: 'Over the past five years, households have increased both their borrowing and their holdings of liquid financial assets . . . the significance of the broad aggregates as monetary indicators has somewhat diminished.' (One can imagine the smile on the face of the official who drafted the word 'somewhat'.) This was elaborated later in another Treasury report: 'Liquidity has grown fast . . . but as long as it is not spent, it cannot cause inflation.'

Policy in the early Lawson years could be characterised as private recognition that the real economy was in bad shape and required a lower exchange rate, and public panic every time this was discovered, leading to protestations of virtue, and higher interest rates which either arrested the exchange rate in its tracks or reversed its direction. The consequent gyrations were certainly confusing to British industry, which had, above all things, been promised a stable financial environment. The NIESR commented in February 1985: 'By the logic of Medium-Term Financial Strategy, fiscal policy is kept tight in order to reduce interest rates – thereby promoting economic recovery. Other things being equal, lower interest rates would certainly be expected to raise demand, though we do not think that the stimulus would be sufficient to outweigh the fiscal deflation needed to reduce interest rates in the first place.'[12]

The pound's 'health' was fully restored by the perceived 'tightness' of the Budget, and interest rates were edged gently downwards from 14 to 11½ per cent by the end of July 1985. The monetary statistics were neither here nor there – indeed M3 was now all over the place, once again rising well above target; the exchange rate had been stabilised, then recovered; further strengthening allowed interest rates to be cut, with the one dollar pound a distant nightmare, and the currency averaging nearly $1.38 in July–September. Relations between Prime Minister and Chancellor, which close observers had described as 'icy' during the January/February sterling crisis, were restored. It might have been the Prime Minister's press secretary who initiated the trouble; it was most certainly the Chancellor who got the blame.

Industrialists and Whitehall officials continued to be worried about the exchange rate and the competitiveness of British industry, but the political emphasis was on recovering from the shock of the 'one dollar pound' and 'one commodity currency' scares. Industry's concerns were well reflected in the report of the House of Lords Select Committee on Overseas Trade in July 1985 – a report that so disturbed Downing Street and the Treasury that the Government information machine was cranked up to contact the press and 'rubbish' the report. Lawson described it as 'a mixture of special pleading dressed up as analysis, and assertion masquerading as evidence.' Lord Aldington, the chairman, was grateful for this, believing it received far more attention than it otherwise might have done.

After calling a distinguished cast of witnesses, the Committee predicted that the balance of payments surplus on oil would disappear by 1990, and called for urgent action to revive manufacturing and stimulate trade in manufactured goods. It said service industry could not substitute for manufacturing 'because many services are dependent on manufacturing and only 20 per cent of services are tradeable overseas'. There was no reason to expect any 'automatic' resurgence of manufacturing and trade when the North Sea oil surplus declined: lost markets would be difficult to regain, and lost manufacturing capacity would take a long time to restore. 'New industries and new products usually grow out of long-established activities and require a long time-scale for development,' it said.

One of the distinguished witnesses who had failed to impress the Committee with his arguments was one Nigel Lawson, on May 15th. He insisted that manufacturing trade would respond to a fall in the 'real' exchange rate as oil ran down – 'some of which has already occurred'. But their Lordships were more impressed by Bank of England evidence attributing only a minor influence to oil when the exchange rate previously rose, and implying little 'automaticity' the other way. In contrast to the impression he had given to other Cabinet Ministers in 1980, however, Lawson was now (as in the Cambridge speech) more inclined to concede that manufacturing 'is, and will remain, the most important source of output and jobs and the more competitive it is the better off we shall be as a nation.' Lawson asserted that new industries and new products would spring up to fill the gap; the Lords, having listened endlessly to witnesses from industry on how things actually worked, commented: 'The Committee do not find the distinction between "sunrise" and "sunset" industries appealing. New products are normally developed out of existing industrial activities and often over long time-scales. They do not simply appear in the manner of a *deus ex machina*. They depend on a healthy and continuing manufacturing base for their gestation.' The Committee were particularly struck by evidence that the UK had a large deficit already – and one which was expected to grow – in one of the few 'sunrise' industries – information technology.

In fact the Select Committee's report was replete with concern that the country was heading for the kind of balance of payments crisis that did indeed appear towards the end of the decade. And when points such as the one about information technology were put to him, Lawson rather lamely said, 'I think it would be better if you asked the witnesses from the Department of Trade and Industry about information technology.' But perhaps the most telling moment in Lawson's evidence was when he boasted that, since 1979, 'real output per head' in manufacturing had grown faster in the UK than in France, Germany and the USA. Total manufacturing output was actually higher in those countries than in 1979 – and a lot higher in the case of the omitted Japan – whereas it was below 1979 levels in the UK. But because of the huge rise in unemployment in the UK, one could arrive at a distorted comparison on Lawson's lines *per head* . . .

But then, the Chancellor was in robust form on this occasion. Having pointed to the benefit of a declining real exchange rate, some minutes later he was deriding conventional measures of 'competitiveness' and pointing to the virtues of 'a rising exchange rate and the great classic example is the German economic miracle'. He forebore to mention that a rising exchange rate was more appropriate to an economy with strong underlying production, and low inflation, than to the UK's case. However, he then acknowledged that the high exchange rate of the early 1980s had been a severe blow to industry, and the exchange market's reaction had been 'exaggerated' – 'That is what foreign exchange markets are like.'

Given that British costs continued to be rising faster than those of competitor countries, Sir Terence Burns rather echoed the fears of the Committee on the same occasion by pointing out, 'The exchange rate has merely gone back to the level it was at for a good part, certainly the first half, of 1984 and a good part of 1983 . . . of course, what has been worse than in other countries has been the growth of manufacturing, and earnings have continued to grow at 8½ p.c., which is rather faster than the growth in other countries. But that is an issue for industry.' (Getting *into* a balance of payments problem was 'an issue for industry'; later in the decade, the 'Lawson–Burns Doctrine' was to be that getting *rid* of a huge balance of payments deficit was 'a private sector problem'.)

The Lords also noted that, if the exports of the future were to come from high technology, 'In high technology we find that the people there are concerned about the lack of engineers, about the lack of skilled people coming forward from our universities, the lack of training of engineers. Japan, we hear, trains six times as many engineers as we do in Britain.'

It was put to Lawson when he was giving evidence:

> We have had a lot of evidence given to us about the impact of exchange rate movements, and high and low exchange rates, on manufacturing ability to compete. But the greatest weight of it is in favour of the importance of stability in the rate at whatever level, and therefore, it is put to us by the CBI and others that the time has come to join the EMS. What are your views on that?

Lawson replied: 'This is a matter which we keep permanently under review . . . there have been great problems caused by the enormous gyrations of the dollar . . . there is no way in which joining the EMS would peg the dollar . . . I do not think . . . there has been a problem, quite honestly, on volatility and fluctuation in the exchange of sterling against Continental currencies. In fact, there has been an astonishing degree of stability.' He added, 'It is a nicely balanced question that of the EMS,' and said he thought 'there would be a greater degree of interest rate volatility than there is'.

The Lords Committee certainly put its finger on the medium- and longer-term problems which were being stored up. Previously Lawson had also had to face the Treasury Committee on April 3rd, 1985, following the Budget. The rate of inflation had been forecast in the Budget papers to rise to 6 per cent in the second quarter of 1985, but to fall to 5 per cent by the end of the year, and to continue, according to the figures in the MTFS, to decline slowly after that. The Chancellor was asked by the then Liberal MP Richard Wainwright what his reaction would be if, by 1988–89, the rate of inflation had not come down in the way he hoped. 'There would be a greater determination to get inflation down, if it seemed to be intractably high in the way you suggested. But that is not the way we see it.' And Sir Peter Middleton, now Permanent Secretary, intervened: 'There would be something seriously wrong with the policy if inflation did not come down.'

It was on this occasion that Lawson made use of a phrase he was to repeat, in the face of some derision, during the inflationary explosion which did subsequently occur in 1988–89. When Wainwright said inflation was now going up, the Chancellor replied, 'There is a blip being forecast, if that is what you mean,' and later, 'One of the reasons why we foresee this blip in inflation during the first half of this year is a series of events which really have their origin in the foreign exchange market.' (Namely the delayed reaction of import prices to the previous year's fall in the pound.)

Lawson gave the Committee the first hint that he would discontinue the practice of publishing the likely 'fiscal adjustment' in the Budget during the autumn, making it clear he felt market discussion of this had contributed to the pound's winter troubles. Also, he showed some consciousness of the unemployment and environmental lobbies by saying that, on the 'infrastructure' of roads, sewers and the water industry, 'We are planning to increase spending quite substantially in real terms over the coming year . . . I am concerned . . . within the context of an anti-inflationary policy which is achieving [a steady reduction in inflation] to see growth in the real economy, a stronger private sector leading to more jobs.'

It was in this evidence that Lawson also gave a hint of the kind of dilemma that was going to hit him several years later over monetary policy and the question of its tightness.

> Certainly it is the case . . . that in judging what is the appropriate financial posture, it is the mix of interest and exchange rates which has to be assessed. Therefore, other things being equal, yes, if the exchange rate goes up, that provides scope for a lower level of interest rates than would otherwise be the case. But we shall, of course, be very cautious in our interest rate policy. We shall not be taking any risks whatsoever with inflation.

Using the exchange rate as an indicator of monetary policy had, of course, come up before the 'Walters' Budget of 1981, when Lawson was Financial Secretary. One of the many oddities of the original, unrevised and unevolved MTFS was that it was an entirely domestic policy, and did not take external factors into account at all. As Richard Brown* has pointed out, this was strange for an economy in which foreign trade accounts for up to 30 per cent of GDP – let alone for one which had pretensions, through the City of London, of being the financial capital of the world. History had suggested that the outside world was very important in its influence on the UK; but, as originally conceived, the outside world was ignored in Lawson's monetary plan.

When the exchange rate began to figure, it was in the context of the fact that, whatever the M3 statistic suggested, monetary policy was exerting unbearable financial pressures on British industry. But under a deregulated financial system, without formal hire purchase controls or restrictions on bank advances (as under the old Bretton Woods system, and indeed, for a time, under floating exchange rates), the criteria for monetary 'tightness' were biased in favour of consumer lending and consumer spending, and against domestic manufacturing production. For example, if a rise in the exchange rate meant, as Lawson said, that interest rates would be lower than otherwise, this clearly alleviated the impact of a 'tight' monetary policy on the consumer. Moreover, the rise in the pound gave the consumer more purchasing power, thereby enabling him or her to spend even more on imported goods, which were becoming cheaper under a higher exchange rate. The corollary of this is that that part of the monetary tightness manifested in a higher exchange rate served to make British industry more uncompetitive, and inhibit the 'recovery'.

Lawson's way of describing exchange rate policy to the Treasury Committee at this juncture was to say, 'We have got a floating exchange rate but the Government does take an interest in what the level of the exchange rate is.' A great interest, he might have added, in the context of the political recuperation from the January/February 1985 sterling crisis.

The outside world was gradually coming to the British Government's rescue over the sterling/dollar rate now. Just as the MTFS had been conceived almost as a plan for a 'closed economy', so the prevailing orthodoxy at meetings of the major industrial countries during the early 1980s had been the assumption that, if only countries put their own houses in order, growth would spontaneously follow. The idea of macroeconomic policy co-ordination between

* 'Prospects for International Macroeconomic Policy Coordination: A British View', Richard Brown, University College of North Wales, Bangor, 1989.

countries was largely rejected in favour of what has been called 'insular monetarism'. The whole idea of OECD style policy co-ordination is that, by taking account of one another's policies, individual countries can avoid damage – thus if the dollar is grossly overvalued, it hurts US domestic industry; but, because of the high cost of commodities priced in dollars, this also arouses inflationary fears in West Germany, the main west European economy, inducing it to conduct deflationary policies which have an unfavourable impact on the whole of Europe. (Indeed, West Germany for several years experienced negligible growth of domestic demand in the early 1980s, and relied on exports.)

Things were gradually changing in the USA during the first half of 1985 however. We have seen how there was some sporadic intervention in the financial markets to push the dollar down. The new Treasury Secretary James Baker was more receptive to suggestions of international co-ordination than his predecessor Donald Regan. George Shultz, then Secretary of State but a former Treasury Secretary and an economist, made a speech at Princeton in which he pointed out the damage being done to US industry by the strong dollar, and urged reductions in the US deficit, interest rates and the dollar. Paul Volcker, the head of the US Federal Reserve, had wanted such a policy for some time – although as head of the Central Bank, he had to blow hot and cold: he did not want any decline in the dollar to get out of hand. Washington was also concerned, from a Nato Alliance point of view, about general sluggishness in the European economy – about what was fashionably termed 'Eurosclerosis'.

There was therefore a growing interest in the USA in policy co-ordination, one of the important points being that, if the US economy did slow down, it was desirable, from the point of view of the world economy generally, that Europe should expand faster to avoid a world recession (which would certainly not do the heavily indebted Third World any good). And as summer approached, the momentum for co-ordination in Washington grew stronger, because, hit by the effects of the strong dollar, US industry was becoming strongly protectionist.

From Lawson's point of view, the idea of international policy co-ordination was attractive, not just to get away from embarrassment over the sterling/dollar exchange rate, but also because if the USA, the world leader, did lower interest rates substantially, this would be beneficial to his own interest rate objectives. Volcker took the opportunity to say in April that the UK had become over-obsessed with reducing its own budget deficit, which, allowing for the cost of unemployment benefits and other recessionary effects, was probably in structural surplus anyway.

At the spring meeting of the IMF key policy-making committee Lawson made it clear that he was happy with the recovery in the pound now taking place. Meanwhile, in addition to allowing sterling to recover to $1.30 or so, funds pouring into London to take advantage of high interest rates were sufficiently plentiful for the Treasury and the Bank to embark on a policy of replenishing the official reserves of foreign currency for the next rainy day. Lawson and the Treasury were cautious about letting interest rates fall, and allowed the new strength of sterling to edge interest rates down in gentle steps.

It was too early for public changes of face on international policy co-ordination, and the Bonn Economic Summit of the G7 in late April produced nothing of substance, although behind the scenes US officials, and some UK ones, were showing increasing interest in the concept of 'target zones' for exchange rates between the major countries, on the lines that France had been proposing for some years. These were thought of as contingency plans, should the dollar fall rapidly.

Sir Ian Gilmour, one of the founder members of the Employment Institute and Charter for Jobs, set up in the early eighties, said the Government had refused to change either its policy or its rhetoric – 'in consequence it has been driven to making large claims for its achievements. If instead of making such claims, you admit that unemployment has gone disastrously wrong, you try to do something about it.' The Chancellor boasted about record investment, although every year should be a record. In fact, said Sir Ian, manufacturing investment was still some 25 per cent down on 1979, the increase was in investment in transport and services: 'Presumably improved facilities were required to handle the rise of around 40 p.c. in manufacturing imports that occurred over the same period.'[13]

But it was one of those phases when the retail price index, reflecting higher mortgage rates and the earlier fall in the exchange rate, was showing an annual rise of 6.9 per cent, and Tony Coleby, assistant director of the Bank of England, told the Treasury Committee: 'Until we have got more convincing evidence that domestic monetary conditions have been brought back under control, we are bound to be rather reserved about the pace at which interest rates might come down.' This judiciously phrased comment was subsequently misquoted by Brian Sedgemore, of the Treasury Committee, in the Commons when he asked Lawson whether he agreed with Coleby that 'domestic monetary arrangements in this country are out of control'. Lawson said they were under control, and certainly had been since the January rise in interest rates, 'despite some ill-informed comment'. In this latter remark, he was taken to be referring to Coleby and the Bank – against the background of the still-embittered atmosphere between Treasury and the Bank over Johnson Matthey, in which, as it happened, Sedgemore was in the lead in provoking both Lawson and the Bank in the Commons.[14]

By early July, the Chancellor was facing calls for more public sector investment from the CBI, the TUC, fellow Cabinet Ministers and the National Economic Development Office. Conservative MPs were concerned about a defeat for the Government at the Brecon by-election; and with the pound at 82 on the sterling index (against an average of 75 in January–March) and DM 3.99 against the German mark (it had averaged DM 3.62 in the first quarter), the pressure for further cuts in interest rates was intense. Lawson referred in a speech to the Government's spending policies as being 'the middle way', and such was the speed with which this remark was interpreted as some kind of Government U-turn, that he then gave a series of interviews emphasising that there was no policy change, but 'we do spend more where it is needed'.

This prompted former Labour Prime Minister James Callaghan to ask in the Commons: 'Is it Government policy to make cuts and represent them as increases, or to make increases and represent them as cuts?'[15] In fact it looked as though pre-Election pressures were already building up, and if the Treasury did have to allow spending to rise, in contrast to the policy of keeping it stable in real terms, Mrs Thatcher and Lawson thought they might as well make the best of it and boast that they were doing something.

By mid-July the Government was told the worst on the retail prices front was over, and with the pound exceedingly strong, it was in a position to offer some comfort to the critics, many in its own ranks, who wanted a relaxation in economic policy. A few days before he was due to appear before the Treasury Committee again, Lawson sanctioned a half per cent cut in base rates, and another one at the end of the month, bringing them down to 11½ per cent, against the crisis level of 14 per cent in January. It so happened that M0 was within its target – but then it had been when the Government was refusing to lower interest rates. The general trend looked like leading to a reduction in mortgage rates too.

With the pound now very strong, there was another revival of interest in the EMS in both Bank and Treasury, but once again the option was turned down by the Prime Minister. M3, the once all-important monetary measure, was now rising at nearly twice the rate ordained for it in the Budget, and at the session with the Treasury Committee Lawson even managed a passing derogatory comment about the media's obsession with M3. This remark prompted one of the Conservative Committee members, who claimed to have been converted to monetarism by Lawson himself, to comment dolefully afterwards, 'The Chancellor no longer believes in the MTFS.'[16]

Lawson had, of course, favoured entry into the EMS exchange rate mechanism when the sterling index was some 13 per cent lower (in January) than it now was in July. Asked, 'Would we have to devalue as an essential part, if we went in, of going in?' he told Labour MP Austin Mitchell 'not necessarily'. When Mitchell added, 'On the present exchange rates?' the Chancellor replied coyly, 'It is a matter of judgment' and, 'At the moment we are not embarking on joining the exchange rate mechanism of the EMS.' He did, however, maintain that the pound had been undervalued in January when the sterling index had fallen to 70. It was significant from the point of view of developments later in the decade, that when asked whether the dollar was still overvalued, and he said it was, he added – 'One only has to look, for example, at the enormous and growing deficit on the American current account balance of payments.'

It was a particularly interesting session with the Treasury Committee, and was formally devoted to the topic of 'International Monetary Arrangements'. During answers to questions Lawson showed that he was moving slowly towards a greater belief in international policy co-ordination, but was not really there yet. He placed more emphasis on the existing system of 'surveillance' and belief that good would result from the 'convergence' of various economies on to a low inflation path; but his senior international monetary official, Sir Geoffrey Littler, sitting alongside him – who was at that time privately in favour of 'target zones' for exchange rates – made it clear that he placed little faith in the existing mechanisms.

This session was also a dry run for the remarkable 'suspension' of M3 as a monetary target which was to come in the autumn. Lawson said quite spontaneously that 'taking the exchange rate into account explains the reduction in interest rates we have just seen,' and, 'I have always made it clear that interest rates will not be held any higher than is necessary to achieve that objective' (bearing down on inflation and 'producing declining inflation'). To the extent that the pound appreciated against other currencies, or the dollar fell, this would enable interest rates to fall further during the year.

Nicholas Budgen, a Conservative monetarist, made the point to Lawson that, 'This recent reduction was mainly as a result of intervention by the Bank and not as a response to market conditions.' He went on: 'You have frequently emphasised the importance of the Medium Term Financial Strategy, of which you were the architect and are now the custodian, and it is right is it not that you have until recently placed most emphasis upon sterling M3?'

Lawson then gave what by any standards was a revisionist view of his own policy. No, he did not think that was right. 'If you look back you will see that, right from the word go. It is true that we inherited an emphasis on M3 . . .'

This was amazing stuff, and certainly startled his interlocutor, among others. Whereas M3 played a role in the Labour Government's policy from the mid-1970s, it was actually Lawson himself, as Financial Secretary, who insisted on elevating it to play the main role in a monetary policy which was itself to play the main role in economic policy. Lawson now took refuge in the footnotes [of the MTFS] the Bank of England had fought for as a safety device, and quoted them to try to demonstrate that he had been consistent all along, and M3 was never that important. He then dropped a pearl: 'As far back as 1980 we issued all those warning statements. The problem has been that the commentators have for the sake of simplicity latched on to M3 to an extent which was wholly unwarranted by the careful language used by the Government.'

This provided great amusement for the politicians and journalists in the committee room who thought they had lived through something quite different, but Lawson was quite unruffled. As for Budgen's further question asking whether reducing interest rates when M3 was expanding at 23 per cent per annum was appropriate, Lawson gave the impression of being amazed that anyone should worry about such a matter. 'So in your complicated judgment one of the indicators is wildly out of the hoped-for path, is it not?' Budgen went on. To which the Chancellor replied: 'Yes, certainly, and not for the first time.'

The Financial Secretary, who had scorned 'intervening, demand-managing Keynesians', felt it necessary to give one of his monetarist disciples a lesson in the facts of life: 'Let me say this, Mr Budgen . . . the real world is very complex, with a very complex financial system. It is extremely difficult to form an accurate judgment of monetary conditions with different dials pointing in different directions. The fact that it is difficult does not mean it is not of the first importance to make a judgment . . .'

Lawson was, of course, contrasting the 'real world' with the monetarist world he had sold to the nation. It was a vintage occasion. Finally, in a desperate search for the kind of simple rule that Lawson had once adopted himself, Mr Budgen suggested that the liquidity and profitability of industry indicated monetary conditions might not be that tight. Lawson replied: 'The proof of the pudding is in the eating . . . we will actually have to see what does happen to inflation over the next 12 months.'

'But, Chancellor, if the theory of the time-lag is correct, even if it is not very accurate, we will not *know* in 12 months' time, will we? We shall know at some time between 18 months' and 2 years' time, maybe after the next election.'

Lawson: 'I suppose things happen a little bit more rapidly now than they did when these sorts of "guestimates" of time-lags were first produced.' What was happening in 12 months' time *would* be 'quite a useful, practical, empirical test' as to whether Lawson or Budgen was right, he said.

Finally, reference to this especially intriguing session of the Treasury Committee in July 1985 would not be complete without an opening remark from Brian Sedgemore, self-appointed scourge of Lawson and the Bank of England: 'Chancellor, we are delighted to see you here today. We thought you might have been too busy sorting out your M3 argument with Mr Coleby of the Bank of England, or possibly digging out fraud at Johnson Matthey, but welcome!'

EIGHT

Election Hero

Summer 1985 – June 1987

If the Chancellor of the Exchequer was having a rough time with economic policy, the Bank of England and the Conservative Party during the summer of 1985, the mood was not exactly euphoric in Number 10 Downing Street either. There was one occasion during July when, goaded by calls for a change in economic policy by other Cabinet colleagues, Mrs Thatcher said she knew 'no other way' and delivered an impassioned lecture on the 'Wetness' of British industry for having failed to respond to the Government's 'supply-side' incentives. Industrialists had raised their own salaries handsomely; were now rewarding their workforces out of guilt; but where was the real investment revival? The latest CBI Industrial Trends survey offered forbidding prospects for the economy in 1986.

The CBI survey meant, of course, that the exchange rate was once again too high – in circumstances where, as the Lords Committee had pointed out, the industrial base was still in bad shape from the cutbacks earlier in the decade. In the opinion polls the Conservatives had fallen behind both Labour and the Alliance, and there were stories of 'betrayal', rumours of 'resignation threats' by Mrs Thatcher, and even suggestions that the Conservatives might want to replace her by John Biffen, then Leader of the Commons. There was perhaps an element of 'midsummer madness' in all this, but it was undoubtedly a nervous time for Mrs Thatcher and her Chancellor. The Prime Minister even made a speech calling for economic expansion; this sounded very much like the kind of talk associated with the bad old Keynesians. In fact she was urging expansion on Japan and West Germany, during a visit to Washington where she appeared to come momentarily under the influence of the new mood there, which was none other than a return to a belief in demand management in international economic policy.

The protectionist mood in Washington had become so fierce that the US Treasury had finally decided that something had to be done about the dollar. But a desired fall in US imports might open up a hole in the world economy – hence the calls for other countries to 'take up the slack'. From April onwards the US Treasury had been in consultation with the Japanese about possible measures to ward off the US protectionist threat. Late in August, the senior US Treasury overseas monetary official, David Mulford, came to Europe to see officials such as Sir Geoffrey Littler and sound them out about the new strategy for a currency realignment. This led to a meeting of the G5 senior officials in London on Sunday, September 15th, which prepared the basis for a dramatic communiqué issued after the G5 Meeting of Finance Ministers and Central Bank Governors at the Plaza Hotel in New York on Sunday, September 22nd, 1985.

Although there was to be much haggling about the details of the agreement and the manner of its implementation, the Plaza Agreement signified a turning point in economic policy and the death-knell of 'insular monetarism'. Any pretence that the market's judgment in the matter of exchange rates could be fully trusted was abandoned. Governments and central banks had learned from the experience of the 1980s that financial markets often 'overshot' – a euphemism for getting things wrong, and failing to produce the optimal outcome so beloved of the writers of pure market theory in the economics textbooks.

In the run-up to the Plaza Agreement, US thinking hardened from a desire to stop the dollar appreciating to a desperate wish to effect a devaluation – although it would not, for reasons of national pride, be called that: the communiqué stated, 'Some further orderly appreciation of the main non-dollar currencies against the dollar is desirable.' Initial European reluctance to participate in Plaza – they thought it was basically a USA/Japan affair, and that the real need was to reduce the US budget deficit – evaporated when there was a renewed surge in the US currency during the summer.

Nigel Lawson enjoyed the drama surrounding the Plaza Agreement, and called a press conference to expatiate on it as soon as he returned to London on the Monday. The events Plaza set in train were to affect his thinking and his policy reactions profoundly: the G5 were secretly aiming at, roughly, a 10 per cent devaluation of the dollar, and had achieved it by the winter. They agreed to intervene in currency markets, and a plan was discussed for sharing out the burden of intervention. Lawson, while signing a communiqué which endorsed intervention to lower the dollar, in the words of one chronicler, 'asserted that Britain took note of, but did not agree to' the intervention proposals.[1] Indeed, the West Germans later said that in the course of the operation of the Plaza Agreement, the British actually contravened the spirit of it by seizing the opportunity to *buy* dollars in order to replenish the UK's official reserves. (When the reserves later *were* replenished, Mrs Thatcher was to object to further purchases of the dollar, regarding acquisitions of the declining US currency as a bad bargain – not value for money.)

The operation of the Plaza Agreement – and of the later 'Louvre Accord', early in 1987, to stabilise the markets – fascinated Lawson. He was host to the G5 at Number 11 Downing Street when the Plaza operation was reviewed during the weekend of January 18th and 19th, 1986, and he was often to refer to his discussions with 'Jim' Baker, the US Treasury Secretary. Indeed, after a slow start, Lawson warmed to his appearances on the world stage, and was to become a star attraction for journalists because of his increasingly informative briefings after G5 and IMF meetings.

If he was to remain on the world stage, however, the Chancellor had to get his act together in a more local theatre. The economic situation looked more and more desperate; the monetary policy on which the economic strategy had been based was falling apart. How was Houdini going to emerge from his latest strait-jacket?

Lawson's big logistical decision of the summer was not to go to the G5 and IMF meetings in South Korea, but to face the music in Blackpool at the Conservative Party Conference. A less beleaguered politician, and a more tireless traveller, could have elected to go to Seoul and return for his speech to the Conference in the same week. Lawson did not relish the prospect, and did not want to be jet-lagged in the face of unrest among the troops. He sent Sir Geoffrey Littler to attend the G5 meeting, and the Economic Secretary to the Treasury, Ian Stewart, to speak on his behalf at the IMF meeting.

The Chancellor's absence from the IMF did not go down well in some quarters, but it was a case of 'first things first'. Sir Geoffrey Littler manifestly enjoyed playing the role of Finance Minister. It fell to Stewart to boast that 'the UK economy itself is now in its fifth successive year of steady growth. Since the trough of the recession in the first half of 1981, United Kingdom GDP has grown at an average rate of just over 3 p.c. per year.' It sounded good that way, better than 'GDP, excluding oil, is even now only 2½ p.c. above the levels we inherited in 1979.' There was a line for connoisseurs in 'growth has not relied excessively on exports. Throughout this period we have been running current account surpluses, although not at an excessive level that could cause difficulties for others.'[2]

Back at home, Lawson started off in light vein in reply to a Conservative

Conference where a surprising number of speakers had demanded more vigorous action to reduce unemployment: '11 Downing Street is all very well, but it is not so easy getting to the shops with small children when the demonstrators are massing in Whitehall. [This was a reference to his wife.] But at least I have to say this: we have no trouble with the neighbours.' The problem was, of course, that his next-door neighbour was exceedingly worried about the economy, and tending to blame the messenger.

Lawson was lucky in that the most important international meeting had already taken place, and he had attended it. He was therefore able to play the role of the international financial diplomatist, and distract attention from comparisons with the time the Labour Chancellor Denis Healey had failed to attend an IMF meeting in 1976 because of political troubles back home.

'Just over a fortnight ago I went to New York for a crucial meeting of the Finance Ministers of the world's major industrial nations, the so-called Group of Five,' he began. ('Crucial' was a favourite journalistic word. There had been one reporter on the *Financial Times* – not Lawson – who used to compete with a rival on another newspaper to see how many 'crucials' he could get into a story.) 'The meeting had been well prepared and Britain had played an important part in those preparations. As a result, we were able to hammer out an important agreement designed to avert the very real danger – and it is a real danger – of an all-out trade war, a war from which Britain, as a major trading nation, has a great deal more to lose than most.'

He added: 'This has brought about for sterling a more sensible pattern of exchange rates in general.' They had been able to reach the agreement not just because they were all concerned about protectionism, 'but because we are all agreed on the economic policies that make sense in the modern world . . . the policies that we are all agreed upon are the policies that we in Britain are following today, while the Opposition parties remain wedded to the failed nostrums of the past.' It sounded good, although what the Plaza Agreement was actually about was a return to the kind of demand management policies that had prevailed before the advent of monetarism. The Chancellor was once again protesting too much.[3]

Lawson then did his best to place the problem on many delegates' minds – unemployment – in a wider context. The European Community was suffering from it; the rest of the world was suffering from it. He then claimed that Britain had nevertheless created more new jobs than the rest of the European Community put together, without pointing out that his figure of 600,000 consisted largely of part-time jobs. He then chanced his arm, six years after Labour had left office, with: 'What we are suffering from today is the new businesses that did not start up under Labour.' But he made no reference to the well-established businesses that were killed by the policies of 1980–81.

This was not all: having declared victory over the unions in his 1984 Mais Lecture, he was now desperate enough to assert: 'The causes of unemployment in Britain today are many and complex but foremost among them is the behaviour of the trade unions.' (Could this have been a reprisal for an incident some time earlier at the National Economic Development Council? Lawson had presented members with a series of charts suggesting everything was 'booming', and Norman Willis, the TUC General Secretary, said a chart was missing – the one for the boom in unemployment.)

The general message was: 'Stand by your trusted friend Nigel and his supply-side policies; it will all come right in the end. Inflation is low and falling, the balance of payments is in healthy surplus, investment in industry is booming and the economy is strong and growing fast.'

Having blamed Arthur Scargill, the miners' leader, for the 'brief setback' in inflation (before the Select Committee, the culprit was the earlier fall in the pound), he said inflation 'is now around 6 p.c. and falling fast. I now expect it to be close to 5 p.c. by the end of the year and below 4 p.c. next year. That is good news for jobs, too.'

He did not spell out the mechanism by which it would be good news for jobs, leaving the audience to deduce, presumably, that 'supply-side' policies would come into their own. The real reason was that the prospect of having inflation once again below 5 per cent was going to give him the opportunity to relax policy and engineer a devaluation of the pound in time to boost the economy before the 1987 Election. What he said was: 'For the first time in a generation we have broken out of the financial prison of spending and borrowing, of inflating and devaluing.'

Spending cuts? These 'have enabled us to spend more where more is needed.' And the Chancellor ended with a rousing 'we will never surrender and we will win.'

Within weeks Lawson was, almost unconditionally, surrendering his monetary policy. At the end of October, in the traditional Mansion House speech on the economy, he coolly announced that, in making policy decisions, he was simply going to suspend the M3 target for the rest of the financial year.

> We can maintain, and are maintaining, progress towards our inflation objective while M3 is growing at a rate well above the top of the range set in this year's Budget Statement. To try to bring it back within the range – which, with the benefit of hindsight, was clearly set too low – would imply a tightening of policy which the evidence of other indicators of financial conditions tells us is not warranted.[4]

M3 was to be an indicator, not a target, although, 'I shall as usual be considering what target to set for M3 for 1986–87 at the time of the next Budget.' It was generally assumed in the City of London that, as a target, M3 was being dropped for good, although it was to have another brief run in 1986–87. Lawson emphasised that he would still bear down on inflation, that Mo would be monitored as an advance warning of the behaviour of money GDP – it was all really perfectly consistent, nothing had changed . . .

He spelled out the basic message which we have seen evolving: the effect on the monetary aggregates of the welcome liberalisation of financial markets, which had brought in its train a new wave of experimentation and innovation, all of which were serving to undermine the measurement of monetary policy. In other words, the liberalisation of the financial markets had meant the liberalisation of M3.

Behind the scenes during the run-up to the Mansion House speech, some officials had again raised the question of whether, in the light of the continuing misbehaviour of M3, the Chancellor wanted to abandon the MTFS, of which M3 had once been the central monetary target. One official said that Lawson in effect elected to 'retain the form but abandon the reality of the MTFS'; Lawson would no doubt say the reverse. The Bank of England, on the other hand, which had always opposed making M3 the sole criterion, and a strict target, wanted to retain M3 but to put greater emphasis on the exchange rate, leading possibly (it was hoped by some officials) to the pound's entry into the EMS – which the Chancellor also supported.

The Bank felt that Lawson was swinging from one extreme to the other in his disregard for M3; but Lawson's new enthusiasm was undoubtedly the exchange rate. He took the opportunity at the Mansion House to refer to the Plaza Agreement:

> We acknowledged that while there is a limit to what can be achieved by concerted intervention on the foreign exchange markets, we were not impotent; and that we should therefore, acting together, lose no time in helping to bring about an orderly depreciation of the dollar against the other major currencies. In the last four weeks, a useful start has been made on this essential process of adjustment.

Lawson now put the exchange rate on a square and equal footing with his Mo indicator. He said Mo had a stable relationship with transactions in the economy (although in Zurich he had said it was 'too easy' to control) and:

> *The other* [my italics] good and early guide to changing financial conditions is the exchange rate. When, as now, signals from the various measures of money become difficult to interpret, the exchange rate inevitably assumes an increased weight in monetary policy decisions. It has a direct impact on the price level and on

> inflationary expectations. Sharp movements tend to coincide with changes in the market's perception of monetary ease or stringency. Large swings in any case cannot be ignored.

Once a certain guide, and now only a guide, Lawson's original monetary indicator was, to his mind, no longer interesting. 'The acid test of monetary policy is its record in reducing inflation,' he said. 'Those who wish to join in the debate about the intricacies of different measures of money and the implications they may have for the future are welcome to do so. But at the end of the day the position is clear and unambiguous. The inflation rate is judge and jury.'

This was breathtaking stuff from the political architect of the MTFS. Opponents of monetarism had always pointed out that an increase in the money supply need not portend a corresponding increase in inflation. Now Lawson was acknowledging that over the past five years M3 had grown by 82 per cent but money GDP by only 54 per cent and prices had risen by 43 per cent. 'It has become increasingly evident that both individuals and companies wish to hold an increased proportion of savings in liquid form.' If anyone had encouraged the debate about the intricacies of different measures of money it had been Nigel Lawson. One might also note that a rise in money GDP of 54 per cent which comprised 43 per cent in prices and 11 per cent in real growth was not totally dissimilar from the kind of ratios which Lawson used to deride under the policy-makers who preceded the arrival of Mrs Thatcher and himself on the scene.

From the Bank of England's point of view, notwithstanding the undoubted embarrassment associated with the central position M3 had had so far, there was a reluctance to conclude that the indicator should therefore lose all significance, and the Bank was, over the next few years, to take M3 rather more seriously than the Chancellor did himself.

For Lawson, any embarrassment associated with the relegation of M3 was negated by the news from his forecasters that inflation should be below 4 per cent by the middle of 1986. This was not a forecast derived from the movement of the money supply, but from conventional old-fashioned examination of the trend of unit costs, the impact of imports prices and so on. But, unabashed, Lawson said: 'Maintaining and improving on that rate through and beyond 1986 depends on continued control of monetary conditions. I am confident that the policies now in place and the techniques of monetary management we are using can ensure that control.'

Although the Mansion House speech might have seemed, on the face of it, a humiliation for Lawson, it was, paradoxically, at about this time that things started looking up for his Chancellorship. Lower inflation would indeed give him scope for a more expansionary policy, and the achievement of a more realistic exchange rate, at just the time when many were in despair. The significance of his abandonment of any pretence at controlling M3 was that he would have even greater scope for creating the Lawson consumer boom than the Treasury's 'better' forecasts were now indicating.

These were presented in the usual November Autumn Statement, a fortnight later. This pointed out that although consumers' expenditure had flattened out after the middle of 1983 (curiously enough, after the General Election of that year) it had recently been showing signs of renewed growth – between the first halves of 1984 and 1985, it had risen by 1½ per cent in real terms. 'As inflation falls over the next year growth in real personal disposable income is likely to pick up further . . . overall consumers' expenditure may rise by some 4 per cent in 1986.'[5]

For all the talk of 'conviction politics', and for all the difficulties between Numbers 10 and 11 Downing Street, Mrs Thatcher and her Chancellor shared even deeper convictions about the need to be re-elected. 1985 had been a rough year for them, and 1986 was going to start even rougher for Mrs Thatcher, because of the Westland crisis. But the forecasts presented by the Treasury at the time of the 1985 Autumn Statement offered them light at the end of the economic policy tunnel, with no obvious signs of trains coming the other way. The prospect of 4 per cent real growth in consumers' expenditure was good by any standards, but especially by the standards of the Howe/Lawson Chancellorships so far. Consumers' expenditure had grown only 5 per cent in the whole of Howe's 1979–83 Chancellorship and it was commonly accepted that the Conservatives had won the 1983 General Election in spite of their economic record.

Whatever Lawson might say about the need for a reduction or slowdown in the rate of growth of real wages, the 1986 forecasts were conveniently based on an acceleration in such growth: the Government had failed to bring the growth rate in wage earnings down to European levels, but price inflation was going to fall during 1986 with lower import prices offsetting the impact of higher unit labour costs – import prices reflecting lower prices for oil and other commodities. GDP was due to grow at a 'normal' rate of 3 per cent, the current balance of payments to be in surplus to the tune of £4 billion or so, and the retail price index was expected to rise by only 3¾ per cent, between the fourth quarters of 1985 and 1986 – against 5½ per cent between the corresponding periods of 1984 and 1985.

This was a more favourable prospect than for some time, and was to become even more so. The missing element was a sure sign of a reversal in the unemployment trend. Lawson had always consistently argued that what mattered politically was not the absolute level of unemployment, but its direction; and having forecast an early reversal in 1983, quite apart from any other considerations, he had some personal interest in a change of trend that was not just accounted for by an expansion of 'special employment and training schemes' or by numerous redefinitions of the unemployment data.

One now sees electoral considerations coming into the public spending plans. The 'stabilisation' policy – freezing the level of public spending in real terms – had not so far been an overwhelming success: indeed, the volume of public spending had risen by nearly 4 per cent between 1983–84 and 1984–85. Although the professed plan was to keep it 'broadly stable' from now on, the Chancellor announced in his Autumn Statement that the target for privatisation receipts was being more than doubled for the next three financial years, and the official document coyly announced that:

> Within unchanged planning totals a significant increase in receipts from the Government's privatisation programme has been matched by increases in departmental programmes . . . within this increased provision, priority has been given to capital spending on roads and renovation of local authority housing; and to spending on health and science. In addition scope has had to be found for demand-led increases in social security.

In fact things were looking up for Lawson in his strategy of containing public spending and thereby finding room for tax cuts. The public, and dissident Conservative MPs generally, were misled by the Government's new tactics of uncharacteristically boasting about various aspects of higher public spending into believing a great reflation was under way. At the very time that such speculation was raging in December 1985, a Treasury official pointed out privately that the worst was over for the Government from the point of view of higher spending on defence and law and order; and, 'Whatever else happens, unemployment is not going to treble again.' Despite the latest 'slippage' in the PSBR target (now expected to be overrun by £1 billion) and other items, the Treasury now saw a fair prospect of containing public spending in real terms; and they were not far out. This did not prevent the official from acknowledging the implications of a decaying public sector infrastructure for future political storms.

It was the consumer-spending side which was to give the principal impetus to the period of above-average growth; this was essential to reverse the unemployment trend, and extremely useful from the point of view of creating a general climate of prosperity for the majority of the population described as 'still in work'. Having been caught out with his specific figures about the likely 'fiscal adjustment' the previous year, Lawson did not reveal this Budget assumption in the autumn of 1985; but provision was there in the figures for a cut in the basic rate of income tax in spring 1986.

The suspension of the M3 target was both symbolic and pragmatic: as one City analyst noted:

> One consequence of relying on Mo instead of M3 will be that bank lending will no longer need to be watched so carefully . . . since the broad money aggregates measure most of the monetary sector's liabilities, bank lending inevitably places upward pressure on measures such as M3. It does not have anything like the same direct effect on Mo, which may be wholly unaffected by a bank-lending explosion. An economic expansion which relies heavily on bank lending will therefore be much less likely to be constrained by the new policy than by the old.[6]

Some months later the American economist Beryl Sprinkel, chairman of President Reagan's Council of Economic Advisers, was seeing Lawson on a visit and said, 'These figures are terrible. I thought you were a monetarist.' Lawson just shifted uncomfortably in his seat, according to one observer.

The Treasury and the Bank knew what the Chancellor was doing in discarding M3, and they were worried about the impact on the financial markets. They therefore adopted a deliberate policy of keeping interest rates high for a while, in an attempt to counteract the (thoroughly reasonable) impression that the Government's monetary resolve had weakened. There was also a revival of interest in the EMS. Since M3 had proved a hopeless guide, the Chancellor himself saw the EMS as the next most desirable form of monetary discipline to impress the financial markets. And opinion within the Treasury was shifting his way, at a time when the Bank of England was still preponderantly in favour too. The ridicule surrounding the dropping of M3 contributed to the feeling within Treasury and Bank that the EMS would provide a credible alternative monetary discipline. Those present at the key autumn 1985 meeting about the EMS included Mrs Thatcher, Willie Whitelaw, Sir Geoffrey Howe, Foreign Secretary, and Leon Brittan, then Secretary for Trade and Industry, as well as the Chancellor and senior Treasury and Bank officials. Mrs Thatcher asked the assembled company one by one for their opinion. All favoured joining the exchange rate mechanism. She turned to Whitelaw last. He said, 'All seven of your advisers have voted "aye".' 'Yes,' she said, echoing Abraham Lincoln, 'Ayes seven, noes one, the noes have it.'

The EMS was to be discussed many times between 1985 and the June 1987 Election: sometimes ministers reviewed the situation by themselves, sometimes officials were present as well. Lawson frequently button-holed the Prime

Minister on the subject, to no avail. Professor Walters would pass through London once a month or so and buttress Mrs Thatcher's emotional opposition with technical arguments; the plain fact was that the Prime Minister's distaste for Brussels and for so many aspects of the European Community – which was to surface more publicly in the 'third term' – meant that she was always against the EMS, although the grounds she adduced might alter from time to time. Moreover, it was not just the influence of Walters on the technical side: there was at least one senior official in both the Treasury and the Bank who would own to reservations about the EMS.

With the dollar itself now falling, the alarm was off concerning the dollar/sterling rate, which averaged around $1.40 in the second half of 1985; and within the context of watching the effective rate, or sterling index, the Treasury and Bank were happy to acquiesce in a fall in the pound/DM rate to a level more satisfactory to British industry – thus the pound averaged DM 3.92 in the third quarter and DM 3.71 in the fourth. But this was still considered too high for comfort by the EMS camp. (There seemed to be an unofficial target range of 85 to 80 (1975 = 100) for the sterling index for most of 1985, and interest rates were in fact kept at 11½ per cent from the end of July onwards.)

It was also considered too high by industry. Despite the optimistic tone of the Autumn Statement, the Confederation of British Industry and the Association of British Chambers of Commerce were concerned about the effect of the relatively high exchange rate on competitiveness, and noted a sharp downturn in export sales and orders, including in the west Midlands, where there were important marginal constituencies, and car and engineering industries heavily dependent on the export trade.

The position at the end of 1985 was that the Government's much publicised 'growth miracle' consisted hitherto of a fall in the economy in 1980 and 1981 followed by a revival in 1982 and 1983, to a point where GDP was simply back to the level of 1979. Growth for the whole economy had then averaged 3 per cent in 1984 and 1985, with 1985 (at 3½ per cent) redressing the balance of the effects of the coal strike of 1984, when growth was 2½ per cent. The average growth rate since 1979 was, at 1 per cent, the slowest since the war, and almost half of this was accounted for by the growth of North Sea oil production. Manufacturing investment and output were still well below the levels of the late 1970s. It was clear from the complaints of industry that a sizeable devaluation was required to boost competitiveness. The official Lawson line was that companies could not be bailed out like this by Government for granting excessive wage claims. But behind the scenes things were stirring.

On November 26th, 1985, Lawson was pressed by Anthony Beaumont-Dark, the Conservative MP for a West Midlands constituency, about the impact of high interest rates and the strength of the pound on manufacturing industry. Lawson replied: 'I have to tell you that in addition to the need to keep interest rates at the right level necessary to ensure that monetary conditions and financial conditions are such to keep pressure on inflation – which can never be taken for granted – I do not believe that there is any salvation for this country through progressive depreciation of the currency, progressive devaluation.' Yet in his meetings with Treasury and Bank officials, a strategy to effect just that was about to emerge.

The opportunity was afforded by the collapse of the OPEC cartel, and a sharp fall in oil prices during 1986, beginning with a fall from $30 a barrel to under $20 in December 1985 and January 1986. This was the reverse, for industrial countries, of the horror of the second oil price shock at the beginning of the decade, offering lower inflation and more scope for economic growth. The position of Britain was slightly different, as both an industrial country and an exporter of oil. We have seen how only a year earlier one foreign exchange dealer had referred to sterling as a 'one commodity currency' and how Lawson had embarked on a policy of trying to play down the significance of oil to the British economy.

What Lawson and his advisers decided was that, in the effort to get the economy moving faster, and offer more of the benefits of that growth to British industry, the UK did indeed require a devaluation of the pound. The last effort to devalue the pound had ended in the fiasco of January 1985, but this time the pound would start from a much stronger position against the dollar, and the US currency itself was falling. The point was that they did not need actively to promote a devaluation – always a dangerous game for the Treasury and Bank. But in so far as the financial markets saw the decline in the oil price as bad for the UK, and speculated against sterling, Lawson and his colleagues would go along with this. Public protestations to the contrary, as delivered to the Treasury Select Committee, were a counterweight to make sure things did not get out of hand.

Within a fortnight or so of Lawson's denial of any intention to devalue, the pound had fallen, on the average index, by 6 per cent. Saudi Arabia's abandonment of efforts to control the oil price had got the markets looking at the implications for the UK; there was also a revival of inflation fears: indeed, a group of the faithful, including monetarists Tim Congdon, City analyst and leader writer for *The Times*, Professor Patrick Minford of Liverpool University and Jock Bruce-Gardyne, had criticised the Government for failing to make further inroads into inflation since the 3.7 per cent rate inherited by Lawson in summer 1983.[7] The Bank of England's December *Quarterly Bulletin* underlined Britain's wage inflation problem.

Politics in Britain during January 1986 was dominated by the Westland affair, during which a simple decision about whether and/or how to arrange a Government-inspired rescue for a helicopter company degenerated into a fiasco in which the competence and integrity of Mrs Thatcher herself was at stake. This added to the general worries about the pound in the foreign exchange markets – as did, 'untargeted' though they might now be, a set of bad money supply figures. And whatever the money supply figures might show, Lawson had now hoist himself on the petard of the inflation figures; the figure to be announced for December was going to show a rise – the 'judge and jury' had not yet been persuaded.

Although Lawson was at nearly all times reluctant to raise interest rates, the concatenation of circumstances in January 1986 was such that his officials presented him with a powerful argument that it was preferable to raise interest rates before the Budget and lower them afterwards, than risk having to raise them at Budget time. The primary concern was inflation rather than the pound, whose fall was secretly welcomed. There was plenty of time for the Treasury and the Bank to discuss such tactics with the Chancellor at the turn of 1985–86. The Lawson family's boiler had broken down in his constituency home, and he spent most of the holiday period in Downing Street. From being a Chancellor whom officials had found difficult to interest in many Treasury proposals in his early days, Lawson, notwithstanding his protestations of 'laziness', was tending to work non-stop, with little sign of outside interests to divert him.

The decision to raise interest rates from 11½ to 12 per cent – the first change for nearly six months – was made just before the Chevening weekend to discuss the Budget strategy on January 11th and 12th. The short-term tactics were to keep interest rates high until they could safely be lowered against the convincing background of better inflation figures; the key to the Budget judgment was the fall in oil prices and the effect on inflation. The problem was that the Government could hardly *announce* that it wanted the pound to fall. Meanwhile the market was pushing interest rates up, and another rise was nearly forced on the Treasury, but Mrs Thatcher told Lawson to wait twenty-four hours, and the pressure eased. Politically, although some commentators were assuming that tax cuts would have to wait until the 1987 pre-Election Budget, there were by-elections coming up, to say nothing of regular opinion polls. It was therefore decided at Chevening to effect, if possible, a token cut of one penny in the basic rate of income tax (to twenty-nine pence), and it was hoped that the fall in oil prices and the consequent beneficent impact on inflation would make this feasible.

The wisdom of the interest rate tactics was borne out by a meeting the following weekend of the G5 at 11 Downing Street, which Lawson enjoyed hosting. James Baker, the US Treasury Secretary, wanted a concerted reduction in interest rates as part of the next stage of the renewed international co-ordination process. The principal Central Bankers favoured a period of stability, and the Governors of the Federal Reserve and the Bundesbank, Paul Volcker and Karl-Otto Poehl, reacted against being dictated to by Finance Ministers. The eventual co-ordinated cut came in early March, in time for the Budget, by which juncture the annual RPI figures were coming down from 5.7 per cent in December to 4.2 per cent by March and 3.0 per cent in April.

The Treasury thought the financial markets were slow to see the benefit to the economy from a falling oil price. Against the background of widespread concern about the effect on the UK's North Sea revenues, Lawson and his colleagues carefully nurtured low-key expectations about the Budget; a fall of one penny in the basic rate of income tax came as a pleasant surprise. In fact, with oil prices by March virtually half what they had been at the turn of the year, forecasts for growth in the world economy were being revised upwards, against the background of diminished inflation constraints for the major industrial economies. Interest rates came down again by 1 per cent to 11½ per cent shortly after the Budget. At an IMF meeting in Washington the following month, Lawson gave enthusiastic backing for the new mood, induced by Baker and officials generally, in favour of more economic co-ordination (based on compatible targets for growth, inflation rates, balance of payments positions and the exchange rates between various major countries). Lawson even said he would accept targets for employment and unemployment, although not much more was heard of this.

The Budget Report in March indicated that, with the effect of lower oil prices and the Budget tax cuts, the expected rise in real income during 1986 was a substantial 5 per cent. While a lot of attention was focused on the loss of oil revenues, Lawson boasted: 'If we can survive unscathed the loss of half our North Sea revenues in less than 25 weeks, then the prospective loss of the other half over the remainder of the next 25 years should not cause us undue concern.'[8]

The eighteen months from the beginning of 1986 to the June 1987 General Election were a remarkable period. As the OECD put it: 'In January and October 1986 interest rates were raised when the decline in the effective exchange rate appeared excessive and it was also warranted by domestic monetary conditions. Sterling was, nevertheless, allowed to fall in response to the oil price collapse, as the adverse impact on inflation was expected to be offset by the effects of lower oil prices.'[9]

This was a basic policy decision reached by Lawson in the face of various options at the turn of 1985–86. With so much underlying concern about the state of the real economy *and* the Government's electoral prospects, Lawson decided to 'go for growth'. Between the fourth quarters of 1985 and 1986 there was an effective devaluation of the pound of 16 per cent; but, with the benefit of the collapse in the price of oil, the impact on domestic inflation was offset, and the annual rate of increase in the RPI fell from 5.7 per cent in December 1985 to 3.7 per cent in December 1986, touching a low of 2.5 per cent in mid-year. In the first half of 1987, in the run-up to the Election, it hovered between 3.9 and 4.4 per cent, but kept well below the politically embarrassing level of 5 per cent.

The alternative was to do what competitor countries such as West Germany and Japan chose, and allow the full benefit of lower oil prices to feed through into lower domestic inflation. But despite all the talk about the ultimate goal of 'zero inflation', Lawson did not seriously consider this option on this one occasion in his 1983–87 period of office when it was on offer. Nor, it has to be said, was he seriously advised to do otherwise. With so much concern about manufacturing output (still below its 1979 levels in 1986) and unemployment (which did not change trend until the second half of 1986), most Treasury officials saw the oil price fall as a golden opportunity to seek the devaluation they thought necessary, without suffering any serious inflationary repercussions.

The beauty of the 1986 devaluation from Lawson's point of view was that it was an essential prelude to the burst of growth in the real economy which led up to the 1987 Election, but there was no great public drama attached to it in the way that affects Labour Governments on such occasions. This does not mean that there was not a fair amount of private drama. An early 1986 re-examination of the EMS question led once again to a Prime Ministerial '*non*', one of the reasons on this occasion being a desire to maintain freedom of manoeuvre in advance of the Election. Relations between Numbers 10 and 11 Downing Street were strained for much of 1986, because there were many nervous moments over the course of economic policy. Mrs Thatcher and Lawson developed an obsession with secrecy after the Westland Affair, and during the Budget preparations even excluded private secretaries from the kind of consultation that would normally require their presence. One aspect of excessive secrecy was the bungling of a tax measure affecting American Depository Receipts (ADRs); this soured relations with the financial community on both sides of the Atlantic for a while, and the Government had subsequently to retreat.

There was a general 'pause' in the world economy during the summer of 1986, which worried those who thought the oil price fall was going to provide a major expansionary influence. World trade picked up again, however, and in any case the British decision to go for growth rather than price stability meant that the Conservatives were stoking things up well for a pre-Election boom.

The key question, however, was: when would the Election take place? This in turn depended on whether Mrs Thatcher and Lawson could reach an accommodation. During the IMF meeting in Washington that September, Lawson had a nervous day when the pound was falling too fast, and he urgently needed a large credit line from the West German Government to restore calm to the markets. This required a certain amount of lobbying of the West German Finance Minister and Central Bank Governor, respectively Gerhard Stoltenberg and Karl-Otto Poehl, both of whom were on the spot in Washington. Poehl had come out publicly in favour of the pound's entry to the EMS the previous year, and the episode raised once again in Lawson's mind the thought of a safe haven for sterling that could be provided within the EMS, especially after the devaluation that had now taken place.

The Germans made him sweat for their support, and got their own back on him for his hectoring manner in G5/G7 meetings. After demanding to see them when Leigh-Pemberton had not got very far with Poehl, Lawson found that the Germans played hard to get. Eventually they received him in their suite at the very smart Four Seasons Hotel and delivered a lecture to him, imposing stringent and unwelcome conditions on the credit arrangements.

The speed with which the pound fell in September and October 1986 was such that even the most ardent 'devaluers' among the Chancellor's advisers felt the time had come for a period of stability. The financial markets, unaware of the basic devaluation strategy, but not blind to poor trade figures and disturbing balance of payments forecasts from such sources as the NIESR, were pushing interest rates upwards; but Lawson used Bank of England intervention, and Bundesbank credits, to stabilise the situation until after the Conservative Conference in Blackpool, when base rates were raised from 10 to 11 per cent (having been unchanged since May). Lawson made another plea with the Prime Minister for EMS entry at about this time, but again to no avail. Sterling had been devalued by some 13 per cent against the average of other currencies during the previous twelve months, and, more remarkably, by nearly a quarter against the German D-Mark (to an average of DM 2.868 in the fourth quarter of 1986). Mrs Thatcher told the *Financial Times* in November 1986 that sterling could not enter the EMS because the British economy 'is not quite strong enough yet'.

It is easy, after the event, to see a smooth pattern in such developments as the 1986 devaluation. But, as we have noted, there were two phases of outright panic – in January and September – when things threatened to get out of hand. From March until the summer, moreover, there was some impatience on the part of the more ardent devaluationists that the pound was actually rising again; this contributed to the spring series of reductions in interest rates. The emphasis on exchange market intervention in September stemmed not just from the obvious desire to avoid a politically embarrassing rise in interest rates before the Conservative Conference: there was also the fact that, in the light of the summer 'pause' to economic growth around the world, a rise in interest rates hardly seemed ideal from a policy point of view. However, interest rates were now to stay at the 11 per cent level until March 1987, when a series of reductions was inaugurated before the Election, even though the 'judge and jury' inflation rate edged back towards 4 per cent, and over.

The September 1986 exchange rate episode was important in the development of Lawson's policy views for two reasons. At a time when the formal obituary of his monetarist policy was about to be written by the Bank of England (and delivered by the Governor in a public lecture), first, the Chancellor had a rather exciting taste of his powers and prowess in exchange market intervention; second, the help he got from the Germans served to reinforce his conclusion, drawn some time earlier, that he wished to put the pound into the exchange rate mechanism of the EMS.

The drama over the sterling crisis of September 1986 was the first of a series of events which prompted the Prime Minister to complain that 'something always goes wrong when Nigel goes abroad.' On this occasion the telephones duly buzzed, but, with the memory of the burned fingers of January 1985, Mrs Thatcher was easily persuaded that it was better to intervene in the exchange markets than risk 'letting the pound find its own level'. Lawson had become intrigued by the whole Plaza exercise of intervention in the exchanges and was now more convinced of the ability of central banks (under suitable direction, of course) to influence the markets.

In his IMF speech during the last week of September (amid the pound's latest drama), Lawson warned that, although the latest monthly RPI figure was down to 2.4 per cent, 'the underlying rate may now be around 3¼ p.c. – in common with other countries, we have to accept that the sharp fall in the oil price and most other commodity prices means that the underlying rate of inflation is not quite as low as that recorded in the latest figures.' He also recalled his Cambridge speech on the necessity for a real exchange rate adjustment, adding, 'Since the oil price halved, we have duly experienced a substantial but on the whole orderly fall in the exchange rate. Inevitably, it will take time to have its full effect on the current account.'[10] The NIESR was now forecasting a series of rising deficits for the balance of payments, in spite of the real exchange rate adjustment. This suggested that, whatever else, it would be damaging, having achieved the fall in the pound, to allow it to be reversed; and thereby were to hang several tales in the following few years. Lawson's 'initiative' at the September 1986 IMF meeting was a call for 'multilateral disarmament among the subsidisers' (of agriculture). Agriculture was one of the many subjects in which the Chancellor showed an interest beyond the call of duty of most Chancellors of the Exchequer, but in this initiative he was literally trying to move mountains – of butter, and many other commodities.

It was apparent during 1986 that Lawson was developing to a fine art the ability to rationalise almost any situation he found himself in. This applied to gyrations of the oil price and the exchange rate: he was always able to cite his 1984 Cambridge speech in which he had stated that declining North Sea oil revenues would necessitate an adjustment in the real exchange rate. The adjustment was not taking place, as he had prescribed, via lower British unit costs – on the contrary: the British wage inflation picture was returning to a familiar old pattern, although masked, for the time being, by lower oil costs.

Mrs Thatcher and her closest advisers were nervous, in the autumn of 1986, about calling an Election in the spring of 1987. Although, in the end, the pattern of Thatcher Governments was in fact to call an Election every four years, the Thatcher entourage was apprehensive – up to a point – about charges of opportunism; and in October 1986 they had their sights on autumn 1987 or even spring 1988. The Treasury view was that things were shaping up nicely for spring 1987: real incomes, as we have seen, were rising fast; public spending had been under such control that there was scope for some convenient pre-Election 'slippage'; the PSBR afforded room for tax cuts, not least because the consumer boom was yielding unexpected largess in the shape of revenue from VAT, but also because the recovery in the British economy was leading to a higher tax-take from Corporation Tax – the smart thing in this area turning out to have been the removal of investment allowances in the first Lawson Budget of 1984.

Those who had worried about the effect on the British balance of payments of the combination of losses of North Sea oil revenue and the earlier contraction of the industrial base were right; but the Treasury was able to advise Lawson and the Prime Minister that the balance of payments problems would be delayed until after the Election, and that the 1986 devaluation provided a welcome respite. The truth was that the 1986 devaluation was, in a sense, the devaluation that had not been allowed to occur in 1984–85; there was still a fundamental competitiveness problem, which would not show up until later.

Mrs Thatcher was apprehensive, for a time, about being remembered in the history books for winning one Election on the Falklands and losing another from a position of a 144 majority. She eventually bowed to the swelling tide of Party opinion that June 1987 was the right time for the Election. For all their propaganda about freezing public spending, Mrs Thatcher and the Chancellor were happy to see the 1986 Autumn Statement envisage an average increase of 1¾ per cent a year in the volume of public spending over the following four years. In this, they had the advantage both ways: public spending was still scheduled to rise more slowly than gross national product, allowing scope, within the fiscal side of the MTFS, for further tax cuts; but departmental ministers could make the most, electorally, of such relaxations as took place.

The traditional autumn series of economic policy speeches was chosen for the consignment of monetarism to the funeral pyre. The Chancellor had included a target for M3 in his March 1986 Budget, despite its suspension the previous autumn (the Bank had wanted M4, to include building societies); the range was generous by previous standards – 11 to 15 per cent – but during the summer M3 managed to expand at an even greater pace than this, on occasion at an annual rate of up to 40 per cent. In a speech to a gathering of bankers after the 1986 Budget, Lawson had claimed that what the Government had really been trying to do all along 'amounted to scaling down the growth of nominal demand . . . an amalgam of two things: the real rate of growth and the rate of inflation.' What he did not add was that he was essentially doing this via interest rates and fiscal policy, and not worrying at all about the growth of credit, which was simply being regarded as a counterpart of the fall in savings.

His 'Lombard Association' speech fleshed out the message of the autumn 1985 Mansion House speech that 'pragmatism' – not to say Election results – 'ruled'.

> We must never forget that monetary targets are a means to an end . . . in the real world no economic relationship is perfect. So monetary targetry was not and never can be a substitute for making an intelligent assessment of monetary conditions, based on all the evidence. That is why the MTFS has always been more than a row of numbers . . . no scientific formula for determining the 'right' size of the PSBR . . . nor . . . any precise relationship between the PSBR and any given rate of monetary growth . . . never suggested that the market could, entirely independently, be left to set the level of interest rates . . . put bluntly, even though the authorities are not the only players in the field, no Government that is interested in controlling the quantity of money can be indifferent to its price . . . I am satisfied that the growth of M3 in recent years reflects a genuine desire on the part of the private sector to increase its liquidity on a lasting basis. So it does not presage higher inflation.

This message was hammered home with some relish by the Bank of England in a lecture by the Governor at Loughborough University in October 1986. In an analysis of the behaviour of the company and personal sectors of the economy during the 1980s, and of the impact of deregulation of financial institutions and the credit mechanism, Leigh-Pemberton said, 'It is . . . perfectly fair to ask whether in these circumstances a broad money target continues to serve a useful purpose.' This question seemed to be being asked on behalf of the Chancellor, who had by now gone from one extreme to the other in his views about M3. The Governor's closest advisers, however, were as concerned about the complete abandonment of M3 as they had originally been about the Chancellor's obsession with it, and managed to insert, 'it would be just as unwise to pay insufficient regard to the behaviour of broad money . . . as it would be to place too much or too precise emphasis upon it.'[11]

By this time the Chancellor himself was placing no emphasis on it. Unemployment had at last begun to turn down – slowly, and from the appallingly high level of 3.3 million, or 11.2 per cent (on highly favourable definitions, after twenty changes which reduced the official count), output was rising again after the summer 'pause', and everything was being thrown into place to make the economy right for the Election. The strong Treasury view was that late spring, early summer 1987 would be fine for the Election, but that there could well be trouble ahead if it was delayed a year or eighteen months.

Leigh-Pemberton delivered his lecture the week after the 1986 Mansion House dinner, at which Lawson had dismissed the idea that M3 or credit growth was responsible for the October rise in interest rates; the Chancellor made a half-hearted reference to Mo, but the emphasis was on the exchange rate:

> Given the precipitate collapse of the oil price, it was inevitable and indeed necessary that the exchange rate should fall so as to enable – after the inevitable delay known as the J-curve – non-oil exports to rise to offset at least the greater part of the fall in oil export revenues. But there are clearly limits to the necessary and desirable extent of that fall.

The November Autumn Statement set the economic scene for the Election. The volume of public spending was going to be allowed to rise by 2 per cent in 1987–88, there being no attempt to rein back higher social security spending (mainly because unemployment had been so high for so long) and local authority 'slippage'.

There were deliberate injections into 'priority' programmes such as the National Health Service. This kind of concession pleased Conservative backbenchers, and the raw increase, unadjusted for inflation, of £7.5 billion extra spending for 1987–88, or £10 billion over two years, made good pre-electoral headlines.

In fact, however, the growth of public spending had now been kept well below the growth of GDP for almost a decade, and the total volume had been virtually flat since 1983–84 ironically, the year when the Chancellor had given up hope of freezing spending, and had put the emphasis on its growing more slowly than GDP: this contributed enormously to the Chancellor's scope for reducing the PSBR, as did revenue from privatisation and sales of council houses (which counted, curiously, as 'negative spending'). On top of this, the buoyancy of tax revenues was also going to help him in the spring, with unexpectedly high takings of Corporation Tax, and extra pickings from the effect of the consumer boom on VAT receipts. The Autumn Statement pointed out that consumer spending in real terms looked like having grown by 5 per cent between 1985 and 1986, and was set to grow by another 4 per cent between 1986 and 1987.

Of a 25 per cent growth in the volume of retail sales between 1979 and the first half of 1987, some four-fifths took place during the period of Lawson's Chancellorship, the bulk of this during the two years before the 1987 Election. As we shall see in the next chapter, the credit aspect of the Lawson consumer boom was becoming increasingly important, mortgage and other lending by banks having risen from a low base; but the final abandonment of Lawson's interest in controlling M3 meant that restraining the credit boom was not even an objective of policy for the political architect of the MTFS. Quite apart from the swelling proceeds of privatisation – by now running at some £5 billion a year – the situation had been reached where, the greater was consumer spending, the higher were tax receipts and the lower the PSBR – the last remaining 'measure' of financial discipline.

Commenting on the condition of the MTFS in December 1986, Gavyn Davies, a specialist adviser to the Treasury Select Committee, said that monetary targets had undergone 'yet another ratcheting downwards in their importance, leaving the government leaning more heavily than ever on fiscal targets and the exchange rate to exert financial discipline. This is obviously a complete reversal of the order of priorities in the original version of the MTFS, in which fiscal policy was supposed to be subordinate to monetary objectives. It also leads to the inevitable and familiar question about the EMS: if the Chancellor is relying on a stable exchange rate to exert counter-inflationary discipline, why stay out of the system which would make that discipline most effective?'[12]

The answer is that Lawson would have been only too delighted to go in.

What is more, increasingly frustrated by the Prime Minister's continual refusals to countenance the EMS, the Chancellor decided to go it alone, by secretly conducting policy so that the pound would shadow the West German D-Mark. That way he hoped to prove to Mrs Thatcher, with a dry run, that she need have no fears about sterling's chances of stability within the EMS.

The new exchange-rate policy became the monetary policy; and, having effectively evolved into a Medium Term Fiscal Strategy, the MTFS's targets for the PSBR became the symbols of financial rectitude, while the lid was blown off mortgage and other personal lending by banks and building societies. In so far as the financial markets were suspicious of the abandonment of monetarism, they seemed, in the spring of 1987, to rank recovery in the political fortunes of the Conservatives – the Party which *said* it believed in financial rectitude – as more important than financial rectitude itself. Thus, although there had been some nervous moments in the exchange markets after the formal abandonment of monetarism in October/November 1986, interest rates did not have to be raised again, and falls in the pound against the German mark were offset by rises against the dollar.

Entry to the EMS exchange rate mechanism would have provided greater certainty for industry about sterling. Lawson, having failed in his latest attempt to persuade Mrs Thatcher, decided after the G5/7 meetings in the Louvre, Paris, on February 21st and 22nd, 1987, on general exchange-rate stability, to try to hold the pound close to DM 2.90, as the next best thing to full membership of the EMS.

The main point of the Louvre meeting was the attempt by the G5 to stabilise the dollar after the devaluation strategy which had been embarked on at the Plaza meeting in New York in September 1985. Lawson, who had developed a good relationship with the then US Treasury Secretary James Baker, enjoyed these meetings, although the truth was that, for the most part, the UK was on the sidelines watching the main participants, the Americans, the Japanese and the West Germans. This did not stop Lawson from taking an active part, and being his usual combative self. While Paul Volcker, the Federal Reserve chairman, did not have much respect for Lawson, Baker admired him, regarding him as a good politician. On this occasion Lawson proved a useful referee in suggesting the vaguer word 'current' for 'present' when the Japanese were unhappy about the formulation of the communiqué committing the G5 to a period of currency stability; the commitment became 'to co-operate closely to foster stability of exchange rate around current levels'.[13]

From the point of view of the Japanese, according to one account: '*Current* implied a somewhat broader span of time, which could make the potentially uncomfortable specification of the exchange rate more nebulous.'[14] Lawson himself, while helping the main participants with their drafting problems, was also working on his own exchange rate agreement. He in effect advised the others to put themselves on hooks, but not obvious ones. 'We can't have a system in which we set up a target for the market to aim at,' he said. He was especially well qualified to advise the Japanese on their use of 'current' because he was in a similar position himself.

The market rates for the pound against the dollar and the mark at the end of the previous week had been just under $1.53 and just over DM 2.79 respectively. Lawson had got the Treasury during 1986 to take discreet soundings about what exchange rate against the mark industrialists felt they could live with; and, in spite of the huge drop (from an average of DM 3.78½ in 1985 to DM 3.18 in 1986) the weight of opinion from companies such as ICI was that even DM 3.20 was too high for most of British industry. Out of this Lawson had come to the conclusion that DM 2.90 was a sensible rate at which the pound could be pegged in the medium term.

The pound had been rising from levels below DM 2.80 in the weeks just before the Louvre, and it continued to go up after the Louvre, when Lawson delicately told the press he did not want to see 'a substantial increase' in its value. There was no doubt that market sentiment towards sterling had turned favourable, and in nursing the pound up to DM 2.90 (and $1.60) Lawson even found the financial markets calling for interest-rate cuts. He was openly contemptuous of such calls, reminding people that it was the very same market analysts who had been calling for an even bigger rise in base rates during the troubles of the autumn. Indeed, Lawson's feeling that he now knew better than the markets about these things was going to make him over-confident in times to come.

From the Treasury's point of view, the scenario was developing favourably for an early Election. The usual pre-Budget weekend gathering of Chancellor and advisers had taken place a month earlier than the Louvre meeting, and the buoyant revenue trends offered the chance of a tax-cutting pre-Election Budget which could also (provided you did not worry about the money supply figures, and Lawson no longer did) be presented as *fiscally* responsible to the City. With the pound strengthening, everything was set for a nice cut in interest rates to coincide with Budget week; and as the pound had been fragile until very recently, neither the Treasury nor the Bank wanted to take any risks with too early a reduction.

In fact the Government could not stave off a reduction in interest rates for very long. The markets were impressed by statistics suggesting that the PSBR was going to turn out lower than forecast; there was gathering speculation on a third Thatcher victory; and post-Louvre, the pound began another phase of being a fashionable currency. Between the Louvre on February 21st and 22nd, and the Budget on March 17th, Lawson and the Bank of England saw the pound rise to over the new secret 'central' rate of DM 2.90, and took massive sums into the official reserves to hold it down, as well as reducing base rates by half a per cent to 10½ per cent on March 10th. Between January 1st and March 31st, the official reserves rose by a fifth to over $27 billion, but this was mainly in the five weeks following the Louvre meeting.

There were two notable omissions to the list of people who knew about the decision to shadow the German mark: they were the Prime Minister, and her then part-time economic adviser, Sir Alan Walters. But Mrs Thatcher had other things on her mind, notably the choice of the date for the General Election; and, in this regard, her Chancellor pleased her handsomely. His Budget included two pence off income tax (to a basic rate of twenty-seven pence), and was still able to project a PSBR of £4 billion for 1987–88, roughly the same as the outturn for 1986–87, which was itself £3 billion lower than the original forecast. Leaving nothing to chance, Lawson went out of his way to raise excise duties in his pre-Election Budget. The Budget was designed with the possibility of a June Election in mind, although the final choice had not been made. If it had, the cut in income tax might have been 3 per cent, just to ram home the good news to the electorate. Base rates were reduced by a further half a per cent two days after the Budget. And Mr Lawson's fourth Budget was an undoubted political success, making him extremely popular with all those Conservative backbenchers he had taken little trouble to cultivate personally.

Putting the final nails in the coffin of his monetarism, Lawson dropped M3 as a target altogether. But, given the nature of his new monetary – i.e., exchange-rate target (anathema to the Prime Minister) – he could hardly announce it in the Budget Report. The focus became 'Money GDP' for which there was a 'planned path' of 3 per cent growth in 1987–88 and 2½ per cent real growth in each of the following three years, accompanied by a declining rate of inflation (4½ per cent in 1987–88, 4 per cent in 1988–89, 3½ per cent in 1989–90 and 3 per cent in 1990–91). The implication was that if inflation was higher, growth would have to be lower; but there was no pretence of reaching the 'ultimate objective' of zero inflation, and the prominence of real growth targets was a far cry from the Budget Reports he signed when he was Financial Secretary.

The only monetary target left was the exceedingly narrow one of M0, which Lawson had described in Zurich as being 'almost too easy to control'. M3? Its effect on inflation?

> The increasing competition in financial markets in recent years has led to rapid growth of private sector liquidity and borrowing. Private sector borrowing has been rising and is now over 10 per cent of GDP . . . these trends are likely to persist, so that broad money growth may continue at around its recent rate, well in excess of the growth rate of money GDP . . . there is no simple relationship between broad money growth and money GDP.[15]

A tax-cutting Budget in the face of what was by now a roaring consumer boom had implications for the balance of payments; but at this stage the Treasury was forecasting a deficit of only £2 billion or so a year (and in the Louvre communiqué Lawson had dismissed this with 'on external account the aim will be broad balance over the medium term'). Lawson was able to point in his Budget speech to the benefits to be expected from the 1986 devaluation – or 'exchange rate adjustment' as he referred to it; but what the Budget forecasts showed was that the devaluation had merely narrowed the gap between exports and the more rapid growth of imports. However, he was now able to point to a 100,000 fall in unemployment since the previous summer, after seven years of a rising trend; in the circumstances he was perhaps pushing things to say that this was 'the largest six-monthly fall since 1973'.

The nearest the Budget speech got to a reference to the new policy of shadowing the D-Mark was to note that the G5 had agreed at the Louvre 'to co-operate closely in fostering a period of exchange rate stability'. Nearly a year earlier, in his speech to the Lombard Association, Lawson had said:

> Over the medium term, maintaining a fixed exchange rate against countries who share our resolve to reduce inflation is a pretty robust way of keeping domestic monetary policy on the rails. But I see no role for an exchange rate target outside a formal exchange rate system, shared by other countries, and supported by a co-ordinated approach to economic management and intervention. And that, for the UK, means outside the exchange rate mechanism of the EMS.

On November 26th, 1986, Lawson had told the Treasury Select Committee that he did not wish to see the pound fall any further after its devaluation of that year – the necessary adjustment to the oil price fall was complete; he wanted to see an exchange rate that 'exercised a financial discipline and was essentially non-accommodating in the face of inflationary pressures'. On Monday, March 30th, 1987, in his post-Budget evidence to the Committee, he said of his earlier evidence: 'Also implicit in my remarks was the view that I did not wish to see a substantial rise in the exchange rate from that level, as it would clearly not make sense to reverse the exchange rate fall that had been the proper response to lower oil prices.'

Now, six weeks into his new secret policy of specifically shadowing the D-Mark, he said:

> A period of exchange rate stability around the parities then prevailing [at the time of the Louvre meeting] had – and continues to have – obvious attractions. In the wake of the Paris Accord I therefore made explicit the view that had been implicit in my pre-Paris remarks. Policy has accordingly been conducted in this light . . . [but] . . . it is not sensible to be more precise than this or to reveal any operational details. No doubt some light will be shed by the passage of time.[16]

The passage of time was short, but the light shed was refracted. Two days later on Wednesday, April 1st, there was a meeting of the National Economic Development Council, at which Lawson said that exchange rates of $1.60 and DM 2.90 were about right, and that British industry could base its plans on these. This was a deliberate move, aimed at spreading the word without formally announcing that these were the rates he had secretly chosen after the Louvre meeting. But when the newspapers referred to these rates the following day, the Chancellor told a press conference that these were in no way targets – they just happened to be, roughly speaking, the exchange rates ruling that week, and all he had been doing was saying in passing what the exchange rates were that day. This did not ring true, and people at the NEDC meeting gave a different version; the Chancellor appeared to be muddying the waters because the Prime Minister had read the press reports and wondered whether, in some way, the Chancellor was trying to interfere with market forces – which he was. But he issued his denial in his usual robust form, en route to the spring IMF meeting in Washington, where he unveiled one of his international initiatives – a plan to relieve Sub-Saharan Africa of a large part of its debt burden.

The Foreign Office and the Overseas Development Administration had been keen for some time to do something to help Sub-Saharan Africa. But, as one of his officials commented: 'Nobody had ever thought of Nigel Lawson losing sleep over Sub-Saharan Africa.' A number of Lawson's associates believe he deserves considerable credit for having seized this issue, and pressed it powerfully in international forums; an alternative view is that he grabbed the issue from the French, in response to a paper from the Bank, saw that the money was never likely to be repaid anyway, and when told 'the French will be upset, we must talk to them' replied, 'that is the point, isn't it?'

The big concern at the April IMF meeting was that the Louvre Accord was under strain, and that, despite massive intervention in the currency markets, US interest rates might have to rise to protect the dollar. This slightly delayed another reduction in UK interest rates, but not for long. The financial markets were by now almost euphoric about the prospect of another Conservative victory, and it looked increasingly as though Lawson and the Treasury had indeed delivered the goods. Foreign money was gushing into London, very heavy intervention was required to keep the pound within reach of DM 2.90, and interest rates were reduced from 10 to 9½ per cent on April 29th, and 9 per cent on May 11th.

The Bank of England was of course party to the Chancellor's policy of shadowing the German mark. When the inflows of funds began to build up, Bank officials at first took the view that these were 'confidence' flows, connected with the presumed imminence of the General Election; the inflow might not persist, it was argued, and could be reversible: therefore it made sense to go on intervening to hold the pound down. But they were well aware that the shift could prove to be more durable, and in the run-up to the Election in May and early June some officials began to ask themselves whether, given the sheer scale of the inflow, this was not something more fundamental. Consumer spending was racing away, but the policy of holding the sterling/mark rate meant that interest rates had to fall, quite apart from the electoral considerations on the Chancellor's mind. The intervention took place when the pound was in the DM 2.96/7/8 and even DM 2.99 range. Although the seeds were undoubtedly being sown for later policy dilemmas, the question of capping the pound at DM 3.00 had not yet come up; indeed, strict shadowing of the central rate of the D-Mark involved keeping the pound a little below DM 3.00 anyway.

The hope of the Chancellor, the Treasury and the Bank of England in spring 1987 was that, by successfully 'shadowing' the D-Mark, they could persuade the Prime Minister to put the pound formally into the EMS exchange rate mechanism later in the year. The Treasury and the Bank are not supposed to take sides in General Elections, but they have to make political calculations, and it was obvious that Nigel Lawson wanted to take the pound in after a successful General Election. Lawson also gave colleagues the strong impression that he wished to be remembered for having succeeded in this European initiative. EMS entry was undoubtedly becoming an important ambition.

In April everything was falling nicely into place for a June Election: Lawson was being acclaimed in City and country for having turned the economy around, and brought years of economic growth. The pound was stable – and how; the PSBR was under control; unemployment was falling and manufacturing output rising fast. In the pre-electoral euphoria it was easy to dismiss the implications of the consumer boom, and the still debilitated industrial base, for the balance of payments or future inflation. As for the discredited totem of M3 – now expanding merrily at 20 per cent a year in the wake of a rapid rise in personal and mortgage lending – who cared? Everything was set for a landslide victory on June 11th, based on a good, old-fashioned consumer boom. The Venice Summit took place in the week of the Election: the Chancellor contented himself with a day trip. The glory, on this occasion, lay elsewhere.

NINE

The Battles of Downing Street

January 1987–July 1989

The months following the June 11th 1987 General Election were the most triumphant of Nigel Lawson's Chancellorship. The man who had been so unpopular in Party and country that he had even been considered a liability on the television screen was now hailed as the architect of the Conservatives' electoral success, and acclaimed by some as the greatest Chancellor since Gladstone. Never previously seen as a serious candidate for the premiership (even by himself), he was now talked about as a natural candidate for Foreign Secretary, in the unlikely event of Sir Geoffrey Howe voluntarily relinquishing the post, and a possible future Prime Minister.

Nigel Lawson as Financial Secretary had gambled on the MTFS, and as Chancellor on its virtual abandonment: that is to say, his monetary policy had shifted a long way from the days when the M3 target reigned supreme, and interest rates and the exchange rate were determined by market forces. On the other hand, the fiscal side of the MTFS had been remarkably successful, even though there had been some well-publicised 'slippage' from the targets during Election year, and the statistics had been lovingly massaged with the aid of the privatisation programme. Restraint in the growth of public expenditure had, within his own preordained terms, enabled him to deliver politically vital tax-cuts; lack of restraint in monetary policy had ensured that, when the credit boom made possible by deregulation eventually materialised, it would not be inhibited by the application of the original 'simple rule' of the MTFS. The adroitly engineered devaluation of 1985–86 had restored enough price competitiveness to British industry for it to be able to participate sufficiently in supplying domestic demand for unemployment first to be checked, and subsequently to fall.

It was a notable political achievement, and, as far as Lawson and the Conservative Party were concerned, it was also a winning formula. Lawson had gambled on allowing his youthful expansionist instincts to come to the fore, and presided over a classic UK-style consumer boom. Why stop now?

There were certainly very few voices within the Conservative Party or the Cabinet urging a sudden change in the policies that had brought – or were at least associated with – electoral triumph. Nor was there any sign, at this stage, of Mrs Thatcher herself manifesting concern with the inflationary tendencies of her widely praised Chancellor.

All of this seems, understandably and perhaps not surprisingly, to have gone to the Chancellor's head. The arrogant streak discernible all along by so many of his opponents was now more apparent than ever. One of his associates commented: 'The fact of the matter is that he became rather cocky, and this undoubtedly affected the way policy was conducted.'

True, there were warning signs that all might not be entirely right with the course of the economy – the explosion of bank credit and mortgage lending was causing increasing concern at the Bank of England; the July trade figures indicating a current balance of payments deficit of half a billion pounds were very disturbing – but such warning signs were lost in the holiday euphoria of August. In any case, they could happily be dismissed as the problems of success: economic growth was impressive; manufacturing output was almost back to the level of the 1970s – what matter if the balance of payments was in deficit? Foreigners, showing a vote of confidence in the Thatcher miracle, were only too happy to finance the deficit by investing in Britain. And was it not sensible that the rapidly expanding British economy should be importing the best of foreign capital goods, in order to supply the investment boom that was a necessary prelude to sustained future growth?

The unfortunate thing was that the industrial boom had not come earlier, when the balance of payments was cushioned by rising revenues from the North Sea. The neglect of manufacturing industry in the early Eighties, and the contempt shown to such critics as the House of Lords Select Committee on Overseas Trade, were going to haunt the latter part of Lawson's Chancellorship. British industry was to prove unequal to the task of supplying the combination of a sustained consumer boom and a belated revival of manufacturing investment. Much was to be made, when things manifestly went wrong in 1988–89, of the Chancellor's excessively liberal attitude to credit; and the Prime Minister would eventually take issue with him for having shadowed the D-Mark. But these, though important, were only tactical issues – and there is room for debate as to whether the policy of shadowing the D-Mark deserved the blame that Mrs Thatcher subsequently ascribed to it.

The truth was that the main damage had been done by the time the 1987 Election took place. This was why the Treasury's advice about the state of the economy in the run-up to the Election was so important. They could almost guarantee that, with the consumer spending-spree in full swing, and the 'poisoned chalice' of the balance of payments deficit not yet palpable, the principal economic statistics would look reasonable in summer 1987. They would not be so sure about the autumn, or the following spring.

The Government was no doubt entitled to revel in its victory for the rest of 1987; and few would have denied Lawson the credit for at least having satisfied the mood of the British electorate. But the basic facts about the economy as Lawson began his own second term as Chancellor were markedly different from the public perception.

A plausible image had been built up of a British economy that could once again hold its head high, on the basis of a productivity 'miracle' which offered the prospect of sustained, non-inflationary growth. Balance of payments problems? Sterling crisis? Mini-budgets? These were horrors of the past, thankfully banished by the 'new realism' with which the economy was now blessed. There were severe flaws in this idyllic picture, however – flaws which the Government simply did not want to know about amid the joys of Mr Lawson's 1987 summer, but flaws which were going to become more apparent in the next two years.

First there had not been a growth 'miracle'. Output had crashed under the monetarist and high exchange rate phase of 1979–81, and had recovered after that – slowly at first, but faster during the latter phase of Lawson's 1983–87 Chancellorship. But studies by, for example, Sir Donald MacDougall and Professor Wynne Godley had demonstrated that the average growth for 1979–87 was less than in many previous post-war phases. And even the productivity comparisons did not show up as favourably as the Government maintained.[1]

More fundamentally, the growth of manufacturing output and manufacturing investment had been especially poor, both by international standards and by past British standards. We saw, in the evidence to the House of Lords Select Committee on Overseas Trade, what a high proportion of the UK's overseas earnings depended on manufacturing trade. But what happened during the period from 1979–87 is that imports of manufactures grew at twice the rate of exports of manufactures, although for a long time the effects were disguised by a rising contribution from North Sea oil. By 1987, with the oil contribution falling, and the industrial base still inadequate to cope with the strains being put upon it, the UK's overall balance of payments was already headed into the red. It was not until 1987 that manufacturing output recovered to the levels of the 1970s, whereas imports had almost doubled.

As Keith Smith has put it:

> The economic growth which began in 1982 and accelerated in the mid-1980s is unsustainable, for it has been based not on investment and the construction of new production capacity, but on a consumption boom fed by an enormous increase in manufactured imports. This growth has been financed domestically by a fall in personal-sector saving and a massive increase in personal debt, and financed internationally by oil exports. Neither of these sources will sustain combined growth of this type. The key point about the 1980s in Britain is that the 1979–81 recession devastated British manufacturing and the subsequent recovery failed to restore it.[2]

Between 1978 and 1986 the UK's exports of manufactures increased by about 50 per cent, but its imports doubled. There was a deficit on manufacturing trade of £5.5 billion in 1986. And this was before the Lawson 'boom' consumption years of 1987 and 1988 which captured the headlines. Instead of growing on average, year by year, the manufacturing base – the net stock of physical capital which is supposed to produce the goods (what Lawson liked to call the 'supply-side') – was still significantly smaller in 1986 than it had been in 1978–79.

This was almost unbelievable for a 'growing' economy, in which technological progress theoretically enables the capital stock to expand year by year. Yet such was the success of the Government's propaganda that it is doubtful whether a majority of the population was aware of how serious the underlying position was. Even now, a sizeable proportion of the electorate might be inclined to attribute most of the troubles of the economy to what has gone wrong *since* the Election of 1987.

Yet the storm cones were already hoisted by 1987. It is just that not enough people were looking out for them. If anything, the preponderant feeling was that, while the Government's economic policies might have caused obvious hardship among the poor, and the 'new realism' had undoubtedly provoked outcries in the public sector – health, education, the infrastructure – at least these were sacrifices that might have been necessary to build up a more entrepreneurial and economically efficient Britain.

In fact the output of the manufacturing sector of the economy was merely on its way back to the levels of ten years earlier; and, whatever the individual success stories of new and expanded businesses, the main testament to economic efficiency lay in the way the captains of industry had feathered their own nests with remarkably high pay awards to themselves.[3]

Rampant inflation of their own salaries put top industrialists in a weak position to resist pressure from below. We have seen how vehemently opposed Lawson himself was to anything smacking of 'incomes policy'. Under his first Chancellorship no serious inroads were made into the UK's endemic problem of wage inflation, with the result that the slightest sign of excess demand was going to cause trouble on the inflation front.

The oil price fall of 1985–86 afforded the opportunity of a move to a lower inflation threshold – which might have led to less embarrassment during the 1987–89 period; but, as we have seen, a conscious choice was made to 'go for growth' at that stage, by using the counter-inflation benefit of lower oil prices to offset the effect of higher import costs from the 1986 devaluation.

This meant, in effect, that Lawson opted to stay around the 5 per cent inflation level, rather than move down to a 2 to 3 per cent rate of inflation, or even lower – the way other industrial countries chose to handle the oil prices bonus of 1986. In a sense Lawson had little option: at the time the pound was overvalued (or even more overvalued than normal) and there were well-founded doubts as to whether there would be sufficient sense of consumer satisfaction to guarantee the Conservatives a good Election result.

One of the themes of this book is that Nigel Lawson did not worry too much about inflation during those formative journalistic years of the 1960s, but was undoubtedly concerned about the high inflation of the 1970s. Indeed, he espoused monetarism as a counter-inflation surrogate for incomes policy, with all the 'wartime casualties' (his own analogy) that brought in the early 1980s.

Despite his claim, after his 'conversion', that there no longer existed a 'trade off' between inflation and unemployment, Lawson acted as if there were during the 1980s.

The Lawson 'policy curve' tells us that whenever inflation was below 5 per cent he was not particularly interested in fulfilling the letter of his monetarist, or monetary policy, commitments; his bias would then be towards expansionary cuts in interest rates and, though vehemently denied, the exchange rate. But given that he and Mrs Thatcher had set so much store by the conquest of inflation ('the judge and jury'), and made a virtue of informing the financial markets of this, he was walking a tightrope along his 5 per cent line; the slightest deviation above this – any suggestion that the 'core' inflation rate was rising above 5 per cent, and he was likely to be in trouble with the markets.

And 'being in trouble with the markets' meant raising interest rates to bring the monetary statistics – or at least inflation – back into line. With a 5 per cent 'core' inflation rate, he was of course vulnerable to any sudden acceleration of wage earnings, or profit margins, or external shocks such as commodity price increases. *A fortiori*, if the inflation rate were to edge up to 6, 7 or 8 per cent he was constrained, should the performance of manufacturing industry and the trade deficit suggest this was necessary, from inducing a devaluation of the pound (which would raise import prices, and the RPI, even further).

What Lawson inherited from himself in the summer of 1987 was a split-level economy. At one level, that of the narrow focus of the MTFS, things were wonderful. The monetary side of the medium-term strategy had proved an almost farcical disaster – inflation did not behave in the way the monetarist model demanded; and so many changes were made to the 'targets' that the Chancellor ended up with an indicator, M0, which his friend Samuel Brittan himself subsequently dubbed a 'pocket money' indicator; and a concept, controlling the growth of nominal gross domestic product, which signally failed to allow for the warning signals of rapid import growth.

But the fiscal side of the MTFS for Lawson was a dream come true. From the period of his conversion onwards he had shown an interest in the 'balanced budget'. With the aid of the proceeds of £5 billion to £10 billion a year from privatisation, and sales of council houses, he was to achieve this. And, paradoxically, the stronger the consumer boom, the 'sounder' his budgeting position would seem, because of the contribution of higher receipts from VAT.

The approach to balance – and eventual surplus – gave him two inestimable political advantages. It diverted attention from the trend of the balance of payments: impressed by the fiscal position, and the 'success' of the MTFS in meeting the targets for public sector borrowing, the market analysts, or 'teenage scribblers' as he called them, were slow to highlight the deteriorating balance of payments trend, and its implications (Dr Gerard Lyons, then at Savory Milln, was a notable exception). And, of course, it gave him some scope for tax cuts – which he also liked referring to as 'tax reform'.

One of Lawson's motives in being such a forceful proponent of privatisation when Energy Secretary was apprehensiveness about the chances of reaching the PSBR targets, given the unexpected pressures on public spending. But, as it turned out, the MTFS strait-jacket did prove to be, from Lawson's point of view, an effective discipline on the rest of the Cabinet's spending plans. The virtual freeze on the total volume of general public expenditure after 1983–84 was essential to the tax-cutting strategy of 1987 onwards.

But the very same freeze on public expenditure also aggravated subsequent economic and social discontents. It was assumed, in spite of opinion-poll evidence to the contrary, that people preferred tax cuts to better public services – or, even, that they did not mind deteriorating public services provided they were soothed with the balm of tax-cuts.

By the summer of 1987 a 'never had it so good' atmosphere had been created in which it was taken for granted that tax cuts would continue. Meanwhile credit was notoriously available from a proliferating variety of financial institutions, with assumptions of future tax cuts stoking up people's perceptions of their borrowing capacity. There was little sense of urgency, or even concern, about the course of the balance of payments, and scant political awareness of the potential upward pressures on a 'core' inflation rate of 5 per cent.

Tax cuts, and consumer credit, are more likely to fuel spending on imports than extra expenditure on, say, roads and railways. Likewise, the recipients of pensions and other social security payments tend to spend more of their incomes on 'essentials' than on imported consumer goods or foreign holidays. But the whole thrust of the fiscal side of the MTFS had been to bear down on such public spending, causing an imbalance in the economy, quite apart from such unpleasant features as discriminating against the already poor and oppressed.

The essence of Lawson's MTFS was that it was counter-inflationary and anti-public spending. In practice the bias against public spending persisted (contrary to the evidence of underlying demand by the public) and the counter-inflation bias was weakened once inflation was at or below 5 per cent. The weakness of the MTFS, and, indeed, of Lawson's general approach to economic policy, lay in its crudeness and narrowness of focus.

For a man of undoubted intelligence, Lawson displayed a fatal lack of subtlety in his approach to the economy. The conduct of economic policy is difficult and complex at the best of times. It is this fundamental point which forces 'pragmatism' on the economic policy-makers of so many countries of the OECD world. Yet officials at such international organisations as the OECD and the IMF and the Bank for International Settlements in Basle often commented that, by comparison with other countries, the British under Lawson would tend to concentrate attention on their latest obsession, in discussing policy, rather than adopt a more rounded approach.

The MTFS itself focused at first on the money supply and public sector borrowing. It was a purely domestically orientated concept, ignoring the fact that the UK is a very open economy, with the foreign trade sector accounting for a quarter of GDP. Moreover, within that domestic orientation, the crucial importance of manufacturing industry to the economy was woefully neglected.

Unlike Japan, which has an industrial strategy looking five to ten years ahead, Britain under Lawson's Chancellorship hardly possessed an industrial strategy at all. It can be argued that previous governments may have overestimated their ability to influence industry – that is one thing. But to have a medium-term strategy which has ignorance and neglect of industrial trends built into it is quite another.

Worse: to the (considerable) degree that the MTFS contained a bias against public sector financial assistance to industry – either directly (Lawson took pride in cutting the budgets for industrial assistance and regional aid) or indirectly, through cuts in education, research and training, the strategy was positively harmful to industry.

The 'single obsession' or 'panacea' approach of Nigel Lawson was remarkable in its lack not only of complexity and subtlety, but also in its inconsistency. The speed with which the objectives and criteria for successful economic policy shifted from M3 to M0, to inflation to budget balances, to budget surplus to shadowing the Deutschmark, was bewildering, not least, one suspects, to the Chancellor himself.

One sphere in which Lawson was entirely consistent from his journalistic days to the late Eighties was in being a 'meritocrat' and an 'anti-egalitarian'. Given the interest which he took in policy from the 'macro' to the most 'micro' level, he was a leading light in the Cabinet which tolerated the shift in British society during the 1980s to a more unequal distribution of income, and to a position where glaring pockets of poverty and public squalor constitute manifest blots on the UK's political and social landscapes.

This was the approach that, under the British electoral system, won the Thatcher Government a third term in summer 1987. There may have been a growing sense of uneasiness about the Galbraithian combination of 'private affluence amid public squalor'; but somehow it was assumed that at least there had been an economic and industrial 'miracle' on the credit side.

Yet, from the point of view of the economy as a whole, that industrial miracle was a mirage. What is more, the problems at the heart of the British economy in 1987 were not only discernible by those who looked; they had also been largely predictable – and indeed were predicted by the House of Lords Select Committee on Overseas Trade, among others. On the one hand the British economy's propensity for more rapid wage inflation than its competitors had persisted; on the other, the contribution of North Sea oil to the balance of payments had ceased rising, peaked and begun to fall, so that it could no longer conceal the underlying deterioration in the export/import balance. Profit margins might be healthy; the stock market might be riding high; there were no doubt scores of individual company success stories – it suited Lawson and his colleagues to generalise from these – but, when all was said and done, there had been insufficient new investment to compensate for the damage wrought earlier in the decade. New investment by manufacturing industry in

1986 was still 16 per cent less than in 1979; and, when allowance is made for scrapping of plant and depreciation, the manufacturing capital stock – the industrial base – was *contracting* in the face of the consumer boom.

The reasonable inflation figures of 1986, and the manifest success, within its own terms of reference, of the fiscal side of the MTFS, had diverted attention from the risks being run with the cumulative effects of financial deregulation. Lawson breezily claimed to have reversed the laws of economics, and dated his precious 'recovery' from the Budget of 1981 and the policy of cutting the PSBR, not raising it. What had happened, however, was that the deflationary impact of lower public sector borrowing was first offset and then more than offset, by what was appropriately called a larger 'private sector borrowing requirement'.[4] The origins of the Lawson credit boom of 1987–89 lie in the fact that, from small beginnings, the entry of the clearing banks into the mortgage market, and the general increase in competition between the building societies and banks, led to a growth in personal and mortgage-related finance that became explosive after a certain point.

This showed up in the economic statistics – among other ways – as a fall in the saving ratio, which came down from 10.4 per cent in 1983 (the first year of Lawson's Chancellorship) to 5.4 per cent in 1987 (the year of the Election). The ratio represents personal saving as a percentage of personal disposable income; most personal saving is contractual – through insurance and pension contributions, and does not alter pattern very much year by year. This big fall in the saving ratio corresponds to the 'dis-saving' or extra borrowing, which took place in the mid-1980s.

The banks and building societies were not only taking advantage of freedom from controls to build up their lending. In the case of the banks, there was the added incentive of the need to find alternative outlets to the business which had 'gone sour' as a result of the Third World debt crisis. Indeed, Margaret Reid has calculated[5] that the retail lending profits of the major British banks in 1987 completely offset their provisions for dubious Third World debt. (Another factor disposing the banks to build up their consumer lending was a loss of their corporate business, as more and more international corporations behaved as their own banks – often, as a result of the Third World debt crisis, with higher credit ratings than the banks themselves.)

At all events, a boom in bank lending and consumer credit occurred during those years of the mid-Eighties when Lawson himself had abandoned most efforts at monetary control. Between 1984 and 1987 the amount of new bank-lending to the private sector per annum nearly trebled, to £42 billion; and of the latter figure about a quarter was nominally related to house purchase. Whether used for house purchase or not, it certainly fuelled the consumer

PL 007198 BIN B2024C SHOP SO

SOUTHPORT A/N/WP HODD CL £14.95 ISBN 0340509783

MR LAWSON'S GAMBLE

21/10/89 KEEGAN,W BOOK PUBLISHED 11/90

QTY REQUIRED [ ]

PL 007198 BIN B2024C SHOP SO

SOUTHPORT A/N/WP HODD CL £14.95 ISBN 0340509783

MR LAWSON'S GAMBLE

21/10/89 KEEGAN,W BOOK PUBLISHED 11/90

QTY REQUIRED [ ]

boom and property price inflation. Bank mortgage credit shot up five-fold in four years, doubling between 1986 and 1987 alone.

Christopher Huhne pointed out that the personal financial liabilities of individuals (mortgages, bank loans etc.) rose from 45 per cent of pre-tax incomes at the beginning of the Eighties to 81.3 per cent at the end of 1987. Without the sharp decline in savings since 1980, consumers' spending would have been 10 per cent lower and GDP 6.4 per cent lower in 1987. During Lawson's first Chancellorship, the general liberalisation of credit interacted with a relatively fixed stock of housing to produce a situation where house prices more than doubled. 'Any Londoner who bought an average house four years ago even with a 100 per cent mortgage is sitting on roughly £60,000 in tax free capital gains, which is probably just about what he or she earned before tax over the same period.'[6] From the point of view of the impact on consumption, the increased purchasing power of existing house-owners would have outweighed the reduction in spending power of 'first-time buyers'.

The NIESR pointed out that of the rise of 5.8 per cent in the volume of consumer spending in 1986, and 5.6 per cent in 1987, only three percentage points of the growth in each year could be accounted for by the growth of real incomes (itself a 'moderately fast' rate of growth), so that nearly half the rise was associated with a fall in the saving ratio. 'The main reason for the change in behaviour in the UK appears to be the liberalisation of financial markets, especially the provision of consumer credit and mortgage lending . . . The growth of consumer credit adds directly to the resources available to households who would otherwise have to delay purchases, especially durable goods.'[7]

The NIESR added: 'The second route by which liberalisation of financial institutions has increased consumption is by making the personal sector more liquid . . . the main reason why this has happened has been the growth of mortgage lending, far exceeding that needed to finance new house purchases.'

While incomes were rising at 3 per cent per annum, the stock of consumer debt outstanding was rising at over four times this rate (at 12.5 per cent per annum in real terms). 'The main reason seems to be an increased willingness of banks and other financial institutions to lend for purposes of consumption; indeed there has been intense competition amongst them to do so.'

The extent of the 1986 and 1987 consumer credit boom took both Government and outside forecasters by surprise. We have seen how, well into 1986, Lawson and other ministers were concerned about the lack of strength of the pre-Election economy. What happened by mid-1987 was that the conscious attempt to ease policy in time for the Election had coincided with the accelerating and cumulative impact of the financial deregulation earlier in the decade. And this, in turn, interacted with the recovery in manufacturing investment that was finally taking place, all those years after the 'supply side revolution' was theoretically inaugurated in 1979.

The first signs of balance of payments trouble did not appear until July 1987, safely after the Election, when it emerged that there had been a current account deficit of over half a billion pounds in May (the publication of the figures being delayed by an industrial dispute). There were some voices in the City expressing concern about the balance of payments trend: Mr Bill Martin, at Phillips & Drew, forecast that, with inadequate domestic industrial capacity, the UK could expect a sharp rise in imports and an annual rate of deficit of £4 billion in the second half of 1987. But, on the whole, the balance of payments trend was not yet causing much concern. On the other hand there were worries about inflation – the money supply figures were bad again, house prices were shooting up, and the retail price index was edging up from 4.2 to 4.4 per cent. And, despite the fact that manufacturing output was only just regaining the levels of 1979, the rapid pace of growth of the economy was worrying officials in both the Treasury and the Bank.

At the same time there was a temporary check to the strong upward pressure on the pound that was to dominate the first year of Lawson's second Chancellorship. This mainly reflected the strength of the dollar at the time, but the pound also eased slightly against the D-Mark. This gave the Treasury and the Bank a perfect moment to suggest tightening monetary policy without damaging the Chancellor's exchange-rate target, and he agreed. Lawson also took some pleasure in taking the markets by surprise on this occasion. Base rates were raised by 1 per cent to 10 per cent on August 7th.

But as far as Lawson was concerned, that was but a minor adjustment to what was essentially his attempt at being remembered as the 'British Erhard'. The emphasis was still on expansion. He was in no sense, after the manner of some Conservative Chancellors before him, about to cut back sharply now that the Lawson consumer boom had won the Party its third consecutive Election victory and himself a considerable reputation. One close associate said: 'By 1987 he thought he knew how to run the British economy and how to control inflation. He was hailed as the architect of electoral victory, the best Chancellor the world had seen. It affected his judgment, and it almost seemed possible to him that he could overrule the Prime Minister.'

The area where he wanted to overrule her was on Europe and the pound's entry into the EMS. Some months before the June Election he had been given some friendly advice on the lines that, if he did not stop hectoring Mrs Thatcher about the EMS and the wonders of its exchange rate mechanism, she might be tempted to remove him from her own political mechanism. Now he was widely described as 'unsackable'.

He proceeded, at the annual IMF meeting in Washington in late September, to deliver a speech in which he advocated a return to a quasi-Bretton Woods system of managed exchange rates. The idea was that the major industrial countries should build on the success of the Plaza and Louvre agreements, and institutionalise and publicise what had hitherto been an arrangement that was so tentative and shrouded in obfuscation that the participants always felt free, when it suited them, to deny that they were committed to it. He even included, at a press conference, the technical proposal that, when adjustments took place in a currency's value, they should not be so great as to take the new 'central' rate outside the existing range of, say, plus or minus 5 per cent around the existing central rate. One official commented simply, 'He has found it easier to run an economy where the exchange rate is fixed.'

The proposal certainly made the kind of splash that Lawson liked to achieve at IMF meetings, although it did not go down too well with several other G7 countries, at a meeting which was marked by some fundamental disagreements on policy. Indeed, with the G7 in obvious disarray over what policies they should be pursuing, and question marks over the viability of the existing exchange-rate pattern, it was an odd time to be building on the G7's 'success' – apart from anything else, the G7 policy disagreements were going to be cited as one of the factors which led, a few weeks later, to the October 1987 Stock Market Crash.

But if the Lawson initiative made a splash in Washington, it opened the floodgates in Number 10 Downing Street. Mrs Thatcher wanted to know what was going on, why had she not been told, how was it that something always went wrong when the Chancellor went abroad? This was not easy to answer: although Lawson and Sir Terence Burns, the Chief Economic Adviser, had been working on the proposal since the spring, they had not included the Prime Minister's office, or the rest of the Treasury and the Bank, in their deliberations until the last minute. What soon became obvious, however, was that the IMF proposals were closely linked with Lawson's EMS ambitions; indeed, one official commented subsequently: 'Reforming the entire world monetary system had become his backdoor route to the EMS.'

Nobody told the Prime Minister that Lawson was shadowing the EMS; but her annoyance with the IMF speech, which marked a public departure from belief in the wisdom of market forces, was to put her more on her guard as to what he was up to with his sterling policy in future months.

The October Crash – 'Black Monday' on Wall Street on October 19th, and a 23 per cent plunge in the value of the London Stock Market on Monday and Tuesday 19th and 20th October, was the next crisis the Chancellor had to negotiate. Although understandably arousing much concern at the time, the

Crash was to be described the following year by Lawson as 'an economic non-event'. Obviously there were fears of 'another 1929', but probably the most important single sentence on economic policy that year was uttered by Alan Greenspan, chairman of the US Federal Reserve, when he said: 'The Federal Reserve, consistent with its responsibilities as the nation's central bank, affirmed today [Tuesday] its readiness to serve as a source of liquidity to support the economic and financial system.' The G7 network of central banks eased monetary policy, and the UK participated in this co-ordinated process, which was in the end so successful that analysts were soon describing the Crash as merely a 'correction', rather than a financial cataclysm. Lawson himself gave a speech at the Stock Exchange in which he noted: 'The view now prevails that the markets had earlier got ahead of themselves.'[8]

One aspect of the Crash was a recrudescence of bad feeling between Lawson and the Bank of England over the question of the privatisation issue of £7 billion of BP shares. Lawson was annoyed by suggestions that the Bank was claiming credit for the 'safety net' formula on which the BP issue took place. The Bank took umbrage at the Chancellor's annoyance. What appears to have happened is that both the Chancellor and the Bank thought that, Crash or no Crash, it was important to give the impression of 'business as usual' and go ahead with the issue. The Bank suggested a 'floor price' (of 90 pence, against the offer price of 130 pence) to reassure worried underwriters in the aftermath of the Crash. Lawson had to be persuaded about this, but eventually accepted the principle, although he insisted on a lower support price (of 70 pence).

The point was that the price of existing BP shares had already fallen in the market, and only the unsophisticated investor would want to subscribe for them at the much higher privatisation price. It is the role of underwriters to take risks. Lawson came under a lot of pressure, especially from American and Canadian firms, to 'pull' the issue – i.e. to withdraw it. Offering a 'safety net' near the existing market price was a way of psychologically reassuring the market, at a very nervous moment, that he did not expect a further sharp fall, without being vulnerable to the accusation that he was bailing out the underwriters at the higher price, with taxpayers' money (he was, of course, still mindful of the Johnson Matthey Bank affair). Whatever their differences over who should receive the credit, the Treasury and the Bank between them appear, in retrospect, to have handled a difficult operation with considerable skill, and not to have cost the taxpayer much. But the episode left each partner believing that the other had behaved badly, and Lawson's outrage at the time hardly seemed worthy of a Chancellor who ended up with considerable credit for having publicly kept his nerve.

Lawson may have been unduly sensitive on this issue because, if it had gone wrong, it could have threatened what were beginning to turn into greater career prospects than he had ever envisaged. But the Election victory, and his new-found popularity with gatherings such as the Conservative Party Conference, were beginning to make him take himself more seriously than even his closest friends remembered.

His speech at the Conservative Conference in Blackpool that year had come, as usual, shortly after the IMF meeting. Not only was Lawson showing a rather broader range of interest than in purely Chancellorial matters: he had also allowed a degree of self-confidence to creep into his speech which was remarkable even by his own standards. Despite the Prime Minister's annoyance over his Washington exchange-rate initiative, he boasted of having represented there a nation whose economy was successful and strong – 'And that is why I was able to take a lead in Washington on moves to reinforce stability in the world's exchange rates. I believe that is what industry wants. And that is what we are delivering.'

The Washington initiative was referred to again in a remarkably confident speech he made that autumn to the annual Mansion House dinner. 'The plain fact is that, as a result of sound policies consistently pursued over a number of years, we are now enjoying the benefits of a virtuous circle. Low inflation, public expenditure under control and sound public finances have led to sustained growth and thus the ability progressively to lower tax rates, which in turn has brought about improved confidence and better business performance.' (He had promised a further reduction in the basic rate of tax 'as soon as it is prudent to do so' at the Conference in Blackpool.)[9]

> As I made clear in my speech at the Annual Meeting of the IMF in September, the system of managed floating that would best serve the needs of the world economy would have as its objective the need 'to maintain the maximum stability of key exchange rates, and to manage any changes that may be necessary in an orderly way' . . . the maintenance of a stable exchange rate for sterling, within the framework of the Louvre agreement, to which we remain committed, has meant a higher level of intervention than used to be the case – most of it, so far, in the direction of increasing the reserves. You will have seen the exceptionally large increase of getting on for $7 billion in October, published yesterday . . . nor should there be any doubt of our commitment to maintain a stable exchange rate, with the rate against the Deutschmark being of particular importance. It gives industry what it wants, and provides a firm anchor against inflation. And we now have very substantial reserves with which to maintain that stability in the future.

The significance of these passages can hardly be overestimated in the light of the position Lawson had now arrived at, and the political problems with the

Prime Minister that lay ahead. He had made his initial proposal in Washington, a proposal with far-reaching implications, implying a return to a quasi-Bretton Woods system of fixed exchange rates (which he sometimes referred to as 'managed floating'), without consulting more than a handful of close colleagues, let alone the Cabinet or the Prime Minister herself. If it was a proposal for managed floating, it was also a programme for unmanaged Cabinet Government – a red rag to a Prime Minister who was generally thought to run the Cabinet like a personal fief (indeed, on one occasion Lawson had told a luncheon gathering that Mrs Thatcher's ideal was 'a Cabinet consisting of one person – herself').

Despite the fact that Mrs Thatcher's displeasure had been communicated to him, he was carrying on the fight in the open. Talked of as in the running for the job of Foreign Secretary, even as a future Prime Minister, he allowed his famous streak of arrogance to come to the fore. The Prime Minister, advised on a part-time basis by Sir Alan Walters on his monthly visits from Washington, believed in the wisdom of market forces. Here was her Chancellor telling the financial world that he believed in the maximum stability of exchange rates, and if the markets could not be relied upon, Finance Ministers such as himself, instructing their Central Banks, most certainly could. The Prime Minister did not like direct intervention in the exchange markets (one of her and Walters's reasons for opposing the EMS). Here was her Chancellor boasting of the way the reserves were piling up as a result of Bank of England intervention under his direction? The Prime Minister's fears about the effect of such inflows on the money supply: 'To prevent there being excessive liquidity in the economy, our policy is to ensure that, over time, any net intervention is sterilised – in other words fully funded.' (Or, put another way, offset by sales of government stock which withdraw the 'excess' liquidity from the system.) Conspiracy theories existed about Mrs Thatcher having directly appointed 'her own man' in the shape of Mr Robin Leigh-Pemberton to be Governor of the Bank. Here was her Chancellor, having reconnoitred the Bank pretty effectively when Financial Secretary, and having been furious over the Johnson Matthey Bank affair, exercising all the control he needed over the institution on macroeconomic policy, and ignoring its warnings of inflationary pressures and excess credit growth in the economy.

In typical Lawson fashion, the achievement of the new obsession – stable exchange rates – had taken over as the main focus of policy. With the post-Election inflows of funds into Britain now becoming a torrent, preventing the exchange rate from rising required cuts in interest rates. And there was a curious sense in which, embarrassing to all policy-makers though it was for a time, the October Stock Market Crash played into Lawson's hands. It gave him an opportunity for lowering interest rates that was independent of the need to do so as part of his exchange rate policy. And he could present lower interest rates as part of a sensible, co-ordinated G7 strategy to avoid the kind of contraction that followed the 1929 Crash, which was on many people's minds at the time.

Thus, in two stages, the 1 per cent rise in interest rates of August was reversed, with rates falling to 9.5 per cent the week of the London Crash, and to 9 per cent on November 4th, the day of the Mansion House speech. Just as the Federal Reserve chairman's statement of reassurance to the markets was itself the most important reaction to the Crash, so these interest rate reductions were a perfectly sensible follow-up in the circumstances of the time. Lawson's comments so soon after the Crash read well in retrospect, although of course policy-makers *have* to keep their sang-froid on such occasions, however nervous they themselves may be. Nevertheless, Lawson came well out of the Crash, and made his contribution to defusing the panic. Lawson stated at the time that the direct effect in the UK 'may not be very large' and pointed out: 'The fact that share prices are at about the same level [after the Crash] as they were a year ago is something that needs very much to be borne in mind when assessing the likely scale of the economic effects of the stock market falls.'

In his Mansion House speech Lawson had no hesitation in pinning part of the blame for the Crash on the market's doubts about the political will of the United States to reduce its budget and balance of payments deficits, and to raise interest rates to the necessary level. 'It is indeed ironic,' he said, 'that an apparent unwillingness of the United States to raise interest rates because of an exaggerated fear that this might tip the economy into recession has led to a collapse on Wall Street, whose recessionary threat is very much greater.' He proceeded to lecture the USA on the need to change its policies, as part of a wider G7 accord involving reductions in interest rates. (This was a lecture which did not go down too well with the US Treasury Secretary James Baker, who felt such public advice, to an audience of international bankers, at a very difficult time, was neither cricket nor baseball.)

The inflationary and balance of payments problems of 1988–89 were to be compounded by the fact that Lawson allowed the pretext of the stock market Crash to be used in justification of his easy-credit policies long after the possible implications of the Crash had ceased to be a threat. Indeed, it may be argued that, if he believed his own rhetoric about the lack of significance of the Crash, he did not need to reduce interest rates on its account for very long. But it is interesting to note that his optimism about the economy was not shared by the NIESR which wrote that November:

> There is general agreement amongst forecasters, including now the Treasury as well as ourselves, that the growth of the UK economy will slow down substantially next year. This expected deceleration is partly the result of the recent fall in the stock market, but also partly the result of the appreciation of sterling this year, especially against the dollar but even against the DM. The appropriate response in this situation must be to cut domestic interest rates. Recent research suggests this would have a significant effect both on investment and on consumer spending, as well as tending to hold the real exchange rate down.[10]

('And how' one might add in the light of the subsequent conjuncture of a belated investment increase *and* a continuing consumer boom.) Thus the NIESR saw interest rate reductions as necessary domestically, and said 'it would therefore be wrong to make reductions . . . contingent on some new "accord" between members of the G3, the G5 or the G7, or contingent on action to reduce the US fiscal deficit. The purpose of cutting interest rates is rather to "prop up" the real economy in this country and to prevent sterling overshooting the level that is sustainable in the longer term.'

In the light of the subsequent upward pressure on the pound in 1988, and downward pressure in 1989, it is noteworthy that Lawson also said in his 1987 Mansion House speech: 'We now have very substantial reserves with which to maintain that stability [of the exchange rate] in the future.' The fact was that both he and his closest Treasury advisers, for all the problems they were to have trying to stop the pound rising in 1988, were very concerned to avoid a sharp drop, and fearful that the pound could go the other way almost any time.

If one abstracts from the stock market Crash, and looks at the kind of picture presented in the Autumn Statement of 1987, one can see how the triumphant Chancellor could convince himself that he was indeed on the verge of 'a virtuous circle' – provided the trend of the balance of payments was ignored. The belated recovery of manufacturing output had helped to produce a year when labour costs per unit of output actually rose less than in many competitor countries (an unusual occurrence). Ever the optimist, Lawson thought he had inflation well under control; and, with the prospect of a PSBR outturn of a mere £1 billion (at a quarter per cent of GDP, even less than the latest target of 1 per cent), he had the prospect of a tax-cutting Budget (on his own criterion of MTFS targets).

Later in the month he was to be heard proclaiming: 'There is, of course, a clear link between sound public finances and a strong economy . . . I do not need to theorise about the benefits that have been brought by this policy, coupled as it has been with a readiness to keep interest rates at whatever level is necessary to curb inflation . . .'[11] Given the way policy was evolving, it might have been more accurate to add: 'but from now on, my interest rate policy will be determined entirely by my desire to stabilise sterling, whatever the consequences may be for consumer spending and inflation.'

The Bank of England was already showing concern about the Chancellor's desire to reduce interest rates further under the umbrella of the G7. It stated in its November *Quarterly Bulletin* that the main purpose of the August rise had been to reverse the falls earlier in the year 'in response to the pressures in the exchange market but which were not fully warranted on domestic grounds.' Disagreeing with the NIESR's analysis, the Bank warned: 'With continuing growth of broad money, domestic monetary developments, like those in the real economy, continue to argue for caution in the conduct of policy. The growth of M0 has shown signs of acceleration . . . the underlying expansion of credit remains strong . . . with a major contribution from lending to persons, particularly on mortgages (where the banks' market share has risen again this year at the expense of the building societies).' The Bank was prepared to go along with the 'confidence' justification for the recent falls in interest rates, but behind the scenes it was arguing against further easing of monetary policy.

There was an intriguing moment during the last week of November when Mrs Thatcher gave an interview to the *Financial Times*. A year earlier she had told the newspaper (notwithstanding all the claims that the UK had undergone 'an economic miracle') that the British economy was not yet strong enough for the pound to go into the EMS exchange rate mechanism. She now said she did not want to be tied down by the EMS, which had 'a deflationary bias'. And, against a background where her Chancellor was 'shadowing' the EMS in the hope that he could eventually persuade her that it was technically feasible to join, she declared 'there is no specific range . . . we are always free.'

Early in December, preliminary indications were that the growth of the economy had been exceptionally strong in the third quarter, particularly in consumer spending. There was again a flood of foreign money into London, and the Bank of England intervened heavily, on Lawson's instructions, to keep the pound below what had become an unofficial ceiling of D-Marks 3.00. The Bank and some senior Treasury officials were worried about the pace of consumer spending and inflationary pressures: although the retail price index was running at just over 4 per cent per annum, the broad index known as the GDP deflator – which measures all price increases in the economy – was edging up to the 4½ to 5 per cent range, and a number of officials were concerned that danger lay ahead if inflation was clearly seen to be heading for the 5 to 6 per cent range.

It was against this background that Lawson sanctioned a further cut in interest rates, to 8½ per cent on December 4th, to try to keep the pound below DM 3.00. Referring later to the three interest rate cuts since the Crash, the Bank subsequently noted coyly that it was 'partly in this context' (the Crash) that interest rates had been reduced.

Lawson himself told the Treasury Select Committee, at perhaps his most brazen, 'obviously interest rates are something which I watch carefully all the time and when I think they ought to go up they go up and when I think they should come down they come down.' His interlocutor, the assiduous Mr Budgen, observed (on the basis of what he had once been taught by no less an instructor than the Chancellor himself): 'I thought they were decided by markets.' To which Lawson replied: 'No, that would be an abandonment of monetary policy and that I am not prepared to do.'[12]

One insider's comment about this period was:

> He really thought he could walk on water. He was not committed to zero inflation. An increasing part of the inflationary pressure came from the restoration of profit margins. Had policy been tighter, a vital improvement in margins, which was necessary to boost industrial investment, might have been prevented. He thought it would be rather clever to pull off the combination of a recovery in profits and investment, plus exchange rate stability.

Another close observer said of Lawson's exchange rate policy during that autumn: 'He was very confident. It was a sort of gamble. He committed himself to the view that, as in the spring, the inflows would not last. He persisted in that view, and the reductions in interest rates encouraged not just consumer borrowing but also corporate borrowing. The mistake conceptually was not to depress consumer borrowing to make way for corporate borrowing.'

What in effect happened was that Lawson and his Treasury/Bank advisers found a justification for pursuing the exchange rate policy through the fragility of the financial markets. But by December officials were deeply worried, there was a large inflow of funds in the first fortnight, and even the Chancellor himself came close to giving up the attempt to hold the rate. Then suddenly the pressure eased, and he was off the hook for a few weeks over Christmas and the New Year holiday.

It was only just over a year earlier, during the IMF meeting in Washington, that Lawson had had to arrange a rescue operation for the pound when the devaluation strategy of the period got out of hand. This was a consideration that weighed heavily on his mind, and the minds of Treasury officials, during the autumn of 1987: quite apart from the Chancellor's particular new 'hook' of below DM 3.00, his Treasury advisers did not want to see the pound rise too far above DM 3.00, only to fall back embarrassingly later. On the other hand, given the strength of the economy – paradoxical in the light of all the concern about the October Crash – they did not want interest rates too low. The Chancellor himself was more cavalier about interest rates and consumer borrowing, while the bias at the Bank of England – well before Sir Alan Walters's views became known in the spring – was in favour of raising interest rates to control the growth of credit; if this meant going above DM 3.00, too bad (that was their advice: they scrupulously carried out their instructions on intervention). It so happened that holding the pound down, difficult though it was, was a lot easier before the turn of the year than after, because the weakness of the dollar itself meant that the Deutschmark was strong. When the German currency itself weakened in the New Year, and the dollar first stabilised and then recovered (after successful G7 action), it was going to prove impossible to hold the pound down against a German currency that was itself falling.

The linguistic philosopher in Lawson came to the fore in an answer to the Select Committee when he was asked specifically whether the fact that the pound had fluctuated close to DM 3.00 meant that 'we are now effectively part of the exchange rate mechanism of the EMS?' He said: 'No, it does not indicate that we are part of the exchange rate mechanism of the EMS.' Nevertheless, within minutes he was adding: 'Germany has . . . a deep distrust of inflation and a very strong anti-inflationary track record . . . therefore keeping the pound in line with the Deutschmark is likely to be over the medium term a pretty good anti-inflationary discipline.'

The Autumn Statement had achieved the difficult feat of referring to the decline in the saving ratio without making any mention of the effects of financial deregulation and the consumer credit boom. In his evidence to the Select Committee the Chancellor ventured bravely, when pressed, to say, 'It is interesting that if you do take aside mortgages you find there has been no growth of personal sector borrowing as a percentage of GDP at all.'

When told: 'You know very well how the banks and other lending institutions virtually beg people to borrow and put forward all kinds of reasons why loans should be taken out – do you think that is a desirable state of affairs?' he replied, 'It is a free country and I believe that lenders should be free to lend and borrowers should be free to borrow.'

This reflected the nub of the growing policy dilemma: Lawson felt proud of the abolition of exchange controls, and of the general philosophy of 'deregulation': yet this was the fundamental cause of the credit boom. And, at this stage, it was not just a case of relying on what Mr Edward Heath was to describe as 'the single golf club' approach of higher interest rates: he was actually trying to lower them whenever possible. To the Chancellor and his associates, the message was quite simple – almost puritanical: if people *did* 'overborrow', they must learn the error of their ways. (This parallel was not yet stretched to apply to the whole country overborrowing.)

As 1988 began and the rows with the Prime Minister and Professor Walters loomed, the Chancellor's policy weapons were therefore constrained by the fact that monetary policy eschewed formal credit controls, and was in any case preoccupied with the exchange rate. Meanwhile fiscal policy, in accordance with his 'supply-side' beliefs, was geared only to reductions in taxation, not to increases. He had explained to the Treasury Committee his devotion to the 'balanced budget' doctrine, and how he was happy with a PSBR of 1 per cent, which was compatible, given reasonable growth, with a falling ratio of national debt to national income. This was the 'modern equivalent' of the balanced budget, he said.

Any speculation about what PSBR was consistent with 'balance' was rendered superfluous, however, by the news that the public sector accounts were in fact heading for surplus. The combination of the squeeze on public spending, and higher revenue (from privatisation proceeds, the effect of the consumer boom on VAT, and taxes on corporate profits) indicated, according to Mr Simon Briscoe, an analyst with the City firm of Greenwell Montagu, that the Chancellor might have a surplus of up to £11 billion to play with in his forthcoming Budget. Briscoe was a former Treasury official, and was the first person outside the Treasury to indicate just how swollen the Treasury's coffers had become.

Given the trend of the balance of payments and inflation, a truly cautious Chancellor would not have been disposed to boost consumer spending and imports even further with tax cuts in the Budget. Apart from anything else, there was the political cycle to consider, on which Lawson had become something of an authority: the early part of a parliament was the natural time for prudence, when there was nothing to lose electorally; tax cuts could be kept for later. But there was another political cycle operating – that of Lawson's own career. He had let it be widely known that he did not wish to serve the whole of the new parliamentary term as Chancellor, and he seemed to friends to be toying with the idea of going off to the lush pastures of the City of London (an important consideration being that he had a young family to support, and his second wife was none too enthusiastic about the glare of publicity in which residents of 11 Downing Street lived). On the other hand, the general boost to his political popularity since the Election gave some of his friends the impression he might wish to stay longer in the forefront of politics, possibly even as Foreign Secretary.

At all events, he decided that a Budget in the hand was worth two in the bush, and that he would take advantage of the fact that the Treasury was awash with revenue in order to make a real impact with tax cuts. In this he was also influenced, from his international connections and observations, by the way that taxation had been dramatically reduced and simplified in the United States. The basic strategy was established at the usual weekend meeting of Treasury ministers and senior officials, which took place at Dorneywood, in Buckinghamshire, then the official country seat of the Chancellor. There was no serious consideration given to the idea that perhaps all this Budgetary largess should be used for extra public spending. And lest anybody should have any thoughts that the money should be channelled towards the poor – through, perhaps, increases in Child Benefit, Lawson made clear in a pre-Budget lecture that 'incentive' and 'opportunity' were still his meritocratic themes, and 'egalitarianism' remained a dirty word in his vocabulary.

When it came, on March 15th, the tax-cutting package was most certainly startling. The basic rate of tax was brought down from twenty-seven to twenty-five pence, and the top rate from sixty to forty pence. There was even some consideration given to bringing the top rate down to thirty-five pence, balanced by the removal of the ceiling on National Insurance contributions, but it was decided the removal of the ceiling would produce too many 'losers'. The Budget was based to a remarkable extent on a tax reform paper which had been published by Professor Mervyn King, of the London School of Economics,[13] and Lawson was at one point heard to comment: 'Why don't people have ideas like this *inside* the Treasury?'

For many Conservative MPs and businessmen, it looked like Lawson's finest hour. It was certainly *theirs*. These were truly dramatic tax cuts – benefiting top income earners by tens of thousands of pounds a year in one fell swoop. An academic study commissioned by the Treasury had concluded that it was difficult to prove any 'incentive effects' from tax cuts, but that did not stop the Chancellor; the cuts were presented as a boost to incentives, that could well finance themselves in terms of greater work effort and higher revenue. (When similar arguments had been used about such 'supply-side' tax cuts in the USA, Lawson had derided them.)

The tax cuts amounted to some £6 billion per annum, with 40 per cent of the reductions going to the top 5 per cent of income earners. The Budget almost coincided with some highly publicised cutbacks amounting to £1 billion a year in social security benefits. And although the Labour Party chose to make Budget Day 'National Health Day', the Government had not yet seen fit to bow to growing pressure for higher public spending in this sphere.

The week before the Budget, Lawson was referred to thus by his journalistic Alma Mater the *Financial Times*: 'It has taken the British media a long time to catch up with the fact that Chancellor Nigel Lawson is a pretty engaging fellow who may even be the next Prime Minister.'[14] And when the Budget tax cuts were duly announced, the reception from the Conservative back benches was truly rapturous.

And yet for Lawson himself it did not seem his finest hour. On the contrary, he spent most of March being extremely angry, and in a bitter feud with the Prime Minister. Senior Civil Servants had to act as nursemaids between Numbers 10 and 11 Downing Street, as the Chancellor, who delivered tax cuts which seemed the apotheosis of Thatcherism, sulked in his tent and muttered resignation threats to his inner circle of friends and advisers. As for his 'historic' Budget, he seemed almost bored by it.

The cause of this malaise lay in the collapse of his exchange rate policy, and a breakdown in his relations with the Prime Minister as a result of a series of humiliating incidents. It all started after the Prime Minister finally rumbled his exchange rate policy – tentative earlier rumblings had been successfully fobbed off. Some officials have suggested that Mrs Thatcher's approach to her Chancellor in these matters was devious, and that she always attacked him through an indirect route. Thus the way she approached the exchange rate policy was not by questioning the wisdom of his targets, but by expressing concern about the mounting pile of dollars that had been accruing to the official currency reserves in the effort to keep the pound down. Her ostensible worry was that here was her Chancellor amassing reserves of a currency that was not a good bet, and generally expected to go down in value over the next few years. Coming from any custodian of sterling, this was perhaps an arrogant approach. But the point was repeatedly expressed, with Sir Alan Walters, on his occasional visits, adding to her concern with dire mutterings about the effect this inflow of funds was having on the money supply. (Lawson's assurance in the November Mansion House speech that these monetary effects would be 'sterilised' was directed as much at Thatcher and Walters as at the international bankers.)

A more likely explanation than deviousness is that Mrs Thatcher was approaching the issue with a certain feminine directness. She did not think the amassing of dollars was 'value for money'. She did not like the thought that the money supply might thus be swollen. This concerned her more than the theoretical abstractions surrounding Lawson's latest obsession with the desired value of the exchange rate. Anyway, she believed market forces should determine that. She was persuaded that Deutschmarks were a better 'buy' than dollars, but still worried about the inflationary implications, and in any case the Bundesbank objected to the scale of the Bank's purchases of D-Marks.[15]

Lawson and his innermost circle of officials had kept the 'shadowing' policy going for a remarkably long time, sometimes by denying its existence, sometimes by explaining particular bursts of intervention in the exchange markets as being necessary under the UK's international commitments dating from the Louvre Accord of February 1987. But once Mrs Thatcher found out, her Chancellor was in trouble. And she found out before his path-breaking 1988 Budget.

The Prime Minister was so furious about Lawson's exchange rate policy that she insisted, after advice from Walters, on certain sections of the Budget speech being rewritten, notably with regard to exchange rate policy. The section on this subject was vague in the extreme, containing nothing like the forcefulness which had characterised the November 1987 Mansion House speech or the first draft of the Budget speech itself.

The Budget was on Tuesday, March 15th, but the demise of Lawson's exchange rate policy occurred eleven days earlier. The public rows and misunderstandings came after the event, and ran on into July. When the pound had dipped temporarily early in February, Treasury and Bank officials wanting a tightening of monetary policy had persuaded the Chancellor to raise interest rates by half a per cent to 9 per cent. But after that the pound had strengthened again, and they had not wanted to encourage it up further through another rise in interest rates. Nevertheless, the point came at the end of the first week in March when, even after massive intervention to hold the pound down, it closed at DM 2.9986, uncomfortably close to what had become the barrier of DM 3.00 where Lawson would be seen to have failed in his self-imposed 'virility test' to manage the exchange rate. The $4½ billion rise in the reserves during March (to $47½ billion) was dramatic by any standards, but especially when it is realised that the bulk of the force driving the pound up was experienced in the first few days. Lawson himself was being impaled on one of his hooks; some officials, knowing that the underlying trend of the balance of payments would be spotted by the market eventually, did not want the pound to rise too far only to fall back; yet they were also anxious to tighten monetary policy, whereas the strength of the pound pointed either to lower interest rates or to more intervention.

The sheer scale of the intervention in those first few days of March was such, however, that it was soon clear to all the advisers around Lawson that they had little alternative but to allow the pound to rise – it was hoped temporarily. This was in the context of the Government's economic philosophy: to lower interest rates did not make sense against the background of the credit boom; but quantitative credit controls were anathema to Lawson; and the idea that perhaps taxes should not be reduced in the Budget – or even that they should be increased – was ruled out by the 'supply-side', tax-cutting philosophy. Nigel Lawson had got to the stage where he believed taxes could only go down, not up. If he had been prepared to rethink his general approach to economic management, he would not have been putting such a strain on the focal point of the exchange rate, and might have exposed himself to less public embarrassment. He chose the glory of being a tax-cutting Chancellor, and suffered the consequence of what was generally interpreted as a public rebuff from the Prime Minister.

Although it was all presented in the press as a great battle, Lawson's advisers felt he had got close, on Friday, March 4th, to realising that 'the game was up' anyway. Throughout February, as the pressures mounted, Lawson was told by officials that he would have to let the pound rise, but he always argued that the problem might go away; he hung on as long as he could. But there were several moments during February when he came close to admitting defeat. It had become obvious to the financial markets that the Bank of England was trying to defend the DM 3.00 barrier; and market operators felt that they were on to 'a one way bet' as the upward pressure on the pound intensified.

The pressure was especially intense on the morning of Friday, March 4th, when the Prime Minister had already expressed her fury at the amount of intervention. Although there were reports of a dramatic meeting of the Chancellor, Mrs Thatcher and the Governor of the Bank of England, at which Lawson was overruled, the sequence of events was different. The Governor was actually away from London that day. Lawson's officials, having talked to the Bank, told him they could not hold the line any longer, and that, if the pressure continued on the Monday, they would have to let the pound rise above DM 3.00. Early in the afternoon Lawson was summoned through the connecting door between Numbers 10 and 11 Downing Street to see the Prime Minister on his own; he was given a humiliating dressing-down by Mrs Thatcher, who had already been on the telephone to the Bank; when he returned, he told his two senior officials '*I* have decided that we can't hold on any longer.' The three then discussed the situation with senior Bank of England officials. The Prime Minister had ruled out further intervention; a *reduction* in interest rates was out of the question, given the strength of demand in the economy – in fact, they needed to *tighten* monetary policy. They agreed on a strategy of letting the pound rise, and raising interest rates later, when, as was hoped, the steam would go out of the upward pressure on the pound. Lawson then returned to Number 10 and told Mrs Thatcher what had been decided.

The change of policy was exploited to the full by the Opposition front bench during Parliamentary Questions the following week, as the pound shot up almost to DM 3.10, provoking worries that the Government was once again adopting the kind of 'strong exchange rate' policy that had proved so damaging to British industry during Lawson's period as Financial Secretary between 1979 and 1981.

In effect, the Prime Minister and her Chancellor spent the next few weeks arguing in public and hardly being on speaking terms in private. Attempts by officials to patch things up and arrange 'agreed forms of words' for public occasions such as Parliamentary Questions only made matters worse. Mrs Thatcher delivered her famous statement 'there is no way in which one can buck the market', which was swiftly transformed in popular parlance to 'you can't buck the market', and the Chancellor made feeble denials that he had ever been following an exchange rate target, when it was perfectly obvious to the Westminster, Whitehall and financial worlds that he had, and that he had suffered a highly visible defeat. As one official commented: 'He had got himself on one of his hooks – on the sharpest of sharp ends.'

There were attempts to suggest that the rows of March were all got up by the press; but they were not. There was visible uneasiness between Prime Minister and Chancellor when they sat together on the Treasury bench in the Commons trying to show a common front; and on one occasion a public 'spat' was witnessed between them in the Members' Lobby, with Mrs Thatcher wagging her finger in her best schoolmistress's manner at her hapless Chancellor. Lawson himself was furious; his friend Samuel Brittan of the *Financial Times* went on television and radio attacking the Prime Minister for undermining her Chancellor's position; from then on, Samuel Brittan was often assumed to be speaking on behalf of the Chancellor, which was by no means always the case.

The relationship between the Prime Minister and her Chancellor was to remain uneasy after this episode. The trouble stemmed partly from Mrs Thatcher's disinclination, when she felt strongly on an issue, to dissemble in the way that is almost commonplace in Whitehall once a 'line' has been agreed. She had not liked the intervention; she was less inclined to try to 'buck' the market than Lawson had become in recent years. And, despite what might have been agreed in advance of Parliamentary Questions as 'the line', she tended to blurt out what she really thought.

The situation was compounded by the fact that Sir Alan Walters, who had not been present on the crucial Friday, but who had certainly advised her some days earlier on the subject, was also someone who tended to blurt out what he thought. At the time he was in the USA, working at the World Bank in Washington and the Johns Hopkins University in Baltimore. There were weeks when he seemed readily available to journalists on the telephone, and poured out a stream of criticism of Lawson's policies. Critical articles by him also appeared in *The Times* and the *Independent* during the early summer. And, to cap it all, Mrs Thatcher decided that the whole affair had strengthened her need for his advice, to the point where he was invited to return to 10 Downing Street on a full-time basis the following year. Whichever way this was presented – 'quite frankly we prefer Alan to be inside the system where we can keep an eye on him' – it could only be interpreted as a move to undermine Lawson.

It was one of those rare episodes in the normally abstruse sphere of economic management which seemed to capture the public's interest. The spectacle of open squabbling by The Neighbours of Downing Street was amusing in itself. But as the months went on, the general public tended to take sides, and by early 1989, when the inflation rate was heading upwards and the balance of payments deficit was running at some £16 billion to £20 billion a year, there seemed to be a popular view that 'she was right and he was wrong'.

It was more complicated than that. On any view of the trend of British industrial costs, underlying competitiveness and the balance of payments, Lawson was surely right to want to try to hold the exchange rate down. Some officials would argue 'yes, but he chose too low a rate'. To which the answer is provided by the subsequent balance of payments figures, and the fears, in the summer of 1989, that the pound might have to fall a lot further in order to restore the country's overseas payments position to equilibrium. Lawson had learned something from the deindustrialisation of 1979–81.

On the other hand, given what was happening to inflation and the balance of payments, Lawson was taking a great gamble with the economy in allowing the consumer boom to carry on in full swing, with no attempt at controls on bank credit, and in cutting taxes so dramatically. The previous year's tax-cutting Budget sent out all the wrong signals, and encouraged people to borrow more. This was compounded by the Budget decision to limit tax relief on mortgages to one property (and its subsequent effect on property prices and borrowing), as opposed to one person or couple, with a starting date five months away. This latter decision provoked a rash of mortgage lending to take advantage of the fact that until August 1988, people could club together and each receive tax relief on their contribution to the purchase of one property.

Both Mrs Thatcher and Sir Alan Walters were right to argue that monetary policy was too loose. Yet, despite their alleged victory over the question of exchange rate intervention, monetary policy continued to be loose, as far as the consumer was concerned, for six months after the March 4th decision. The fact was that, although the pound was allowed to rise, interest rates were actually reduced three times – from 9 per cent at Budget time to 8.50 per cent two days later, 8 per cent on April 11th and 7½ per cent on May 18th. It was not until the end of June that they were brought above the levels ruling before the Budget. Meanwhile Mrs Thatcher rubbed her Chancellor's nose in his defeat at a Number 10 seminar in May.

'What we wanted,' said one official, 'was higher interest rates with the same exchange rate. But this was not on offer. For a time we could only have achieved higher interest rates with a higher exchange rate.' There was, in fact, an upward revaluation of the pound against the average of all the major currencies of 6 per cent between 1987 and 1988. Officials tried to rationalise this by saying that a higher exchange rate indicated a tightening of policy. In fact, while making industry less competitive, it actually *loosened* policy from the consumer's point of view, by enabling him or her to buy more foreign goods for the same quantity of money.

Meanwhile mortgage and bank lending continued apace for much of 1988. Lawson subsequently said that the £40 billion of extra lending by banks and building societies during 1988 was the main cause of excess consumer demand, not his Budget tax cuts. The point was that, from the point of view of what the domestic economy could cope with, the consumer lending was obviously too great and the tax cuts should not have taken place at all.

Professor Walters had great fun sniping from the sidelines during the early summer, because policy undoubtedly remained too loose. In the old days hire-purchase restrictions would have been tightened, credit controls imposed, and even taxes raised in a July 'mini-Budget' – the balance of payments deficit was already running at an annual rate of £12 billion, against a Budget forecast of £4 billion, and the underlying acceleration in inflation was beginning to show up in the retail price index, which rose above 5 per cent during the summer, and reached 6.4 per cent by October.

Although Professor Walters only came into public view after the episode of bursting through the DM 3.00 ceiling, the shadowing of the Deutschmark was to be firmly fixed in Mrs Thatcher's mind as the time when things really began to go wrong. 'It was in fact shadowing it very, very closely,' she subsequently said of the pound and DM episode, 'and that's where we picked up inflation.'[16]

In fact the pick-up in inflation came well after the policy had been found out, and was due to a combination of excess demand in the economy (fuelled by rapid credit growth, as a result of the cumulative effect of financial deregulation) and a faster increase in average earnings. As Tim Congdon, a well-known City monetarist, has pointed out: 'UK net mortgage advances in the second quarter of 1988 were over 50 per cent higher than a year earlier and gave further impetus to the house price explosion. By June 1988 the annual rate of increase in house prices . . . had climbed to almost 30 per cent.

At the same time the prices of houses in West Germany rose by under 5 per cent.'[17]

The mix of loose monetary policy and tax cuts in circumstances of a dramatically deteriorating balance of payments was something for which the Chancellor must take responsibility. By the time of the autumn meeting of the International Monetary Fund in West Berlin, when the deficit was of increasing concern in the financial markets, Lawson produced the novel doctrine that it did not matter because 'the current account deficit is entirely the result of private sector decisions.' But base rates were raised no fewer than ten times between June and November, from 7½ to 13 per cent.

The IMF secretariat had itself suggested it was odd that the UK was not prepared to use fiscal policy (i.e., higher taxes) as a policy instrument. Lawson said 'private sector behaviour is by its nature self-correcting over time ... there is a limit to the amount of debt which the private sector will be willing – or can afford – to undertake. Once that limit has been reached, the savings ratio will rise again.'[19]

Yet he could give no indication of when this limit might be reached, or when the balance of payments deficit might start to improve.

The policy now appeared to be that interest rates would have to be kept high not only to help private sector behaviour to be 'self-correcting' but also to persuade overseas holders of funds to keep their money in London to finance the payments deficit meanwhile. Between the March Budget and the Autumn Statement of November 8th, 1988, the official forecast for the balance of payments deficit for 1988 was revised from £4 billion to £13 billion, falling to £11 billion by 1989. When the Budget Report for 1989 was published on March 14th, 1989, the current account deficit for 1988 was estimated at £14½ billion, and the same figure was forecast for 1989. By the time the OECD reviewed the British economy in June 1989, its forecast, based on Treasury figures, was £18 billion for both 1989 and 1990, with no sign of an improvement. During 1988 the volume of imports rose by 13.4 per cent and of exports a mere 0.7 per cent.

While dismissing in public any suggestions that the balance of payments trend posed even a difficulty, Lawson was energetic behind the scenes trying to persuade official statisticians to find faults with the payments figures, so that they could be revised downwards in time for the March 14th, 1989 Budget. They were unable to give him much satisfaction.

Despite the prospect of an unprecedented Budget surplus of £16 billion, his 1989 Budget had to be an exercise in the kind of old-fashioned demand management he had for so long eschewed. Calls from people such as the former Cabinet Minister John Biffen for higher public spending were of course ignored. But the wishes of those extremists such as the Institute of Directors who wished to see a further dramatic reduction in taxation were also brushed aside. A mere £2 billion of the 'available' revenue was used for tax cuts – roughly half in the form of changes in the National Insurance system aimed at removing the 'disincentive to work', and half in the form of a failure to index excise duties in line with inflation.

This latter point was an indication of just how great the constraints on Lawson's freedom of action had become. The man who had in 1979 been so enthusiastic about nearly doubling VAT, with the effect that had in putting several percentage points on the RPI – was now, with inflation heading for 8 per cent again, reluctant to risk the most marginal extra impact. The truth was that the 1989 Budget was dominated by fears about inflation and the balance of payments, and the 'glory' of the Budget surplus was overshadowed by the rising concern in the City about the inadequacies of economic policy. Indeed, so concerned was the Chancellor now about the inflation trend that, although he persistently argued through the winter that 13 per cent base rates were sufficient to bring about the necessary 'correction' of consumer demand, he was forced to raise them to 14 per cent on Wednesday May 24th, 1989, in order to defend the pound. This brought interest rates to their highest level since the dark hour of the January 1985 sterling crisis. Moreover, the pound was in fact being defended at a higher level than the rates he had thought appropriate for British industry when he originally embarked on his ill-fated Deutschmark policy. But that was because any further fall in the pound, however necessary on competitiveness grounds, would aggravate the inflation trend.

By midsummer 1989 the inflation rate was 8.3 per cent and even 'good' balance of payments figures were running at an annual rate of £15 billion to £16 billion. The Chancellor might complain that, without the effect of the mortgage rate increases on the RPI, the underlying rate was lower. But with most people this cut little ice, because housing costs are one of the most important items in their cost of living. It was going to take a long time to bring inflation down to within the Lawson 'policy curve' range of under 5 per cent; and it was difficult to calculate how, without a major devaluation of sterling, the balance of payments position was to be restored. Yet such a devaluation was being desperately warded off, because it could easily bring the published inflation figure up to 10 per cent, which would finally destroy what little credibility the Government still had with its counter-inflation policies.

One occasionally heard the argument from Lawson's colleagues that the pace of growth of output and demand in 1987–88 combined had been much stronger than forecast (especially of demand); but that did not meet the objections that, given the deterioration in such important indicators as inflation and the balance of payments, corrective action should have been taken sooner, and further fuel should not have been stoked on the fire in the 1988 Budget.

While miracles are always possible, it seems to this writer that Lawson had gambled and lost. He had first gambled on monetarism and the Medium Term Financial Strategy; the latter had produced the tax cuts on which, if he had resigned after the 1988 Budget, he could have gone out in a blaze of political glory – leaving it to curmudgeonly critics to point out that the tax cuts had been achieved at the expense of a neglect of the poor, the weak and the social infrastructure which had unpleasant features at the time, and threatened potentially dire consequences for the future.

Whether or not monetarism worked (and it did not) his 'conversion' of the 1970s now seemed to his colleagues to have been an act of opportunism, to please a Mrs Thatcher who had had some kind of mystical conversion herself, but who needed a technical expert she could trust. Lawson's friend Jock Bruce-Gardyne subsequently described the idea that Lawson was 'the original, unreconstructed monetarist axeman' as 'always a gross misreading of his character'.[20] (Bruce-Gardyne had always professed more sincerely held monetarist beliefs himself.)

It has to be remembered that Mrs Thatcher's use of the advice of Professor Walters (whom she inherited from Sir Keith Joseph) goes back to the days when Lawson was only Financial Secretary. Her subsequent resort to Walters showed that she needed someone who could give her economic advice independently of the Chancellor, the Treasury and the Bank. But what reinforced her need for this advice, and led to the invitation to Walters to return, was the fact that she lost trust in her Chancellor after the General Election of 1987, for which he had delivered her the perfect economic electoral recipe.

She lost trust essentially for two reasons. The first was the secret shadowing of the Deutschmark, to which for a long time she was not privy. The second, and not unassociated with the first, was that, after June 1987, when the general adulation seemed to go to her Chancellor's head, Lawson threatened to become too powerful.

The combination of the Election-winning consumer boom, and the tax-cutting Budget of 1988, led people to speculate that Nigel Lawson, the man who had seldom been taken seriously as anything other than Chancellor, could be Foreign Secretary – even Prime Minister. Lawson had been one of the 'Gang of Four' backbenchers who were Mrs Thatcher's political henchmen in the Opposition days of the 1970s. And she had continued for a long time to find him a political asset, whom she respected, despite the ups and downs of his Chancellorship. He was, for example, someone who was not frightened to argue with her, or tell her she was talking nonsense. He even, on one occasion, got away with telling her to 'shut up' during a meeting of a Cabinet Committee.[21] But suddenly being seen as a possible rival – even a potential successor – was something different.

In crude political terms, therefore, Lawson during his second Chancellorship was 'riding for a fall'. There was a brief episode of midsummer madness before the Parliamentary recess of 1988 when Number 10 Downing Street sounded out Conservative backbenchers on the question whether Lawson and the Foreign Secretary Sir Geoffrey Howe should be shifted from office (with eyes on the next Election, and a younger team); but the time was not, as the Government persistently said about EMS entry, ripe. Despite the row over exchange rate policy, backbenchers were prepared to back their Chancellor – indeed, to a large extent, *because* of that row. There was a sense in which, at that stage, Tory backbenchers thought Lawson had been unfairly treated by the Prime Minister, and were angry about the interventions of Professor Walters. But that was before the politically embarrassing increases in mortgage rates.

A year later, however, in June 1989, the reports started appearing again that Mrs Thatcher was thinking of a kind of 'night of long knives', in which both Chancellor and Foreign Secretary would be replaced. This time, with interest rates at 14 per cent and the economy in manifest trouble, Lawson's image as a super-Chancellor was somewhat tarnished. On the other hand, there was considerable sympathy on the back benches for his persistence in advocating EMS entry – which he and Sir Geoffrey Howe were now doing at every opportunity, and in public – and the general view was that it was better for Lawson to 'see this through'; indeed, it was thought that it could have a catastrophic effect on the financial markets if the Prime Minister ditched her Chancellor now. Nor were Conservative backbenchers too happy with this phase, reminiscent of March 1987, when the Prime Minister appeared to be distancing herself from her Chancellor, and publicly attributing current troubles to the Deutschmark episode.

Sir Alan Walters was now alternating in three-weekly periods between Downing Street and Washington. He had been asked by Mrs Thatcher to stop talking so openly to the press, but the general pot of discontent was stirred by reports of 'private' City lunches at which he was going around criticising the Chancellor. There were so many of these reports that, to believe what was said, Walters never stopped lunching. With Mrs Thatcher offering only reluctant support to her Chancellor in public – egged on by a more confident

Labour Front Bench containing John Smith, the Shadow Chancellor, and Gordon Brown, a forceful spokesman on Treasury matters, with the polls going very much their way – Lawson's position seemed decidedly uneasy in the weeks before an expected Cabinet reshuffle in July. There was a report on BBC TV News at nine o'clock one evening that Howe and Lawson were safe, but the Number 10 Downing Street spokesman Bernard Ingham telephoned the BBC at 9.05 p.m. to ask whether it had a better reading of the Prime Minister's mind than he did.

It was a fascinating political situation. Mrs Thatcher openly speculated about the agonies of having to reshuffle her Cabinet, and was then persuaded to make a statement in the Commons saying she gave 'full, unequivocal and generous backing' to her Chancellor. But her own position was becoming mortal too. The Conservatives did badly in the June elections for the European Parliament, and this strengthened the hands of the pro-European Chancellor and Foreign Secretary, who urged her to soften her anti-European tone for the Madrid meeting of the European Council of Ministers in late June.

Lawson himself, though angry in private, adopted a dignified, almost statesmanlike tone in BBC interviews and before the Commons Select Committee, continuing to fight the EMS cause, while offering olive branches to the Prime Minister over the timing of entry – not before the complete abolition of exchange controls in the European Community on July 1st, 1990. He also backed Mrs Thatcher by being hostile to rapid progress towards full economic and monetary union – stages two and three of the 'Delors Report' – and in showing great concern about loss of British sovereignty in fiscal and monetary matters.[22] (He had started this line of attack in a speech to the Royal Institute of International Affairs earlier in the year, which had appeared to be aimed at pleasing Mrs Thatcher; but its tone had the effect, if anything, of heightening tensions between the Treasury and other European countries, at a time when Lawson's primary short-term concern was still the EMS.)

Lawson had repeatedly said he did not want to serve two terms as Chancellor; and after the 1987 Budget and the EMS row he hedged his bets about future office by sounding out the possibility of a job in the City of London. He turned down one or two offers, but might have liked the chairmanship of the National Westminster Bank had it been offered. It was widely thought that Rupert Murdoch would like him to edit *The Times*, but he repeatedly told friends and colleagues that this did not appeal.

Friends and colleagues alike thought that he wanted to see things through at the Treasury now, and not depart when the economic news was not good. But the big question was: how long would it take for the inflation and balance of payments positions to be manifestly better? The strategy of holding off a necessary devaluation of the pound until the inflation figures were below 5 per cent again was obviously a risky one, especially when there was increasing awareness of what the Government was up to. Lawson, knowing what was at risk, was now taking personal supervision of the Treasury's intervention in the foreign exchange markets, arriving in his office at 8 a.m. to 'play the markets' as a colleague put it. He had once told an interviewer that, as Chancellor, he had given up playing poker because 'certainly, in the life I lead, there is sufficient risk'.[23] Exchange market intervention had been the *casus belli* of his problems with the Prime Minister. It had become his new obsession, and his ultimate reputation as Chancellor might well hang on its success. Did he really understand the market-place in whose judgment he had once believed?

The Cabinet reshuffle took place on Monday July 24, and Lawson duly remained in place, although the Foreign Secretary Sir Geoffrey Howe, also an enthusiastic champion of the EMS, was sacked. The French newspaper *Le Monde* said, of Lawson, that one does not change the helmsman in the middle of the storm. This captured the general feeling.

But the helmsman suffered two blows to his dignity, one more serious than the other. In order to pacify Sir Geoffrey, who had put up an unaccustomed display of truculence over his loss of the Foreign Secretaryship, Mrs Thatcher offered him Dorneywood, the house Lawson had been using as his own official country residence for several years. More seriously, in a very controversial move, she promoted John Major, hitherto Number Two to Lawson as Chief Secretary to the Treasury, to Sir Geoffrey's job of Foreign Secretary.

Major's promotion seemed finally to put paid to any vestiges of hope Lawson might have of becoming Foreign Secretary, at least under Mrs Thatcher. But it also meant that, if he so chose, Lawson could resign from the Chancellorship at a time to suit himself, not the Prime Minister. The general belief remained that he would want to see things through, and certainly not depart before the economy was looking perceptibly better. The year-on-year inflation figures were expected to fall in the autumn, but an acceleration in wage inflation raised doubts about how long it would be before inflation was back within Lawson's 'policy curve' range of under 5 per cent.

There was also the question of the continuingly large current balance of payments deficit, and its financing. Nigel Lawson had gambled on a supply-side miracle to cope with such irritating distractions. The problem with miracles is that they are, by definition, somewhat elusive.

GLOSSARY

BROAD MONEY Money used for day to day transactions *and* money held in various forms of savings.

DEMAND MANAGEMENT The discretionary use by the Government of changes in the level of taxation, public spending, and interest rates in order to affect the level of output and employment and/or the rate of growth of the economy.

DEREGULATION The process by which, from 1979 onwards, direct controls on the financial system were abolished, enabling banks and other financial institutions to compete more freely to attract and lend deposits.

ECONOMETRIC Relating to the building of mathematical models of the economy, which show the relationships between economic variables and sectors, and try to predict, from past experience, the future effect of events and policy changes.

EUROPEAN MONETARY SYSTEM (EMS) A system of exchange rate management within the European Community (EEC), involving the pooling of some official currency reserves. Most currencies are allowed to diverge no more than 2¼ per cent either side of a central rate, but the lira and peseta have a wider band (6 per cent either side).

EXCHANGE CONTROLS Official limits on the amounts of currency that can be moved in and out of the country; abolished in the United Kingdom in 1979.

EXPANSIONISM A bias in favour of expanding the economy whenever possible. An expansionist fiscal policy is biased in favour of lower taxes and/or higher public spending.

GROSS DOMESTIC PRODUCT (GDP) The total value of all the output and services in the economy. GROSS NATIONAL PRODUCT is GDP plus the value of net income from overseas investment.

HOT MONEY Funds invested on a very short-term basis in sterling (often daily), and likely to flow out at the first signs of a collapse of financial confidence.

INCOMES POLICY An attempt by Government to limit, sometimes statutorily, the size of pay settlements in the private sector as well as the public.

INTERNATIONAL MONETARY FUND (IMF) The overseer of the international monetary system, set up by the leading non-Communist industrial powers in 1944; it holds important meetings twice a year, at which member governments from over 140 countries are represented.

KEYNESIAN A word used to describe the approach to the economy of followers of the great economist John Maynard Keynes, who believed that DEMAND MANAGEMENT is both feasible and desirable.

MACROECONOMICS Economics as it affects the whole economy, as opposed to –

MICROECONOMICS The study of the economic behaviour of individual sectors. Of course, each affects the other.

MINIMUM LENDING RATE (MLR) 'Bank Rate', or the rate at which the Bank of England lent funds to the banking system in its capacity as lender of last resort; although MLR was abolished in 1981, the Bank continues to have dealing rates at which it performs the same function. After the abolition of MLR, bank base rates became the principal criterion for the level of UK interest rates.

MONETARISM The belief that control of the MONEY SUPPLY, however defined, is both a necessary and a sufficient condition for controlling inflation, and that DEMAND MANAGEMENT is irrelevant and damaging to economic progress.

MONEY GDP GDP as it occurs, by contrast with REAL GDP, which is adjusted for inflation.

MONEY SUPPLY The amount of money added to the accumulated stock in any one period.

> MONETARY BASE (NARROW) Commercial banks' deposits with the Bank of England. These amount to about 1½% of –
>
> MONETARY BASE (WIDE) which also includes notes and coins resting in commercial banks ('till money') and notes and coins in circulation with the public (about 90 per cent of wide monetary base), which together constitute –
>
> M0
>
> M1 – M0 plus bank deposits which can be withdrawn on demand ('"sight" deposits').
>
> M3 – M1 plus 'time' deposits (whose interest rates are geared to the length of time for which they are deposited).
>
> M4 – M3 plus deposits with building societies.

NARROW MONEY Money readily available for current transactions.

PUBLIC SECTOR BORROWING REQUIREMENT (PSBR) What the Government sometimes has to borrow, to make up for any discrepancies between its spending and tax revenues.

VELOCITY OF CIRCULATION The speed with which money circulates, or GDP divided by the money supply. It is essential to MONETARISM that this is stable, or at least predictable, so that increases in the money supply can be equated with subsequent increases in prices. The KEYNESIAN belief is that life is more complicated. This is what Mr Lawson discovered after abandoning Keynesianism for Monetarism.

NOTES

1 Lawson the Expansionist

1 *Observer*, Interview with Kenneth Harris, March 10th, 1985.
2 *Sunday Times*, Interview with Susan Crosland, March 11th, 1984.
3 K. Harris, op. cit.
4 K. Harris, op. cit.
5 *Spectator*, February 14th, 1970.
6 *Daily Telegraph*, March 17th, 1987.
7 *Guardian*, September 5th, 1983.
8 D. Kynaston, *Financial Times – A Centenary History*, Viking, 1988.
9 *Sunday Telegraph*, March 24th, 1963.
10 *Sunday Telegraph*, February 26th, 1961.
11 *Sunday Telegraph*, April 29th, 1962.
12 *Sunday Telegraph*, June 18th, 1961.
13 *Sunday Telegraph*, May 7th, 1961.
14 *Sunday Telegraph*, February 19th, 1961.
15 *Sunday Telegraph*, April 2nd, 1961.
16 *Sunday Telegraph*, September 30th, 1962.
17 *Sunday Telegraph*, April 2nd, 1961.
18 *Sunday Telegraph*, March 11th, 1962.
19 *Sunday Telegraph*, September 30th, 1962.
20 ibid.
21 *Sunday Telegraph*, March 24th, 1963.
22 *Sunday Telegraph*, March 11th, 1963.
23 ibid.
24 *Sunday Telegraph*, March 11th, 1963.
25 *Sunday Telegraph*, April 7th, 1963.
26 ibid.
27 *Sunday Telegraph*, April 21st, 1963.
28 ibid.
29 ibid.
30 *Sunday Telegraph*, April 28th, 1983.
31 ibid.
32 *Sunday Telegraph*, April 28th, 1963.
33 *Sunday Telegraph*, May 12th, 1963.
34 *Sunday Telegraph*, June 9th, 1963.
35 *Sunday Telegraph*, June 23rd, 1963.
36 *Sunday Telegraph*, July 7th, 1963.
37 *Sunday Telegraph*, August 8th, 1963.
38 *Sunday Telegraph*, September 8th, 1963.
39 *Sunday Telegraph*, February 4th, 1962.
40 ibid.
41 *Sunday Telegraph*, February 17th, 1963.
42 *Sunday Telegraph*, October 29th, 1961.
43 *Sunday Telegraph*, April 15th, 1962.
44 *Sunday Telegraph*, September 29th, 1963.
45 *Sunday Telegraph*, July 15th, 1962.
46 *Sunday Telegraph*, July 29th, 1962.
47 *Sunday Telegraph*, September 8th, 1963.
48 ibid.
49 ibid.
50 ibid.

51 *Sunday Telegraph*, December 2nd, 1962.
52 *Sunday Telegraph*, September 3rd, 1961.
53 ibid.
54 *Sunday Telegraph*, October 13th, 1963.
55 *Financial Times*, November 13th, 1982.
56 Sir Michael Fraser, quoted by Susan Crosland, *Sunday Times*, March 11th, 1984.
57 *Financial Times*, February 10th, 1965.
58 *Financial Times*, February 24th, 1965.
59 *Financial Times*, March 10th, 1965.
60 *Financial Times*, March 17th, 1965.
61 *Financial Times*, April 21st, 1965.
62 ibid.
63 ibid.
64 ibid.
65 *Financial Times*, June 9th, 1965.
66 ibid.
67 *Financial Times*, September 22nd, 1965.
68 *Financial Times*, October 27th, 1965.
69 ibid.
70 *Financial Times*, May 5th, 1965.
71 ibid.
72 ibid.
73 ibid.
74 ibid.
75 *Financial Times*, December 15th, 1965.
76 ibid.
77 ibid.
78 *Financial Times*, October 6th, 1965.
79 *Financial Times*, November 3rd, 1965.
80 ibid.
81 ibid.
82 *Financial Times*, March 31st, 1965.
83 *Financial Times*, December 29th, 1965.
84 *Financial Times*, June 9th, 1965.
85 *Spectator*, January 7th, 1966.
86 ibid.
87 *Spectator*, January 14th, 1966.
88 Interview with Robert Harris on Thames Television's *This Week*, February 2nd, 1989.
89 *Spectator*, January 14th, 1966.
90 *Spectator*, January 21st, 1966.
91 *Spectator*, February 4th, 1966.
92 *Spectator*, February 11th, 1966.
93 *Spectator*, March 4th, 1966.
94 *Spectator*, June 24th, 1966.
95 *Spectator*, March 25th, 1966.
96 *Spectator*, April 1st, 1966.
97 *Spectator*, July 15th, 1966.
98 *Spectator*, April 8th, 1966.
99 *Spectator*, July 22nd, 1966.
100 Clive Ponting, *Breach of Promise*, Hamish Hamilton, 1989.
101 *Spectator*, July 29th, 1966.
102 ibid.
103 *Spectator*, September 14th, 1966.
104 ibid.
105 *Spectator*, December 23rd, 1966.
106 *Spectator*, March 3rd, 1967.
107 ibid.
108 ibid.
109 ibid.
110 *Spectator*, February 17th, 1967.
111 *Spectator*, February 24th, 1967.
112 ibid.
113 ibid.
114 ibid.
115 *Spectator*, November 29th, 1968.

2 The Conversion

1 *Sunday Times*, May 11th, 1984.
2 Interview with author, spring 1982.
3 Interview with Susan Crosland, *Sunday Times*, March 11th, 1984.
4 *Encounter*, August 1974, 'New Inflation, Old Obsession'.
5 ibid.
6 Clive Ponting, *Breach of Promise*, Hamish Hamilton, 1989.
7 Speech at Conservative Central Office, November 27th, 1975.

8 *Observer*, March 17th, 1985.
9 *Spectator*, May 16th, 1970.
10 *The Times*, February 2nd, 1977.
11 ibid.
12 *The Times*, April 29th, 1976, and *Hansard*, April 4th, 1976.
13 *Hansard*, April 1st, 1976.
14 ibid.
15 *Hansard*, November 10th, 1977.
16 *Spectator*, January 7th, 1978.
17 Letter to *The Times*, August 4th, 1977.
18 *Spectator*, January 7th, 1978.
19 *Hansard*, March 13th, 1978.
20 *Spectator*, January 7th, 1978.
21 Adrian Hamilton, 'North Sea Impact', International Institute of Economic and Social Research, 1978.
22 *Spectator*, January 7th, 1978.
23 ibid.
24 *Financial Times*, February 8th, 1978.
25 Interview on Thames Television's *This Week*, February 2nd, 1989.
26 *Observer*, June 25th, 1978.
27 *The Times*, August 17th, 1978.
28 *Observer*, March 17th, 1985.
29 ibid.
30 *The Times*, August 17th, 1978.
31 ibid.
32 *Observer*, March 17th, 1985.
33 *Daily Telegraph*, March 17th, 1987.
34 Rt. Hon. Nigel Lawson, 'The New Conservatism', Centre for Policy Studies.
35 ibid.
36 ibid.
37 ibid.
38 ibid.
39 ibid.
40 ibid.
41 *Guardian*, August 1980.
42 Rt. Hon. Nigel Lawson, 'The New Conservatism', Centre for Policy Studies.
43 ibid.
44 ibid.
45 ibid.
46 ibid.
47 ibid.

3 Lawson as Quasi-Chancellor: the Medium Term Financial Strategy

1 *Financial Times*, May 21st, 1979.
2 *Financial Times*, September 15th, 1981.
3 Jock Bruce-Gardyne, *Ministers and Mandarins*, Sidgwick & Jackson, 1986.
4 From an interview on Thames Television's *This Week*, February 2nd, 1989.
5 ibid.
6 William Keegan, *Mrs Thatcher's Economic Experiment*, Harmondsworth: Penguin, 1984.
7 HM Treasury, August 17th, 1979.
8 Jim Prior, *A Balance of Power*, Hamish Hamilton, 1986.
9 Evidence to the Treasury Select Committee, 1980.
10 Speech to *Financial Times* Euromarkets Conference, January 21st, 1980.
11 House of Lords Select Committee on Overseas Trade, 1985.
12 William Keegan, *Britain Without Oil*, Harmondsworth: Penguin, 1985.
13 *Sunday Telegraph*, March 11th, 1962.
14 J. C. R. Dow and I. D. Saville, *A Critique of Monetary Policy*, OUP, 1988.
15 Speech, May 8th, 1980.
16 Jim Prior, op. cit.
17 Alan Walters, *Britain's Economic Renaissance*, OUP (New York), 1986.
18 William Keegan (1984).
19 *Sunday Times*, April 5th, 1981.

4 Lawson as Quasi-Chancellor: the Zurich Speech and the 1981 Budget

1 Speech to Zurich Society of Economists, January 14th, 1981.
2 Alan Walters, op. cit.
3 Evidence to the Treasury Select Committee, October 1982.
4 Dr Jurg Niehans, *The Appreciation of Sterling – Causes, Effects and Policies*, Social Science Research Council, 1981.
5 Letter to *The Times*, March 31st, 1981.
6 Wynne Godley, *Observer*, September 18th, 1988.
7 Professor Sir Alan Walters, in *Keynes and Economic Policy*, edited by Walter Eltis and Peter Sinclair, Macmillan, 1988.
8 Alan Walters, op. cit.
9 David Smith, *The Rise and Fall of Monetarism*, Penguin, 1987.
10 *Financial Times*, January 15th, 1981.

5 Energy Secretary and the 1983 'Inheritance'

1 *Financial Times*, September 15th, 1981.
2 *The Times*, September 15th, 1981.
3 *Financial Times*, October 1981.
4 *The Times*, October 1981.
5 CBI Conference on Energy, September 29th, 1981.
6 ibid.
7 *Guardian*, September 30th, 1981.
8 *Sunday Telegraph*, November 1981.
9 Speech to London Committee of the Scottish Chartered Accountants, November 26th, 1981.
10 Speech to University of Surrey Energy Conference, April 15th, 1983.
11 Speech to Selsdon Group, October 15th, 1981.
12 Speech to The Association of Economic Representatives of London, January 27th, 1982.
13 Speech to the Institute for Fiscal Studies, 1981.
14 ibid.
15 Speech to The Association of Economic Representatives of London, op. cit.
16 Leo Pliatzky, *The Treasury under Mrs Thatcher*, Blackwell, 1989.
17 *Keynes and Economic Policy*, edited by Walter Eltis and Peter Sinclair, Macmillan, 1988.
18 Professor Sir Alan Walters, *Britain's Economic Renaissance*, OUP (New York), 1986.
19 William Keegan, *Britain Without Oil*, Harmondsworth: Penguin, 1985.
20 Evidence to the House of Lords Select Committee on Overseas Trade, 1985.
21 ibid.

6 The Floating Chancellor

1 Speech to Institute for Fiscal Studies, March 1981.
2 Leo Pliatzky, *Paying and Choosing*, Blackwell, 1985.
3 Conversation with author, November 1st, 1983.
4 Speech by the Rt. Hon. Nigel Lawson to the IMF in Washington, September 29th, 1983.
5 *The Times*, W. Rees-Mogg, June 13th, 1976.
6 Bank of England, *Quarterly Bulletin*, 1983.
7 *Observer*, October 30th, 1983.
8 Evidence to the Treasury Select Committee, December 19th, 1983.
9 ibid.
10 'The 1984 Budget', the Institute for Fiscal Studies.
11 Kit McMahon, reported in the *Observer*, March 4th, 1984.

12 'The Next Ten Years: Public Expenditure and Taxation into the 1990s', HMSO, 1984.
13 *Observer*, April 15th, 1984.
14 Bank of England, *Quarterly Bulletin*, June 1984.
15 *National Institute Economic Review*, August 1984.
16 *Financial Times*, June 21st, 1984.
17 *Daily Telegraph*, March 29th, 1984.
18 *Hansard*, July 31st, 1984.
19 Speech by the Rt. Hon. Nigel Lawson to the IMF, September 25th, 1984.
20 *Daily Telegraph*, October 15th, 1984.
21 IMF Speech, September 25th, 1984.
22 Interview with US syndicated columnist, George F. Will, December 1984.
23 Speech by the Rt. Hon. Nigel Lawson at the Mansion House, October 18th, 1984.
24 *Sunday Times*, December 30th, 1984.

7 The Sterling Crisis of January 1985 and its Aftermath

1 *National Institute Economic Review*, November 1984.
2 Hugo Young, *One of Us*, Macmillan, 1989.
3 *Sunday Telegraph*, January 20th, 1985.
4 Letter to *The Times*, January 1985.
5 Letter to *The Times*, January 1985.
6 Evidence to the Select Committee on the Treasury, January 28th, 1985.
7 Stephen Fay, *Portrait of an Old Lady*, Viking, 1987.
8 Margaret Reid, *All Change in the City*, Macmillan, 1988.
9 *Financial Times*, July, 1984.
10 *Hansard*, June 1985.
11 Financial Statement and Budget Report, 1989.
12 *National Institute Economic Review*, February 1985.
13 *Observer*, May 12th, 1985.
14 *Hansard*, May 1985.
15 *Hansard*, July 1985.
16 Evidence to the Select Committee on the Treasury, July 1985.

8 Election Hero

1 Yoichi Funabashi, *Managing the Dollar: From the Plaza to the Louvre*, Institute for International Economics, 1988.
2 Speech to IMF Conference, Seoul, October 1985.
3 Speech to Conservative Party Conference, October 1985.
4 Speech at the Mansion House, October 18th, 1985.
5 Autumn Statement, November 1985.
6 Gavyn Davies, *Mr Lawson's 'New' Monetary Policy*, Simon & Coates, October 1985.
7 Centre for Policy Studies, December 1985.
8 Budget Speech, March 1986.
9 OECD's *Economic Survey* 'United Kingdom', July 1987.
10 Speech to IMF Conference, Washington, September 1986.
11 Speech at the Mansion House, October 1986.
12 Second Report from the Treasury and Civil Service Committee, 1986–87, December 10th, 1986.
13 Funabashi, op. cit.
14 Funabashi, op. cit.
15 Financial Statement and Budget Report, March 1987.
16 Treasury Committee 'The 1987 Budget', April 22nd, 1987.

9 The Battles of Downing Street

1 Ken Coutts and Wynne Godley, 'The British Economy under Mrs Thatcher', *Political Quarterly*, July 1989. Sir Donald MacDougall, 'Fifty Years On: Some Personal Reflections', British Academy, December 8th, 1988.
2 Keith Smith, *The British Economic Crisis*, Penguin, 1989.
3 John Rentoul, *The Rich Get Richer*, Unwin, 1988.
4 Victor Keegan in the *Guardian*, January 4th, 1988.
5 Margaret Reid, *All Change in the City*, Macmillan, 1988.
6 C. Huhne in the *Guardian*, November 16th, 1988.
7 *National Institute Economic Review*, February 1989.
8 Speech by the Rt. Hon. Nigel Lawson at the Stock Exchange, October 26th, 1987.
9 Speech by the Rt. Hon. Nigel Lawson at the Mansion House on November 4th, 1987.
10 *National Institute Economic Review*, November 1987.
11 Speech by the Rt. Hon. Nigel Lawson to American and Canadian Chambers of Commerce, November 24th, 1987.
12 Evidence to the Treasury Select Committee, December 9th, 1987.
13 Professor Mervyn King, 'Prospects of Tax Reform in 1988', LSE Financial Markets Discussion Paper No. 10, 1987.
14 *Financial Times*, March 11th, 1988.
15 Philip Stephens, *Financial Times*, July 21st, 1988.
16 BBC *World Service*, May 19th, 1989.
17 Tim Congdon, 'Monetarism Lost', Centre for Policy Studies, May 1989.
18 Speech by the Rt. Hon. Nigel Lawson to the IMF in Berlin, September 28th, 1988.
19 ibid.
20 Jock Bruce-Gardyne, *Sunday Telegraph*, 1987.
21 Julian Critchley, *Mail on Sunday*, 1988.
22 Treasury Committee Report on the 'Delors Report', June 19th, 1989.
23 BBC Radio, quoted in the *Guardian*, August 22nd, 1983.

INDEX